Theatre and Performance in Contemporary Scotland

"*Theatre and Performance in Contemporary Scotland* maps the impact of the many major dramatists and companies that have emerged from Scotland in recent decades, showing how they have forged and developed a distinctive cultural and theatrical identity. The book is, simply, inspirational: it allows readers to think anew about how theatre can intersect with the political—and how great art can affect a whole society."

—Patrick Lonergan, *Professor, University of Galway, Ireland*

"This is the book I have been waiting for. It offers a rigorously insightful encounter with a rich range of Scottish theatre and performance practices in the post-devolutionary context. Thinking through the relationships of cultural production and cultural identity extends its relevance well beyond one nation, though I admit a particular pleasure in sharing it with my peers—students and colleagues alike—across Scotland."

—Deirdre Heddon, *Professor, James Arnott Chair in Drama, University of Glasgow, UK*

"*Theatre and Performance in Contemporary Scotland* covers its admirably wide-ranging ground lucidly and authoritatively. It balances rigour and readability in a vivid and engaging style and is an important contribution to the field by a leading international scholar. Combining fresh insights with appropriate personal perspectives, it is essential reading for anyone with an interest in any aspect of contemporary theatre."

—Ian Brown, *Emeritus Professor in Drama, Kingston University and Honorary Senior Research Fellow in Scottish Literature, Glasgow University, UK*

Trish Reid

Theatre and Performance in Contemporary Scotland

palgrave
macmillan

Trish Reid
Reading, UK

ISBN 978-3-031-61190-2   ISBN 978-3-031-61191-9 (eBook)
https://doi.org/10.1007/978-3-031-61191-9

© The Editor(s) (if applicable) and The Author(s) 2024

This work is subject to copyright. All rights are solely and exclusively licensed by the Publisher, whether the whole or part of the material is concerned, specifically the rights of translation, reprinting, reuse of illustrations, recitation, broadcasting, reproduction on microfilms or in any other physical way, and transmission or information storage and retrieval, electronic adaptation, computer software, or by similar or dissimilar methodology now known or hereafter developed.
The use of general descriptive names, registered names, trademarks, service marks, etc. in this publication does not imply, even in the absence of a specific statement, that such names are exempt from the relevant protective laws and regulations and therefore free for general use.
The publisher, the authors and the editors are safe to assume that the advice and information in this book are believed to be true and accurate at the date of publication. Neither the publisher nor the authors or the editors give a warranty, expressed or implied, with respect to the material contained herein or for any errors or omissions that may have been made. The publisher remains neutral with regard to jurisdictional claims in published maps and institutional affiliations.

Cover illustration: Nerea Bello, Mairi Morrison, Helen Katamba and Belinda Odenyo in Julia Taudevin's, Move (directed by Julia Taudevin, Disaster Plan, 2021) reproduced with kind permission from Brian Hartley

This Palgrave Macmillan imprint is published by the registered company Springer Nature Switzerland AG
The registered company address is: Gewerbestrasse 11, 6330 Cham, Switzerland

If disposing of this product, please recycle the paper.

This book is dedicated to the memory of my nephew Martin Llyod, who left too soon, but was in his own way a very talented Scottish performance artist.

Acknowledgements

This book has been a relatively long time in the making and there are many people I need to thank for their ongoing support and advice. Firstly, my thanks go to Palgrave and particularly to Alice Carter who has cajoled me through the final stages of the project with unfailing good humour. The support of colleagues at Kingston University, and latterly at the University of Reading, has allowed me to complete the project, while retaining something like an acceptable work-life balance. My special thanks go to Jonathan Bignell and Ian Brown, with whom I have had many helpful exchanges and whose comments on my final draft were extremely perceptive and very helpful indeed.

I am also indebted to the wider scholarly community with whom I have shared and tested ideas over the last several years. In particular, I have enjoyed the support of colleagues in the Political Performances Working Group of the International Federation of Theatre Research, the Theatre and Performance Research Association, and Contemporary Drama in English. Special thanks to Adam Alston, Siân Adiseshiah, Vicky Angelaki, Julia Boll, Jacqueline Bolton, Paola Botham, Claire Cochrane, Cristina Delgado-García, Marrisia Fragkou, Lynette Goddard, Steve Greer, Sam Haddow, Catherine Hindson, Nicholas Holden, Nadine Holdsworth, Nicola McCartney, Martin Middeke, David Pattie, Ben Poore, Mark Robson, Graham Saunders, Liz Tomlin, Eckhart Voigts, Clare Wallace and Marilena Zaroulia. Thanks to David Greig and David Harrower for providing rehearsal scripts.

Finally, my thanks go to Dee Heddon and Patrick Lonergan for their kind endorsements of the book, and to my family Andy, Grace and Tom Lavender, without whom I would not be the happy woman I am today.

Trish Reid

Contents

1	**Introduction**	1
	Scottishness Redefined	6
	Contexts	9
	The Epistemic Community	12
	Structure of the Book	16
	Lanark	20
	References	28
2	**Key Contexts**	31
	The Citz	35
	Traverse 85	39
	Other Voices, Other Rooms	45
	Other Voices	51
	Plays and Playwrighting in the 1990s	54
	Conclusion	62
	References	64
3	**Other Stages**	69
	Tramway	76
	NRLA, Behaviour, Take Me Somewhere	79
	Performance Companies	84
	Festival City	96
	References	98

4	**A New Model for a New Nation**	101
	2006	106
	Since 2006	120
	Conclusion	131
	References	133
5	**Engaging Audiences**	137
	Performances in and of the Rural	143
	Theatre for Children and Young People	152
	Reclaiming a Politics of Sincerity	162
	References	168
6	**Plays and Playwrighting**	173
	Established Voices	178
	Newer Voices	192
	The Old Guard	200
	References	204
7	**New Imperatives**	209
	Scenes for Survival	213
	Financial Pressures	216
	New Imperatives	220
	Epilogue	233
	References	234
	Index	237

List of Figures

Fig. 1.1 Sandy Grierson and Jessica Hardwick in David Greig's *Lanark* (directed by Graham Eatough, Royal Lyceum Edinburgh, 2015) reproduced with kind permission from Eoin Carey — 23

Fig. 2.1 Joyce Falconer as La Corbie in Liz Lochhead's *Mary Queen of Scots Got Her Head Chopped Off* (directed by Alison Peebles, National Theatre of Scotland, 2009) reproduced with kind permission from Peter Dibdin — 49

Fig. 3.1 George Anton as George Anton in Untitled Projects' *Paul Bright's Confessions of a Justified Sinner*, 2013. Reproduced with kind permission from Tommy Ga-Ken Wan — 70

Fig. 4.1 Matthew Pidgeon as James III in Rona Munro's *James III: The True Mirror* (directed by Laurie Sansom, National Theatre of Scotland, 2016) reproduced with kind permission from Tommy Ga-Ken Wan — 130

Fig. 5.1 Ian Cameron as Wrinkle and Andy Manley as Cotton in *White*, 2011. Photograph by Douglas McBride reproduced with kind permission from Catherine Wheels Theatre Company — 154

Fig. 6.1 Fletcher Mathers, Leah Walker, Georgette McMillan and Kirsty Stuart in Zinnie Harris' *The Duchess (of Malfi) after John Webster* (directed by Zinnie Harris, Royal Lyceum Edinburgh and Glasgow Citizens', 2019) reproduced with kind permission from Mihaela Bodlovic — 178

Fig. 7.1 Belinda Odenyo in Hannah Lavery's *Lament for Sheku Bayoh* (Directed by Hannah Lavery, National Theatre of Scotland, 2020) reproduced with kind permission from Mihaela Bodlovic — 223

CHAPTER 1

Introduction

Early in David Greig's *Caledonia Dreaming* (1997), in a scene titled 'The Yes Yes Campaign', a chorus reflects on the uses and value of the word 'yes'. The 'timpanist in the Royal Scottish National Orchestra' says yes, and when he does 'he thinks of mountains' we are told (1997: 16). Someone's mum says yes, when asked for the use of her car and someone else's dad, 'when he's on the phone to his brother in Aberdeen' says 'aye', which makes him happy, happier than using standard English we assume (17). A little more ominously, a mother says yes when a policeman arrives at her door asking whether she has a son called Kevin. Overall, though, the forward-looking, future-focused potentials of the word are emphasised:

> It's a happy word to say.
> For years we've had to say …
> No. No way. No way Jose.
> Stop. Hold on. Don't do that.
> But not now.
> We're the yes yes campaign.
> We demand new questions
> Questions whose answer is …
> Yes Yes. (1997: 18)

The question of Scotland and its imagined future which this chorus enacts, is one that has preoccupied Scotland's theatre artists in recent decades. The reference to dreaming in the title of Greig's play is particularly apposite in this context, and the notion of the Scottish theatre and performance sector as a whole engaging in such an activity, finds expression again in the Joyce McMillan collection *Theatre in Scotland: A Field of Dreams* (2016). As arguably the country's leading theatre critic, McMillan has been an astute and perceptive chronicler of the Scottish theatre revival of the last thirty years, and has been among the first to raise her voice in protest when the sector appears under threat from funding cuts. In common with many cultural commentators, she has also sought to highlight and unpick connections between Scotland's developing performance culture and the wider trend in Scottish politics in which calls for a greater degree of autonomy in the governance of the country have been prominent. This link between cultural activity and politics in the broadest sense is a central concern of this book not least because a narrative of chicken and egg has developed around this relationship, in which increased cultural confidence in Scotland is understood as both the driver and the consequence of demands for increased political autonomy. In *The Literary Politics of Scottish Devolution* (2020), Scott Hames describes this 'story of cultural vanguardism in which writers and artists play the starring role in the recuperation of national identity, cultural confidence and democratic agency' as 'The Dream' (2020: xii). This comment rather conveniently brings us back to Greig's play.

Caledonia Dreaming is an energetic ensemble piece that intersperses short scenes between named characters with choral sections of the kind described above. It deals with themes of dissatisfaction, personal aspiration, and the power of the imagination, in a setting described as 'some kind of Edinburgh, on a summer night, at some recent time' (3). Among other things the play is notable for being the first time Scotland appears as a specific location in Greig's work, but while its title suggests otherwise, it contains few moments as explicitly linked to contemporary Scottish politics as the one described above, which seems unequivocally to be addressing the question of Scottish devolution, and the upcoming referendum of September 1997. Instead, *Caledonia Dreaming* explores its characters' aspirations—with Greig's customary ironic humour—substantially through their shared obsession with the iconic Scottish actor Sean Connery, who operates as a present absence in the play, and as a kind of synecdoche for a newly aspirational Scotland. As the play begins, the hyper-masculine actor and prominent supporter of Scottish independence is rumoured to be ensconced at the Caledonian Hotel on Princes Street, his usual residence during visits to Edinburgh. It is to this hotel that Greig's eclectic group of characters initially gravitates.

Darren, a restless lad from the peripheral Oxgangs housing estate, hopes to become Connery's personal assistant, thereby breaking free of his working-class roots. Eppie, a disgruntled middle-aged housewife from the posh suburbs, longs to inject new meaning into her life by reliving a youthful encounter with the legendary actor. A Labour member of the European Parliament, Stuart, thinks Connery would be the ideal candidate to front his campaign to bring the Olympics to Edinburgh, and Jerry, the doorman at the Caledonian Hotel, dreams of enlisting Connery's help in launching his singing career. To this mix Greig adds Lauren, an English sex worker who becomes embroiled in Stuart's political manoeuverings, and a taxi driver named Lawrence who acts as a foil in various scenes but does not appear onstage or speak. As the action progresses the characters' lives become increasingly interconnected and they drift, by this time somewhat the worse for wear, first towards the hotel and then to the Heart of Midlothian, a pavement mosaic located outside St Giles Cathedral on Edinburgh's High Street. Here they finally catch a glimpse of the great man as he drives past in a limousine, and their rapt responses confirm his status as a kind of uber-Scottish blank canvas onto which every and all aspirations can be projected:

> **Eppie** He looked familiar.
> **Lauren** He looked welcoming.
> **Darren** He Looked like my dad.
> **Stuart** He looked like he was in charge.
> **Jerry** He didn't need to speak. (83)

A celebratory tone dominates and even as Stuart, the most morally and ethically compromised of Greig's characters, urinates against a wall and collapses in a drunken heap, a note of optimism persists: 'See from down here. I see things. I see how it could be' (84). *Caledonia Dreaming* ends with Stuart's ambition of bringing the Olympics to Edinburgh realised and in a moment of hyperbolic Scottishness, Connery reciting Robert Burns' 'A Man's a Man for a' That' to cheering crowds at Murrayfield stadium. Long before this point the shackles of realism have been cast off. It is not that Greig's play critiques the world-as-is, but rather that it gestures optimistically towards the world-as-might-be. The imperative, it seems to suggest, is to dream.

Commissioned by 7:84 Scotland and directed by the company's then artistic director Iain Reekie, *Caledonia Dreaming* premiered at the Traverse in Edinburgh and transferred to the Tron in Glasgow in the summer of 1997. It was later revived at the Edinburgh Fringe in August 1999. As the brief summary above indicates, Grieg's play eschews the ideological clarity associated with the earlier output of 7:84 Scotland as exemplified in its flagship inaugural production, John McGrath's *The Cheviot, the Stag and the Black, Black Oil* (1973). In that seminal socialist play, the history of the repeated exploitation of the Scottish Highlands over centuries, is used to expose contemporary class inequalities with the explicit aim of redressing them. Beyond its episodic structure, and as Clare Wallace notes, 'a particular sense of resilient optimism' *Caledonia Dreaming* appears to share little with *The Cheviot* although the ensemble itself, which is the basis for Grieg's play, and in which actors perform multiple roles, echoes the performance mode of the earlier play (2013: 73). The ensemble also models a kind of polity—especially in the chorus sequences that punctuate the action—but it is hardly the socialist collective staged in *The Cheviot*. Greig focuses instead on the personal aspirations of a notably diverse group of individuals. In doing so he privileges, admittedly with his tongue in his cheek, what Scott Hames, following the sociologists Alex Law and Gerry Mooney, has usefully termed 'a trans-class people-nation' construction of Scottish identity, a kind of vernacular and inclusive nationhood, that eschews and even effaces class conflict (2020: 303). This discursive framing of contemporary Scotland as a pan-class national fraternity constituted in relation to a set of distinctively Scottish values, is something I will return to repeatedly in this study, particularly in relation to how the theatre reflects and inflects this notion, and indeed plays a role in its construction. For now, though, we can notice that a number of the inevitable tensions and likely elisions inherent in such a project are highlighted in Grieg's play by Stuart, as he searches for a candidate qualified to front Edinburgh's Olympic bid:

> Scotland is modern — yet old.
> Urban — yet rural.
> Friendly — yet canny.
> Strong — yet compassionate.
> Who is it?
> Who's Scotland. That is the question we need to answer. (41)

After disqualifying a number of other contenders, including Billy Connolly and Irvine Welsh—who he accuses of making 'himself wealthy on our ugliness'—Stuart decides that Connery is the answer to his question (41). It is noticeable that for Stuart Scottishness is an inherently masculine quality. No female candidates are considered.

The absurdity of Stuart's conclusion, as David Pattie has noted, can be thought of as demonstrating that 'one actor, no matter how famous' cannot resolve the obvious tensions inherent in any inclusive definition of Scottishness, and conversely, that 'no one image of Scottish identity can carry the weight of national aspiration' (2013: 202). And yet the fantasy persists, and Stuart's dream of bringing the Olympics to Edinburgh, and of Sean Connery playing a central role in the Opening Ceremony, are realised in the play's final scene. Perhaps the best we can say is that Sean Connery operates as an empty signifier in *Caledonia Dreaming* and in that capacity as a metaphor for Scotland itself. Obviously, the particular timing of this production has significant bearing on its meaning and its optimistic tone. Devised with the company during a UK General Election campaign, *Caledonia Dreaming* was performed in the immediate aftermath of the New Labour landslide in May 1997, a victory which transformed Tony Blair's manifesto commitment to a pre-legislative referendum on Scottish devolution into a concrete reality. On Thursday 11 September of that year, just over 74% of Scots voted yes to the establishment of a Scottish parliament, and over 63% to that parliament having tax-raising powers: Yes/Yes won the day. The play is the product of a very particular historical moment.

By 1997 Greig was already being touted as part of an emerging generation of Scottish playwrights whose distinctive voices were seen as embodying a new and outward-looking cultural confidence (Zenzinger 1996). Moreover, as indicated above, the perceived distinctiveness of Scottish culture, of which theatre was one element, was the basis on which demands for constitutional change were built in the 1990s. In this context, artists and writers were of peculiar importance. Indeed, according to some commentators, 'cultural devolution' was nothing less than a necessary precursor to political devolution. Without a groundswell of cultural activity, the argument went, it would be impossible for Scotland to conceive of itself as a modern, outward-looking nation worthy of its own parliament (Hames 2020; Smith 2011; McCrone 2005; Ryan 2002). The existence of a distinctive Scottish cultural identity was not only the ground on which demands for devolution were made but, as Greig's play demonstrates, also its promise. The question of what kind of Scotland the Scottish people might want to build in the post-devolutionary period is one Greig foregrounds in a play that refuses easy answers. Instead, as Mark Fisher notes, *Caledonia Dreaming*:

> ... throws out a load of ideas about people, cities and nations, independence, devolution and union, not to mention a cultural icon who is half-milkman, half-James Bond, and leaves the audience to take what it wants. (1997)

Rather than 'charting a history of exploitation, or raising a call to action', as Clare Wallace observes, Greig's play offers a determinedly multi-dimensional rendering of Scottishness that 'ranges from burgeoning patriotism to cultural cringe' and includes a politician on the make, a sex worker, a middle-class housewife whose politics are disturbingly authoritarian and, in Jerry the doorman, a victim of racial violence (2013: 72). Greig's Scotland is far from perfect, then, but it has arrived at a moment of opportunity, and is encouraged to respond with optimism.

Scottishness Redefined

In an article written in November 1997 in the immediate aftermath of the referendum result, Greig and his fellow playwright David Harrower responded to the shifting political landscape by positioning themselves, and their sector, as ideally placed to participate in constituting the post-devolutionary nation:

> Scotland has voted to redefine itself as a nation. To redefine ourselves we need to understand ourselves, exchange ideas and aspiration, confront enduring myths, expose injustices and explore our past. The quality, accessibility and immediacy of Scottish theatre make it one of the best arenas in which these dialogues can take place. (Greig and Harrower 1997: 15)

In the years that followed, as the following chapters demonstrate, a significant number of Scottish theatre and performance makers embraced their role as active agents in the discursive reproduction of nationhood. For some, Scotland's new constitutional settlement and the opportunities it offered for re-imagining the country became a central preoccupation.

Their work, in its many and myriad formations, endeavoured to articulate a specifically Scottish national citizenship and to enable its existence as a functioning political category. This book focuses on theatre and performance in a period when a rise in nationalist sentiment has been the defining political trend in Scotland. Consequently, questions of how citizenship is conceived and performed are of central significance. In this sense, my focus is typically on the interstices between discourses of performance, politics and citizenship.

In a 2015 essay, 'Performance at the Crossroads of Citizenship', Janelle Reinelt makes a persuasive argument for the efficacy of performance as mode for the exploration of democratic citizenship in the twenty-first century. I am similarly concerned in this study to understand performance as a mode of political engagement which can contribute meaningfully to the interrogation of discourses of identity and belonging. Consequently, I have found Reinelt's essay very enabling, not least because, as she notes, recent developments in performance studies have meant the 'term "political theatre" has become increasingly weakened or even discarded by some scholars' (2015: 34). Reinelt attributes this weakening to three factors which are worth rerehearsing here. Firstly, she cites a loss of faith in the possibility of any kind of effective opposition in the post-Cold War era of globalisation and neoliberal assimilation. Secondly, she identifies a tendency towards universalism in relation to our shared understanding of human rights which works to efface identity categories—including class, gender and race—that call for different treatment in order to achieve justice or equality. Thirdly, Reinelt notes the influence of Hans Theis Lehmann's *Postdramatic Theatre* (2006), on theatre and performance studies. Lehmann's intervention, she argues, has had the effect of turning much scholarly 'attention inward to the processes of the theatrical apparatus itself and its internal politics', and away from the connection between the theatre and the political realities outside its walls (2015: 35). Lehmann does, of course, encourage this focus. 'It is not through the direct thematization of the political that theatre becomes political' he argues, 'but through the implicit substance and critical value of its *mode of representation*' (2006: 178 emphasis in original). In response to these trends, Reinelt proposes a re-thinking of theatre's relationship to the political. Drawing on the work of the philosopher Etienne Balibar, and in particular his concept of *worksites of (and for) democracy*, she argues for a new understanding of theatre as a situated embodied social practice that retains the potential to function as a 'worksite for democracy and citizenship' because of its capacity to imagine, interrogate and reinvent modes of citizenship for uncertain times (2015: 42). Balibar helpfully uses the term worksite 'in order to emphasize a *pragmatic* dimension' that accommodates 'trial and error', or to use the theatrical term, rehearsal (Balibar 2004: 198).

While her defence of theatre's political utility is robust, Reinelt is careful not to overstate its reach. She notes that a realistic approach involves:

> … seeing theatre as a part of a multiple and hybrid social engagement, peopled by a variety of publics, and making its contribution not as a huge standalone event or artefact, but rather as a communication node within a network of highly varied and sometimes contradictory nodes that together make up public discourse. Its efficaciousness is not solitary – theatre cannot change the world – but it can and sometimes does work towards change alongside the other multiple avenues of public expression. (2015: 48-9)

Reinelt's emphasis on situatedness is pertinent in the context of the present study, because my focus covers a period in the theatre and performance history of Scotland when work was often made in response to a set of rapidly changing political imperatives that foregrounded questions of sovereignty, identity, citizenship, and the constitutional settlement within the UK.

Constitutional change can have unforeseen consequences. The New Labour administration that set the process of devolution in motion with the referendum of 1997, certainly did not anticipate its own rapid electoral decline in Scotland. In fact, the proportional element of the voting system established with the new Scottish Parliament was designed explicitly to prevent an overall majority for any party. In 1997, the Labour government was confident that devolution would neutralise the nationalist threat to the Union. Indeed, many Scottish unionists supported devolution in the 1997 referendum with the expectation that it would act as a permanent barrier to the formation of an independent Scottish state. We now know that devolution did not satisfy nationalist demands, nor did it prevent large numbers of voters shifting their allegiance from Labour to the SNP. The election of a majority Scottish National Party (SNP) government in 2011, triggered—with the approval of Westminster—an Independence Referendum in 2014. This resulted in 55% of voters expressing a desire to remain part of the UK. The 45% who voted 'yes' to independence were not discouraged, however. The campaign itself was marked by a large increase in support for independence and in the subsequent Westminster election of 2015, the SNP polled 50%. To complicate matters further, in the 2016 Brexit referendum, Scotland voted decisively to Remain in the EU while a UK-wide majority voted to Leave. That each and every Scottish local authority area voted Remain, added to an already strong sense of grievance. The Tory government that called the EU referendum, had won only one seat in Scotland in the 2015 general Election. The Scottish Parliamentary elections of May 2021 concluded with the SNP winning a fourth consecutive term in government. Subsequently, the resignation of Nicola Sturgeon as First Minister in February 2023, the cloud of scandal that surrounded it, and the bitter contest for a new SNP leader that followed, complicated matters further. At the time of writing, the Labour Party is confident of regaining a foothold in Scotland at the next UK General Election, by regaining 10–20 seats, but its committed Unionist stance remains problematic in electoral terms because, in spite of recent SNP trials and tribulations, support for independence remains stable. Polling averages from August 2023 place 'Yes' at 47.9% and 'No' at 52.1%.

Contexts

Part of the work of this introduction is to map the key forces and events—political, social, economic and cultural—that have shaped contemporary Scotland and contributed to the developing sense of distinctive cultural identity referenced above, however precarious the cultural sector currently feels. In this context, the collapse in support for the Conservative Party in the second half of the twentieth century is an important part of Scotland's story. In the 1997 general election, which New Labour under Tony Blair won by a landslide, not a single Conservative MP was returned by a Scottish constituency to the UK parliament. This statistic becomes all the more remarkable when we consider that as recently as 1955 the Conservatives held 36 seats in Scotland to Labour's 34. There are many reasons for the rapid post-war decline in support for the Conservative Party in Scotland, but among the most significant, in the narrative constructed by Scottish artists and commentators, is the election of a Conservative government under Margaret Thatcher in 1979 and the economic hardships that followed in the 1980s.

By the 1990s, Thatcherism was routinely figured as alien to Scottish political and cultural values, and the mass rejection of it by Scottish voters was in itself seen as an assertion of cultural difference. Defining oneself as a Scot had become a way of expressing a specific political position and perhaps more importantly of distancing oneself from a set of values that had increasingly become associated, however unfairly, with 'Englishness'. The eminent Scottish sociologist David McCrone makes this point concisely:

> National identity and political values are connected, so that to say that one is Scottish is to say that one has left-of-centre values; and to say that one is British is to assert distinctly more right-of-centre views, largely the opposite of the meaning in England. (McCrone, 2001: 27)

In Scotland during the 1980s, the social, political and cultural landscape was dominated by Thatcherism, or perhaps more precisely, by Scotland's emphatic rejection of Thatcher's aggressive brand of neoliberal capitalism. Thatcher's electoral victories appeared to evidence the ascendancy of certain neoliberal beliefs not only over the collectivist ideals of the European post-war consensus—built around trade union representation and the Welfare State—but also over more traditional British conservative values. With the benefit of hindsight, it is possible to see that certain unpleasant—from a Scottish perspective—aspects of Thatcherism, including an increase in overt materialism and social atomisation, were part of larger global trends and thus not limited to the UK. However, it remains important in the context of this study to emphasise the extent to which hostility to neoliberal ideas became personalised in Scotland. Thatcher very quickly became a hate figure. In 'popular Scottish mythology' as Richard Findlay notes, 'the eighties match the thirties as the Devil's decade' (Findlay 2004: 341). This is hardly surprising. The Conservative majorities of the 1980s were built on the party's relative popularity in England and on a non-proportional electoral system that allowed the Conservatives to secure an overall majority of 144 seats in 1983, for instance, while polling 42.1% of the popular vote. Moreover, at no point during the eighteen years of Conservative government that followed Thatcher's election in 1979 did the Tories enjoy a majority in Scotland (or Wales). On the contrary the narrative of Scottish Conservative support during this period is one of rapid decline. In their best showing in 1979, they secured 22 of Scotland's 71 seats. In 1992 they won 11, a performance outranked in awfulness only by their failure in 1997 to secure a single Scottish parliamentary seat.

The significance of this trend to the devolution debate was that it functioned as a reminder of Scotland's inability to prevent the repeated re-election of Conservative governments. Resentment solidified around the notion of a 'democratic deficit' in which Scotland's voice was silenced by the voting preferences of the larger English electorate. Scotland's powerlessness in preventing the implementation of unpopular Thatcherite policies was experienced as a further indignity. The idea that Scotland's lack of political autonomy exposed it to English exploitation was not entirely new, of course. In the 1970s the SNP had campaigned for independence on the grounds that Scotland's North Sea oil revenues were being siphoned off by vested interests in Westminster, for example. But in the 1980s the economic agenda was more defensive, focusing on the continuing decline of the heavy industries such as coal, shipbuilding and steel that had defined industrial Scotland for generations. This inexorable downward spiral, which many blamed on Conservative policy, served only to fuel Scotland's sense of grievance and to strengthen the desire for some form of self-government as an antidote to Tory indifference. In addition, the privatisation of nationalised industries, which was a key policy under Thatcher, was deeply unpopular in Scotland and the decision to pilot the controversial Poll Tax north of the border convinced many Scots that they were being used as a laboratory for Tory experimentation and moreover that they were being punished for their continued refusal to vote Conservative. Again, McCrone summarises:

> In Scotland, the attack on state institutions – the nationalized industries, the education system, local government, the public sector generally, even the Church, institutions which carried much of Scotland's identity – was easily perceived as an attack on 'Scotland' itself. (McCrone, 2001: 122)

During the 1980s, then, a sense of difference between Scottish civic society and that of its larger southern neighbour took firm hold, at least in Scotland. Among the longer-term effects of Thatcherism on Scottish playwriting, was a focus on the damaging effects of an absence of solidarity. This trend is exemplified in Mike Cullen's *The Cut* (1993), in which a power struggle between workers at a Scottish colliery explodes the us/them binary that had characterised industrial relations in the pre-Thatcher era. In Cullen's play, and again in Gregory Burke's *Gagarin*

Way (2001), the secure and immutable masculine working-class culture on which notions of solidarity had been built has disintegrated. It is now every man for himself.

The Epistemic Community

This book is a study of theatre and performance in contemporary Scotland that foregrounds its relationship with Scottish society largely in the period after the establishment of the devolved Scottish parliament in 1999. This is an acknowledgement of the fact that while it is possible to over emphasise the importance of particular dates in the development of theatrical cultures—not least because such dates are typically drawn from outside theatre itself—devolution was justified in Scottish political argument not merely as a constitutional or technocratic fix to state structures, but as a fundamental claim for the recognition of Scotland's cultural distinctiveness. In addition, as Adrienne Scullion observed in 2001, the establishment of the devolved parliament altered Scotland's 'understanding of and relationship to government' and encouraged 'a more immediate sense of responsibility and empowerment on the part of the electorate' (Scullion 2001: 373). For these reasons, 1999 is as significant for cultural production as for developments in the political and social spheres. In the event, the consolidation of a sense of particularity and autonomy has challenged and benefited the country's theatre workers in a number of ways. Funding mechanisms have changed, and Scottish theatre has undergone a period of redefinition as it seeks new and meaningful ways of engaging with its audience in a newly energised environment.

Since it is based around a particular selection of key productions, plays, companies and practices this study does not claim to provide an exhaustive account of theatre and performance in contemporary Scotland. It does aim to look beyond plays, playwrighting and theatre buildings however, and in this sense, it differs from existing book length studies such as Ian Brown's *History as Theatrical Metaphor* (2016) and Mark Brown's *Modernism and Scottish Theatre Since 1969* (2019). One of my arguments is that a focus on conventional drama fails to capture the diversity of practice that makes up theatre and performance in contemporary Scotland. This study is intended to fill a gap therefore, insofar as it brings this diversity of practice into one place and foregrounds its interconnections and dependencies. Even so, like any study it leaves gaps, and these are bound to be significant. No doubt my choices will be disputed by some, who may quite rightly have made a different and equally valid selection. In any case, the fact that the rich and diverse practices of theatre and performance in Scotland today cannot be adequately surveyed in a single volume is surely cause for celebration. Several questions frame the arguments presented in this book. What can the theatre culture of post-devolutionary Scotland reveal about the possibilities of performance as a nation-building practice? How might its practices interrogate and re-imagine the idea of the nation for twenty-first-century Scottish audiences? How, and to what extent, has devolution created new opportunities for Scottish theatre and performance makers?

Scotland is a small country with a population of around five and a half million. Its cultural sector is consequently relatively limited in size. In analysing their practices and outputs, I understand Scotland's theatre and performance makers—who form only one part of this sector—as a kind of 'epistemic community', a grouping defined in sociology as 'a network of professionals with recognised expertise and competence in a particular domain and an authoritative claim to policy relevant knowledge within that domain or issue area' (Haas 1992: 3). This term has its roots in Ludwik Fleck's notion of the *thought collective* developed in his book *Genesis and Development of Scientific Fact* (1935) and Michel Foucault's adaptation of the Greek term *episteme*, in *The Order of Things* (1966). The epistemic community's reliance on expert knowledge, which it validates within the group, is what differentiates it from other interest groups. I use the term to describe how theatre artists, scholars and critics have organised themselves to promote particular practices within the framework of post-devolutionary Scotland, and often to create innovative work. An obvious example of this epistemic community in action is its influencing of the model on which the new National Theatre of Scotland (NTS) was founded in 2004. In 2000, the recently elected Scottish Government committed to funding a national theatre company but refrained from specifying what form the company should take. In the following year, however, a working group set up by the Scottish Arts Council (SAC) to explore available options reached a clearer conclusion, recommending the new company be buildingless and to all intents and purposes nomadic. Crucially, the SAC working group was influenced by a report published in 2000 by the Federation for Scottish Theatre (FST) under the chairmanship of Hamish Glen, the then artistic director of the Dundee Repertory Theatre. The model for a buildingless national company was outlined in the FST report. The innovative structure of the NTS thus emerged from the Scottish theatre community itself, in what amounted to a significant influencing of cultural policy.

This book stems from a conviction that the renaissance in theatre and performance in Scotland that has marked the last several decades is worth celebrating. It would be disingenuous, however, not to acknowledge that the country's culture sector, like that of its southern counterpart, is currently 'facing a "perfect storm" of long-term budget pressures, reduced income generation, and increased operating costs' (Culture Counts, 2023). A 2021 report from the Federation of Scottish Theatre to Holyrood's Culture Committee provides more detail:

> Public funding for the arts is relatively small and in decline. Total funding for the arts in Scotland is much less than 1% of the total budget. Since 2010, funding in cash ... including Creative Scotland is expected to increase from £59M to £66M. That is real-terms cut of £8.3M, or 12.5% ... More than two-thirds of our regularly funded members received the same cash award from Creative Scotland for 2018-21 as they received for 2015-8, and for several this is the same cash amount as their grant in 2010 when Creative Scotland took over responsibility for funding. This is a real-terms cut of more than 25% in ten years and its impact on sustainability is palpable. (Scottish Parliament Committee on Culture, Tourism, Europe and External Affairs 2021)

The funding situation has not improved, although the sector has been vocal in defending itself. In early 2023 the Scottish Government announced a £6.6 million cut to Creative Scotland's budget, which was reversed after more than 15,000 people signed a Campaign for the Arts petition. However, this change of plan was always subject to confirmation in autumn budget revisions. Much to Creative Scotland's dismay, in September the government u-turned again, reinstating the cut. By this time, of course, the funding had already been allocated, and Creative Scotland was obliged to use its national Lottery reserves to plug the gap. Although in periods when the public purse is particularly under pressure it may not seem unreasonable to expect reserves to be utilised, Creative Scotland's Chief Executive Iain Munro insisted Lottery reserves were 'not intended to substitute for Scottish Government funding', and that if reduced funding levels were maintained into 2024–2025, around half of the current Regularly Funded Organisations (RFOs), 2000 jobs and nearly 3.5 million audience members would be at risk (Scottish Television News 2023).

July 2023 saw the publication of *Disappearing Act?*, a report commissioned by Scotland's six leading independent producing theatres: Citizens Theatre, Dundee Rep, Pitlochry Festival Theatre, Royal Lyceum Theatre Edinburgh, Traverse Theatre and Tron Theatre. In the absence of any 'prospect of a return to historic levels of government funding' the report recommended the adoption of a 'federal' approach and the creation of a 'new company that will support and co-produce popular shows that are expected to tour within Scotland and then go on for further commercial exploitation in other parts of the UK and internationally' (2023: 10). Without these producing theatres, it might be added, successful shows as various as *The Slab Boys* (1979), *Sunshine on Leith* (2007), *Pride and Prejudice (sort of)* (2018) and *Moorcroft* (2022) would not exist.

The report's recommendations were not universally welcomed and produced a mixed response from trade unions and other organisations. While Equity welcomed the federal approach so long as it increased opportunities for its members, a spokesperson for BECTU—the Broadcasting, Entertainment, Communications and Theatre Union—objected to the implication that 'greater casualisation and driving down costs is the way to deliver a successful venture' (BECTU, 2023). In a statement published in the *Scotsman*, the Society for Scottish Playwrights, registered its concern 'about the lack of detail surrounding the aspiration to "share resources" across companies' and confirmed that it would be working with partner unions to seek 'clarity on how this might operate, and what cuts or job losses could result' (Ferguson, 2023). What is so 'infuriating about all of this' as Joyce McMillan rightly points out, 'is that the sums involved in making the difference between a struggling and desperate theatre sector and a thriving and expanding one are so vanishingly small, in relation to overall public spending' (2023). In spite of repeated statements from the Scottish Government about the value of the arts and culture, and about the importance of projecting an image of Scotland as a confident and cultured small nation, chronic under-investment in artists and the arts continues seemingly unabated and austerity continues to be an influential discourse despite its evident failures.

Structure of the Book

Because of the importance of the final decades of the twentieth century to the dynamics of the political and cultural changes that shaped contemporary Scotland and altered its relationship with itself and the rest of the UK, I follow this introduction with a chapter that focuses on key developments in the practice, and extensions in the vocabulary, of Scottish theatre in this period. I include an account of the remarkable tenure of Giles Havergal, Philip Prowse and Robert David MacDonald as co-artistic directors of Glasgow's Citizens' Theatre which was effectively transformed under their leadership, as Michael Coveney observes, into a theatre of 'European orientation' bearing 'no relationship whatsoever to the great upheavals in British theatre since the mid-1950s' (Coveney 1990: 4). I argue that the Citizens' played a key role in the re-theatricalisation of Scottish theatre, while also demonstrating through its pricing policy that theatre is an art form of high cultural value that should be made accessible to all.

As Thatcherism began to dominate the cultural landscape, and the ideology of the market began to be applied to all aspects of cultural life, the mood of theatre workers in Scotland and across the UK became increasingly negative. Then as now, however, they also looked for and contrived creative solutions and the next section of my opening chapter turns to an example of such innovation. A key moment in this narrative, I suggest, was the 1985 season at the Traverse in Edinburgh where three plays premiered—Peter Arnott's *White Rose*, Chris Hannan's *Elizabeth Gordon Quinn*, and Jo Clifford's *Losing Venice*—that collectively challenged the orthodoxy of Scottish drama by looking outward towards other dramaturgical forms and theatre cultures, and by revising some well-established tropes. The 1980s also witnessed the emergence of a number of important female voices into what had hitherto been a male-dominated field, and I also consider their impact. Prominent among them was the poet Liz Lochhead, whose playful and imaginative use of the Scots language in combination with her feminist reworking of the traditional Scottish history play was to have lasting influence. A discussion of the mixing of foreign and native impulses in the work of the influential company Communicado, which produced Lochhead's celebrated *Mary Queen of Scots Got her Head Chopped Off* (1987) is also included, before I turn my attention to David Greig and David Harrower who came to prominence the 1990s and achieved significant presence in the international repertoire.

In the final decade of the twentieth century, the reinvention of political Europe in the aftermath of the fall of the Berlin Wall in 1989 was an important context which fed into their ongoing examination of political and cultural Scotland, providing a different worldview than that which had dominated the country in the 1980s. This shift in focus and perspective is particularly apparent in Greig's early plays which in the 1990s established him as the leading playwright of his generation. Whether writing directly about Scotland, in plays such as *Caledonia Dreaming* and *Victoria* (2000) or dealing with more cosmopolitan subject matter in *One Way Street* (1995) or *The Speculator* (1999) Greig's plays consistently explore the possibilities inherent in a bold and aspirational approach to the future and the dangers of over-reliance on the assumptions and prejudices of the past. Meanwhile, Harrower's acclaimed debut *Knives in Hens* (1996) premiered at the Traverse in Edinburgh and established him as a very distinctive voice. The chapter concludes with a discussion of Chris Hannan's *Shining Souls* (1996), which to my mind is among the most luminous and affecting Scottish play of recent decades.

With the impetus towards international engagement in mind, my third chapter considers the impact of the establishment—with Peter Brook's *Mahabharata* in 1988—of Glasgow's Tramway as a venue on the international touring circuit. While I understand Tramway as important in extending access for Scottish audiences to experimental international work, I also want to think about the strong tradition of experimental performance art in Scotland itself and the emergence of a vibrant live art scene at the Third Eye Centre, the CCA and the Arches in Glasgow. An additional aim of the chapter is to better understand the ecology that supports the development of experimental performance in Scotland. Innovative and experimental companies have become an increasingly important part of the developing theatre and performance culture of post-devolutionary Scotland, as have various festivals of live and performance art including the National Review of Live Art, Behavior, and Take me Somewhere. The chapter includes discussion of the work of several of the most significant performance companies including Suspect Culture, Gridiron, Vanishing Point and Untitled Projects, and of the Edinburgh Festivals and their place in the developing ecology of Scottish theatre.

By common consent, the most significant event in Scottish theatre in the last twenty years has been the establishment of the NTS, and the company is the focus of Chapter 4. Beginning with an explication of the campaign for its establishment and the precise circumstances that led it to be constituted in its innovative buildingless form, I consider the remarkable consensus achieved by the Scottish theatre community in lobbying for this model and in levering extra money from the new Scottish Government. Since it began producing work in 2006 the NTS has been a focal point for the epistemic community that willed it into being, and although the relationship has not been without tension, the company has largely delivered on its promise to increase opportunities for producers, artists and audiences throughout Scotland. The flexibility of the buildingless model will be considered through discussion of the company's extraordinarily successful first season, which included *Home* (2006), Anthony Neilson's *Realism* (2006) and Gregory Burke's by now legendary *Black Watch* (2006). The international success of John Tiffany's production of Burke's play will be given particular attention because it raises interesting questions about the performance of contemporary Scottish identity at home and abroad, and the persistence of a number of long-established and not entirely productive stereotypes. The chauvinism of certain aspects of this production will be contrasted, however, with the inclusive agenda of the company in its work elsewhere, both in the extensive opportunities it has offered female theatre practitioners and in the large number of small-scale and site-specific community-based projects it has produced. Taken together these projects have succeeded in reflecting and inflecting the experience of Scottish people in the communities in which they live and the NTS represents, therefore, a cultural achievement of both national and international significance.

Against the backdrop of the progressive civic nationalism that has come to dominate Scottish politics since devolution, my fifth chapter considers how theatre has both contributed to the developing notion of Scotland as a progressive polity, but also challenged and interrogated this notion. I begin by considering the NTS's extensive education, community and outreach programmes with particular focus on how they have conceptualised and problematised, boundaries and borders in post-devolutionary Scotland. I am especially interested here, in local and/or inclusive performance projects typically created in areas of the country outside the urban centres of Glasgow and Edinburgh, that engage with lived realities and histories of Scotland's diverse communities. Examples include *Five Minute Theatre* (2011), *Ignition* (2012–13) and *Granite* (2016) David Harrower's *Calum's Road* (2011) and Kieran Hurley's *Rantin* (2013). In thinking about how notions of identity and community are constructed and expanded through theatre and performance—and given its importance in developing audiences—I also give an account of Scotland's vibrant children's theatre scene, which has produced internationally acclaimed productions via companies such as Catherine Wheels and Visible Fictions. Finally, I turn my attention to work that has been conceived specifically for working-class audiences, and which purposefully continues the strong traditions of popular theatre that were established in Scotland in the twentieth century.

Chapter 6 is dedicated to the recent resurgence in Scottish playwriting, which has been accompanied by an aesthetic renewal, I argue, integrating forms drawn from feminist dramaturgies and popular modes, as well as the poetic traditions of Gaelic culture and the more overtly political and didactic traditions that animated Scottish theatre in the 1970s. Major post-devolutionary plays by established playwrights including Peter Arnott, David Greig, David Harrower, Rona Munro and Anthony Neilson are discussed alongside those of a newer group of writers especially, Zinnie Harris, but including Henry Adam, Gregory Burke, Rob Drummond, Kieran Hurley, Muireann Kelly and Morna Pearson. Scotland continues to produce and offer a home to talented theatre and performance makers, but new work whether innovative or derivative, is unlikely to emerge let alone achieve lasting influence without robust funding arrangements. In my concluding chapter, I give space to examination of the mechanisms via which Scottish theatre is currently (under)funded. My exploration of precarity in this context is developed via a case study of the NTS's lockdown project *Scenes for Survival* (2020). I also consider work that has been created in response to new and urgent imperatives including concerns about racial injustice and its histories, gender politics, artificial intelligence and the climate emergency. Scotland does not exist in a vacuum and a more robust engagement with its past and present in relation to historical and continuing injustices is most welcome.

I want to bring this introduction to a close with another example of the epistemic community of Scottish theatre in action because it is my contention that Scotland's theatre-makers will likely continue to work across boundaries and generations to create acute and imaginative responses to socio-political realities, and to the continuing funding crisis. This final section also models my approach to the material covered in this book, which where possible privileges my own subject position as a spectator, and also attempts to conjure the felt experience of theatre going. In addition, I aim to understand any given production in relation to its own political, social and creative moment, but also other moments with which it is in conversation. In this way I hope to foreground understandings of theatre as an embodied live practice which retains the potential to generate new ways of thinking about social, political and national life.

Lanark

It is the evening of 24 August 2015 and, as the city bustles around it with the sound of Edinburgh's various summer festivals, an audience at the Lyceum Theatre is contemplating a large projection of light playing on water. It might be a river, or the sea, or possibly even a very large puddle. At approximately 7 p.m. a man tumbles into frame, falling like Don Draper in the title sequence of *Mad Men*, or a suicide from a bridge. The image dissolves, and soon a figure we assume is the same man is standing on the balcony of a sleazy art-house cinema bar, in a dark, damp city where, we soon learn, the sun shines weakly for only three minutes a day. These are the opening moments of David Greig's stage adaptation of Alasdair Gray's seminal novel *Lanark: A Life in Four Books* (1981)—retitled *Lanark: A Life in Three Acts* (2015).

Even before the projection appears, the atmosphere in the theatre is charged with goodwill and expectation. This is among the major theatrical events of the year and the evening is in some ways a celebration of Gray, Scotland's favourite polymath, who is currently ill in hospital. Perhaps there is also a slight undercurrent of trepidation however, because *Lanark*, which became an instant classic at the time of its publication, is truly a mighty work of the imagination, and arguably the most influential Scottish novel of the late twentieth century. A marvel of typography complemented by the author's own illustrations, it is complex, formally experimental and nearly 600 pages long. It is fantastical, containing parallel realities. It is also idiosyncratic, famously difficult to summarise and consequently, the audience suspects, rather difficult to stage. An earlier attempt by TAG Theatre Company in 1995 had met with a mixed response (Edwards 1996: 37–38). Nonetheless, this new adaptation is highly anticipated. A co-production between the Lyceum, Glasgow's Citizens Theatre and the Edinburgh International Festival (EIF), it is additionally supported by the Scottish Government's Edinburgh Festivals Expo fund which was 'established in 2007 to help maintain the global competitive edge of the festivals, to increase funding available to Scottish-based artists and practitioners and to encourage creative collaborations'

(Scottish Government 2012). 2014's Expo funded EIF show had been Rona Munro's critically acclaimed *James Plays* trilogy for the NTS. The stakes are high, then, but the Lyceum audience has reason to be confident because an impressive creative team has been assembled around the project.

In the first place the show's writer, David Greig, is Scotland's most celebrated contemporary playwright. In addition to full-length plays such as *Europe* (1994), *The Speculator* (1999), *San Diego* (2003), *Dunsinane* (2010) *The Events* (2013) and *Two Sisters* (2024), he has written short plays, radio plays, musicals, plays with songs such as *Midsummer* (2008) and *The Strange Undoing of Prudencia Hart* (2011), and a number of adaptations including *Bacchae* (2007), *Charlie and the Chocolate Factory* (2013), *The Suppliant Women* (2016) and *Solaris* (2019). He is joined on *Lanark* by the director Graham Eatough and the composer/sound designer Nick Powell. The show thus reunites three founding members of Suspect Culture, which during its lifespan—1993 to 2009—had been Scotland's leading experimental theatre company producing intelligent, cool and widely admired shows such as *Airport* (1996), *Mainstream* (1999), *Lament* (2002) and *8000m* (2004). Also on board is designer Laura Hopkins, whose previous work in Scotland includes *Black Watch* and *Peter Pan* (2010) for the NTS, but who has also worked with Frantic Assembly and The Wooster Group. The lighting design is by Nigel Edwards, best known for his work with Forced Entertainment, and the task of rendering Gray's distinctive visual style falls to Imitating the Dog's video artist Simon Wainwright. The ensemble cast features Sandy Grierson as the eponymous hero. A performer of great physical skill, Grierson's reputation has been built substantially via his long association with the Glasgow-based performance company Vanishing Point whose work has a distinctly European flavour. The inclusion of Gerry Mulgrew, co-founder of Communicado Theatre, in the cast further emphasises the link to European ensemble traditions and Mulgrew's fatherly presence sends a further signal, if one were needed, that the production is consciously reflecting on the cultural legacy of the 1980s, the decade in which *Lanark* first appeared and in which Communicado was founded. As audience members set aside their programmes and the show begins, it seems timely to reflect on the obvious differences, and interesting parallels, between the moment of *Lanark's* original publication and the condition of Scottish theatre in 2015.

Gray's first and most famous novel took decades—from the late 1950s—to complete, but at the time of its eventual publication in 1981 Scotland was undoubtedly in the doldrums, suffering from the combined effects of the election of the Thatcher Government in May 1979 and the irresolute outcome of the referendum on Scottish devolution in the same year. The Scotland Act of 1978 allowed for a referendum on the establishment of a Scottish Assembly, but an amendment stipulated that more than 40% of the total registered electorate would need to approve the proposal, as well as the usual 50% + 1. In the event, 51.6% supported the proposal, but with a turnout of 64%, this represented only 32.9% of the registered electorate. The Act was subsequently repealed.

In Scotland, some feared these failures would leave artists condemned to describing a dwindling amnesiac culture, a kind of second-hand nationhood defined by neurosis, defeatism and inadequacy. The challenge for novelists and playwrights was to find ways of creating new stories to live by: of narrating a more self-confident nation into being. Against this backdrop, Gray's enormously iconoclastic, playfully allusive and deliberately subversive book had an immediately invigorating effect. *Lanark* is a composite of four books in which a realist narrative (books one and two) is juxtaposed with a fantasy one (books three and four) in the order 3,1,2,4, which disrupts any sense of linear time. Unfolding against a bleak post-war backdrop, the semi-autobiographical realist sections follow the awkward, sensitive and asthmatic working-class artist Duncan Thaw as he grows up in Glasgow's relentlessly grim east end, suffers countless petty agonies, sexual frustrations and injustices, attends art school, and struggles to find meaning in life. Marked by disillusionment and frustration, this narrative climaxes with Thaw's suicide by drowning. The fantasy sections unfold in a kind of apocalyptic near future in the parallel city of Unthank. Here, marooned with no memory of his former existence, Thaw recasts himself as Lanark and attempts to escape from a deeply strange, dystopian and often frightening city that is constantly on the brink of social and environmental collapse. Unthank's inhabitants suffer from strange medical conditions and disappear without warning. Lanark himself struggles to remain human and finds parts of his body becoming scaly and 'dragonish' (Fig. 1.1).

Like the novel on which it is based, Greig's play complicates matters by beginning with Lanark's arrival in Unthank. Titled 'Act Two' this section is followed by 'Act One' in which Thaw's life story in post-war Glasgow is narrated more or less chronologically. The evening ends with a return

Fig. 1.1 Sandy Grierson and Jessica Hardwick in David Greig's *Lanark* (directed by Graham Eatough, Royal Lyceum Edinburgh, 2015) reproduced with kind permission from Eoin Carey

to Unthank in 'Act Three' where Lanark is cast as the unlikely saviour of the city. An interlude titled 'Curtain Call' is inserted between acts one and three echoing Gray's use of an 'epilogue' in the middle of Book Four of the novel. In each case the realist episode is sandwiched between Unthank sections and is thus effectively enfolded in allegory. The audience is invited to draw comparisons between the hellish world of Unthank and the decaying landscape of post-industrial Glasgow. In this sense, the show, like the novel, is about the transformative power of the imagination. It is also about the transformative potential of art. When asked by his father what he intends to do with his life the teenage Thaw answers, 'I want to compose a modern *Divine Comedy* and illustrate it with drawings in the style of William Blake' (Greig 2015: 106). This statement is met with laughter, and is tinged with irony, of course, because Duncan's grand ambitions lead to little more than abject failure and suicide. His single attempt at a major artwork, the decoration of a church ceiling, is never completed and the church is later demolished. The achievement of Gray's book, however, is to come much closer to reaching Thaw's goal, and moreover, to inspire others to undertake similarly ambitious projects. As Greig and Eatough note in their forward to the published play text, this 'in the end, is the gift Alasdair gave us: he forced us to try the impossible' (Greig 2015: 6).

Since its publication *Lanark* has been read by many Scottish artists as a kind of call to arms. Rejecting, or at least complicating, prevailing realist, romantic and sentimental models, *Lanark* presents a vision of Scotland that is fragmented, alienated, in crisis, urban and decidedly non-essentialist. Writers as diverse as Iain Banks, A L Kennedy, Ali Smith, Alan Warner and Irvine Welsh have cited it as a major influence. This inspirational aspect of the book seems a deliberate strategy. In one passage in particular Gray appears to be entreating Glasgow's artists to imagine their city into being:

> "Glasgow is a magnificent city," said McAlpin. "Why do we hardly ever notice that?" "Because nobody imagines living here," said Thaw... "Think of Florence, Paris, London, New York. Nobody visiting them for the first time is a stranger because he's already visited them in paintings, novels, history books and films. But if a city hasn't been used by an artist, not even the inhabitants live there imaginatively. (Gray 1981: 243)

What Thaw is describing here is an unarticulated city awaiting an arts practice that will allow its inhabitants to see themselves. In the decades following the publication of the novel this aspiration was extended to cover Scotland as a whole and was also contained in Gray's motto—paraphrased from the Canadian poet Denis Lee—'work as if you live in the early days of a better nation'. Gray—who died in 2019—may have been audacious, deluded even, in his hope of making life follow art, but a measure of the success of his idea in the political realm is that the phrase was one of several inscribed on the Canongate Wall of the new Scottish Parliament building in 2004. In the period between 1979 and the successful referendum on devolution in 1997, it became commonplace for Scottish critics to assert that 'in the absence of an elected political authority the task of representing the nation' was 'repeatedly devolved' to its artists (Whyte 1998: 284).

Back in the Lyceum theatre, around four hours after tumbling into the frame, Sandy Grierson, who we might recall is playing both Lanark and Duncan Thaw (whom we now know to be versions of the same person) stages a wilful rebellion. He loses his line, is prompted, loses it again and is eventually handed the script by the stage manager. The technicians are perplexed. Grierson seems surprised to find that he is the lead character in the play 'about politics, and philosophy and morality and Scotland' (191). He flicks forward through the play text:

Lanark	What happens?
Monboddo	What do you mean?
Lanark	What happens to me in the end?
Keith Troy	You die.
Lanark	What happens to Unthank?
Eric Viper	Unthank is destroyed.
Sheila Poots	It's a tragedy.
Kate Whizz	In the theatrical sense.
Eric Viper	You're a tragic hero.
Sheila Poots	You have a deep inner flaw which stops you from achieving your ends. In your case your inability to be happy stops you finding love.
Lanark	I don't find love?!
Sheila Poots	No.
Lanark	After all this I don't find love? ...
	A moment
Lanark	I demand to speak to the writer! (191)

During this sequence, the audience's reaction moves from confusion and embarrassment through knowing chuckles to uproarious laughter as a productively liminal space is created by Greig and his collaborators. At this moment the boundaries between book and play, actor and role, stage and auditorium, onstage and off, reality and illusion become decidedly blurred.

When told his request to meet the author is 'physically impossible' Lanark '*grabs the book*' and writes in it: 'Lanark leaves the author's head. Lanark meets the author' (192). He then returns the book to the stage manager and:

Everything goes dark.
A long weird moment.
Suddenly eyes open on stage.
Breathing.

> *We are inside a head.*
> *The eyes open and look at a painting.*
> *They look around a studio.*
> *Lanark sits in a chair.*
> Lanark   Mr Gray?
> *Head nods.* (192)

Unsurprisingly Lanark is unable to convince Gray that a conventionally happy ending would improve the play. The author insists death 'is the best ending' because without 'death even love turns slowly into farce' (195). Lanark is allowed one small success, though. He is particularly unhappy about the removal, in the stage adaptation, of a dream sequence from late in the novel in which he goes hillwalking with his son Alexander. He is told this scene was cut because it was too sentimental but responds by tearing out the pages from the novel and handing them to the stage manager. Despite further protestations he insists on playing it: 'This is an adaptation, isn't it? ... adapt!' (196). The resulting scene is very beautiful and very moving.

This sequence in all its complexity demonstrates how performance can challenge perception, and complicate understanding of the relationships between fiction, the self and the world. In this sense it calls to mind Laura Cull Ó Maoilearca's notion that performance does not merely submit itself to philosophical analysis but can constitute 'its own kind of thinking' (2012: 3). It also draws our attention to the affective capabilities of contemporary scenographic practices. Wainwright's video design is central to the effectiveness of the inside-of-his-head moment. In drawing all of these elements together the production aligns itself with current trends in contemporary theatre practice, of course, but its epic scope, and the consequent magnification of theatre's signifying possibilities, resists the possibility of a critical reductionism that would delimit it as merely a Scottish show about the state of Scotland. Instead, from a distinctly Scottish perspective, *Lanark* asks questions of broad significance—about hope and despondency, consumerism and alienation, art and technology, localism and environmentalism, for instance—and can thus be understood as interrogating some of the contradictions and limitations that continue to haunt Western culture. It can certainly be understood as a major Scottish artwork the creation of which relied on the drawing together of expertise, validated in the Scottish theatre sector over the last several decades, and consequently the work of a functioning epistemic community.

Lanark: A Life in Three Acts was widely praised for its ambition and the confidence of its execution. For Joyce McMillan the production was 'wholly at one with the bold, mysterious and infinitely searching spirit of Gray's novel', for instance, while Alex Eades pronounced it 'wildly surreal and beautifully executed' (McMillan 2015; Eades 2015). The programming of the show in the 2015 EIF alongside two other Scottish co-productions—*Paul Bright's Confessions of a Justified Sinner* (Untitled Projects and NTS) and *Dragon* (NTS, Vox Motus and Tianjin Children's Art Theatre)—also tells us something about how Scottish theatre was made in 2015 and the confidence with which it was promoted. Not too long ago the single space allocated to Scottish production in the EIF programme was known apocryphally, as the 'death slot'. The moment also problematises the EIF's reputation, perhaps only partly deserved, for being 'derogatory in its treatment of Scottish culture and elitist in its implicit validation of certain arts over others' (Harvie 2003: 12). *Dragon* was, after all, a children's show.

In the closing moments of *Lanark: A Life in Three Acts*, a Chamberlain, dressed in '*full costume, with a tricorn hat, wig and cane*' arrives carrying a red velvet cushion on which is placed a small scroll (204). 'Dear Lanark' the scroll reads, 'in exactly four minutes time you will die' (ibid.). Lanark accepts this news stoically, other than to note that he 'ought to have had more love' (205). 'That' responds the Chamberlain 'is everyone's complaint' (ibid.). Lanark is ready. He wishes us 'Goodbye', dawn breaks. The stage direction reads, '*The sun. Brightness. Whiteout.* GOODBYE' (205).

This image of hope and its accompanying promise of renewal recurs in a variety of forms in Gray's book. It is symbolic of a small nation that has in the past few decades become increasingly forward focused. In the course of this study, I draw on contemporary scholarship in the field of theatre and identity politics to examine significant developments and interventions in Scottish theatre, and to show that it has been remarkably responsive to, and resonant with, important shifts in Scotland's wider cultural landscape. My aim is to chart the processes—institutional, artistic, cultural and economic—through which Scottish theatre has expanded its own performance vocabularies while simultaneously coming to prominence in national and international contexts. It is largely, if not exclusively, a story of success.

References

Balibar, Etienne (2004) *We the People of Europe? Reflections on Transnational Citizenship*. Princeton, N.J., Princeton University Press.

BECTU (2023) Available at: https://bectu.org.uk/news/bectu-responds-to-report-into-future-of-scotlands-producing-theatre-sector

Brown, Ian (2016) *History as Theatrical Metaphor: History, Myth and National Identities in Modern Scottish Drama*. Basingstoke, Palgrave Macmillan.

Brown, Mark (2019) *Modernism and Scottish Theatre Since 1969: A Revolution on Stage*. Cham, Switzerland, Palgrave Macmillan.

Coveney, Michael (1990) *The Citz: 21 Years of the Glasgow Citizens Theatre*. London, Nick Hern Books.

Cull, Laura (2012) *Theatres of Immanence: Deleuze and the Ethics of Performance*. Basingstoke, Palgrave Macmillan.

Culture Counts (2023) 'Response to the Constitution, Europe, External Affairs and Culture Committee's Scrutiny of the Scottish Government's Culture Budget for 2024–25'. Available at: https://www.parliament.scot/-/media/files/committees/constitution-europe-external-affairs-and-culture-committee/correspondence/2023/54-culture-counts.pdf

Disappearing Act? (2023) 'A Data-Led Review and Recommendations for Urgent Actions to Safeguard a Credible Producing Theatre in Scotland'. Available at: https://img1.wsimg.com/blobby/go/367c61ea-5574-4c59-b292-eff50683746b/Disappearing%20Act%20report%20final%20published.pdf

Dudley Edwards, Owen (1996) 'Cradle on the Tree-Top', in Randall Stevenson and Gavin Wallace (eds.) *Scottish Theatre Since the Seventies*. Edinburgh, Edinburgh University Press, pp. 34–48.

Eades, Alex (2015) 'Lanark'. *The List*, 24 August.

Ferguson, Brian (2023) 'Unions Accuse "Big Six" Venues of Putting Jobs at Risk and Endangering Future of Scottish Theatre'. *Scotsman*, 1 August.

Findlay, Richard (2004) *Modern Scotland: 1914–2000*. London, Profile Books.

Fisher, Mark (1997) 'Enter the Connery Factor'. *Herald*, 3 June.

Gray, Alasdair (1981) *Lanark: A Life in Four Books*. Edinburgh, Canongate.

Greig, David (1997) *Caledonia Dreaming*. Unpublished Rehearsal Script.

Greig, David (2015) *Lanark: A Life in Three Acts*. London, Faber and Faber.

Greig, David and David Harrower (1997) 'Why a New Scotland Must Have a Properly Funded Theatre', *Scotsman*, 25 November.

Haas, Peter (1992) 'Introduction: Epistemic Communities and International Policy Coordination', in *International Organization*, 46:1, pp. 1–35.

Hames, Scott (2020) *The Literary Politics of Scottish Devolution: Voce, Class, Nation*. Edinburgh, Edinburgh University Press.

Harvie, Jen (2003) 'Cultural Effects of the Edinburgh International Festival: Elitism, Identities, Industries'. *Contemporary Theatre Review*, 13:4, pp. 12–26.
Howard, Philip (2016) (ed.) *Theatre in Scotland: A Field of Dreams: Reviews by Joyce McMillan*. London, Nick Hern Books.
Lehmann, Hans-Thies (2006) *Postdramatic Theatre*. Translated by Karen Jürs-Munby. London, Routledge.
McCrone, David (2001) *Understanding Scotland: The Sociology of a Nation*. Second edition. Edinburgh, Edinburgh University Press.
McCrone, David (2005) 'Cultural Capital in an Understated Nation: The Case of Scotland'. *British Journal of Sociology*, 56:1, pp. 65–82.
McMillan, Joyce (2015) 'EIF Theatre Review: Lanark'. *Scotsman*, 25 August.
McMillan, Joyce (2023) 'Cult of Austerity Is Endangering the Future of Vital Scottish Theatre Companies and Damaging the Fabric of British Life'. *Scotsman*, 4 August.
Pattie, David (2013) '"Who's Scotland?": David Greig, Identity and Scottish Nationhood', in Wallace, Clare (ed.) *The Theatre of David Greig*. London, Bloomsbury, pp. 194–210.
Reinelt, Janelle (2015) 'Performance at the Crossroads of Citizenship,' in Janelle Reinelt and Shirin Rai (eds.) *The Grammar of Politics and Performance*. London, Routledge, pp. 34–50.
Ryan, Ray (2002) *Ireland and Scotland: Literature and Culture, State and Nation 1966–2000*. Oxford, Oxford University Press.
Scottish Government (2012) 'Edinburgh Festivals Expo Fund'. Available at: http://www.gov.scot/Topics/ArtsCultureSport/arts/Key-projects/EdinburghFestivalsExpoFund
Scottish Parliament Committee on Culture, Tourism, Europe and External Affairs (2021) 'Submission for Federation of Scottish Theatre'. Available at: https://archive2021.parliament.scot/S5_European/Inquiries/CTEEA_S5_19_AF_11.pdf
Scullion, Adrienne (2001) 'Self and Nation: Issues of Identity in Modern Scottish Drama by Women', *New Theatre Quarterly*, 17:4, pp. 373–390.
Smith, Alexander (2011) *Devolution and the Scottish Conservatives: Banal Activism, Electioneering and the Politics of Irrelevance*. Manchester, Manchester University Press.
Scottish Television News (2023) 'Arts Groups "Extremely Disappointed" After £6.6m Funding cut U-Turn'. 29 September. Available at: https://news.stv.tv/scotland/creative-scotland-extremely-disappointed-after-governments-6-6m-funding-u-turn
Wallace, Clare (2013) *The Theatre of David Greig*. London, Bloomsbury.
Whyte, Christopher (1998) 'Masculinities in Contemporary Scottish Fiction'. *Forum for Modern Language Studies*, 34.2, pp. 274–285.

Zenzinger, Peter (1996) 'The New Wave', in Stevenson and Wallace (eds.) *Scottish Theatre Since the Seventies*. Edinburgh, Edinburgh University Press, pp. 125–137.

CHAPTER 2

Key Contexts

Before embarking on an analysis of theatre in post-devolutionary Scotland, it is useful to look back over earlier decades at the practices and preoccupations that laid the groundwork for the rapid diversification that has characterised the sector in the twenty-first century. Scottish theatre looks quite different today than it did forty years ago. Writing in 1996, Randall Stevenson noted the extent to which 'specifically Scottish issues – *differentia* of language, history, life – greatly [had] contributed to the growth of Scottish drama in the 1970s', but also that the conditions in which that drama had flourished had since been quite drastically altered (Stevenson 1996: 17). In the 1970s playwrights including Bill Bryden, Donald Campbell, Stewart Conn, Hector MacMillan and Roddy McMillan experimented productively with varieties of contemporary vernacular Scots but did so largely, if not exclusively, within a realist and leftist paradigm. This trend is exemplified in works such as Bryden's *Willie Rough* (1972), McMillan's *The Bevellers* (1973) and Tom McGrath and Jimmy Boyle's *The Hard Man* (1977), all of which drew their energy from the creative use of working-class Scots while retaining a focus on masculine concerns. As Ian Brown has noted, the discourse of Scottish playwriting in the 1970s was dominated by 'the male, the heterosexual, the central belt, the urban and the industrialised' (Brown 2007: 287). Thought of in this context John McGrath's *The Cheviot, the Stag and the Black, Black Oil* (1973)—with its Highland setting, and its 'assembly of

© The Author(s), under exclusive license to Springer Nature Switzerland AG 2024
T. Reid, *Theatre and Performance in Contemporary Scotland*, https://doi.org/10.1007/978-3-031-61191-9_2

songs, stories, scenes, talk, music and general entertainment'—although widely held to be the key Scottish play of the decade was, formally at least, the exception rather than the rule (McGrath 1981: x) That said, the years immediately leading up to and following the disappointment of the referendum on devolution in March 1979 and the election of the Thatcher government in May of the same year fed into a shift in the focus and vocabulary of Scottish playwriting as the new decade arrived.

A number of factors contributed to this expansion. The extraordinary linguistic confidence and comic inventiveness of John Byrne's demotic Scots in his *Slab Boys Trilogy* (1978, 1979 and 1982), was to have an enormous impact, for instance, as was the emergence of a number of female playwrights, including Marcella Evaristi, Sue Glover, Liz Lochhead and Rona Munro, who experimented with a wider range of dramaturgical strategies. In Munro's *Fugue* (1982), for example, the central character Kay's split personality is externalised as two actresses compete for control of her psyche. Munro's dramaturgy thus implicitly questions the efficacy of realism as a mode for representing female experience. The establishment of Glasgow's Tramway as an international stage with Peter Brook's *Mahabharata* in 1988 was also among the developments that contributed to the internationalisation of Scottish theatre.

The background against which Scottish theatre developed in the 1980s was Thatcherism, of course, and while this book seeks to identify and examine those aspects of Scottish theatre that make it distinctive, it would be disingenuous to imply that Scottish theatre workers were alone in experiencing the 1980s as hostile to their aspirations. Throughout the decade, across the UK, the sector was subjected to a series of rhetorical, economic and political pressures that were almost entirely perceived by the arts community as a low-brow attack by a hostile government. Consequently, the language of theatre workers in the 1980s became one of crisis, expressed both as a strong sense of dissatisfaction with the present and, as Jane Milling notes, as nostalgia 'for the lost radical left-wing alternative theatre of the 1970s' (2012: 33). Even though, as Milling has shown, the funding situation was not quite as bleak as this rhetoric implies, a reading of subsidised British theatre in the 1980s as under perpetual attack and distorted by a continuous assault on its core values, nevertheless achieved a kind of orthodoxy. By 1994, Baz Kershaw was arguing that 'British subsidized theatre in the 1980s, in common with other cultural institutions, was subject to massive pressures which aimed to make it more market and consumer oriented' (1994: 156). Similarly,

Elaine Aston observed that from the perspective of 'many feminist practitioners, the economic squeeze on political theatre in the 1980s was in part responsible for the displacement of issue based, political theatre and the rise of a theatre which prioritised style over (political) content' (1999: 14).

The 1980s certainly witnessed the introduction of a language of 'value for money' in arts funding, a rhetoric which had been largely absent since the establishment of the Arts Council of Great Britain in 1946. Perhaps more worryingly, as Milling also notes, the Conservative government signalled its willingness to politicise arts appointments in 1981 by forcing Richard Hoggart out of his role as Vice Chairman of the Arts Council (2012: 38). Although never explicitly party political, Hoggart had co-founded the Centre for Contemporary Cultural Studies at Birmingham in 1964 and had been identified with the Left throughout his career. Subsequently, funding bodies began to speak of 'investment' rather than 'subsidy', to express instrumentalist as opposed to essentialist views about the way theatre should function in society, and in general terms to engineer, or attempt to engineer, a transfer of power in the arts from producers to consumers. The high Tory former editor of *The Times*, William Rees-Mogg, was appointed Chairman of the Arts Council in 1982 and continued to argue this position throughout his tenure. By 1988, he was openly playing a populist hand.

> We are coming to value the consumer's judgement as highly as that of the official or expert ... The voice of the public must ... be given due weight ... [and] the way in which the public discriminates is through its willingness to pay for its pleasure. (Arts Council of Great Britain 1988: 2–3)

In Scotland, debates around funding for the arts were complicated by a growing perception that England was on a different political path. As Donald Smith notes, the impact of 'the new Arts Council emphasis on management, marketing, sponsorship and self-earned income' was somewhat eased in Scotland 'by local authorities coming to support the cause of improved theatre facilities' (Smith, 1998: 293). Between 1980 and 1992 new theatres were built at Pitlochry and Dundee; Glasgow Citizens, the Royal Lyceum and Perth Rep were refurbished; large receiving houses including Her Majesty's in Aberdeen and the King's in Edinburgh were upgraded; and new spaces were developed at Tramway, The Arches and the Tron in Glasgow and at Edinburgh's relocated Traverse.

For better or worse, a growing awareness of a political gap between Scotland and England, which persists to the present day, quickly manifested as a sense of cultural superiority. Richard Weight explains:

> The more the English revelled in the benefits of Conservative rule, the more the Scots and Welsh saw them as a nation of callous, selfish individuals. In contrast they saw themselves as people with a unique sense of community and compassion; a belief which the nationalist parties encouraged. (2002: 589)

Despite the consensus that quickly emerged in opposition to Thatcherism, however, Scottish theatre-makers, and artists of other kinds, did not respond in ways that could be described as uniform or predictable. On the contrary, the decade was marked by remarkable diversity and richness in cultural output as energies that were denied appropriate expression in the political domain transferred into the field of arts and culture. Paradoxically, as Cairns Craig concluded towards the end of the decade, 'instead of political defeat leading to quiescence, it led to an explosion of cultural creativity' (Craig 1989: 5). The decade witnessed the consolidation of important literary figures such as Liz Lochhead and Edwin Morgan, as well as the emergence of a new avant-garde of Scottish novelists, most notably Iain Banks who debuted with *The Wasp Factory* (1984), and the mighty James Kelman whose *Bus Conductor Hines* (1984) and *A Chancer* (1985) brought a very distinctive Glaswegian realism to the fore. As noted in the introduction to this study, another revival, that of a kind of fantastic gothic romance, was pioneered by the publication of Alasdair Gray's *Lanark* (1981) and so a 'return to magic', as Douglas Gifford puts it, was offered in parallel with realism (Gifford 1996: 17). Alongside the Scottish novel, the theatre quickly developed as a vibrant and unruly vehicle for Scottish self-representation. As Scotland's opposition to the core values of Thatcherism solidified, theatre-makers began to deal increasingly with issues of marginalisation and disenfranchisement. Richard Todd stresses 'the compelling connection between the remarkable efflorescence of indigenous cultural activity that began to take place in 1980s Scotland and a crisis arising out of an almost desperate response to external political events' (Todd 1996: 134).

The aim of this chapter is to provide a selective overview of the aesthetic responses employed by Scottish theatre-makers in the 1980s and 90s in order to better understand how these trends fed into the revival that was to follow. The emergence of a more confident and experimental performance culture in these decades is also part of Scotland's story and will be discussed more fully in the next chapter, but for now, I want to concentrate on theatre. As stated in the introduction to this book, because of the limitations of space, my account cannot hope to be comprehensive and inevitably a significant number of important plays, playwrights and productions are not mentioned here. This is unavoidable. The work I touch on can be identified as enabling an expansion in the vocabulary of Scottish theatre and consequently as influencing the generation of Scottish theatre-makers that emerged and came to maturity in the new century. I want to begin with a discussion of the remarkable and arguably unique mixing of foreign and native impulses among the Glasgow Citizens.

THE CITZ

From 1969, under the co-artistic directorship of Giles Havergal, the designer/director Philip Prowse, and later the playwright/translator Robert David MacDonald, Glasgow's Citizens Theatre—hereafter the Citz—developed a strikingly visual style, which loudly proclaimed *mis-en-scène* as an art form, and typically gave more weight to directorial and design choices than dramatic text. Although their seat pricing policy remained radically inclusive, and they ran immensely popular annual Christmas shows, the joint artistic directors disdained overtly political theatre of the kind favoured by many theatre practitioners in the 1970s. Indeed, throughout its remarkable tenure, which lasted until 2003, the triumvirate did little to disguise its distaste for what it considered the moribund English text-bound tradition.

The Citz company presented a repertoire unlike any other in the UK in which European dramatists, including Brecht, Büchner, Dürrenmatt, Genet, Goethe, Gogol, Goldoni, Ibsen, Schniztler, Sartre, Pirandello and Racine, featured heavily. The theatre also offered English and Irish plays. 'Jacobean plays and the work of Noel Coward … enjoyed particular prominence' as David Hutchison has noted, as did Oscar Wilde and George Bernard Shaw (Hutchinson 1996a: 59). The pronounced internationalism of the Citizens' aesthetic project, which was both confrontational and sexy, and its distinctively daring and cerebral dramaturgical policy, were exemplified in productions of Shakespeare's *Hamlet* (1970), *Anthony and Cleopatra* (1972) and *Troilus and Cressida* (1973). Adrienne Scullion sketches some of the detail:

> Elsinore stripped back to an essential black-box set with actors in black loincloths and short cloaks; and angry, youthful prince; A player King with undertones of paedophilia ... A heady 'ethnic' drumbeat underscoring an equatorial location; a male actor as a dangerous and forbidden Cleopatra. A louche Achilles lying provocatively with Patroclus under the knowing gaze of a semi-naked Helen. (2004: 172)

The programme for *Hamlet* also signalled the dawn of a new era. Foregrounding the centrality of the ensemble to the new aesthetic, the acting company was listed in alphabetical order with no roles assigned, and actors not performing in *Hamlet* but elsewhere in the season were included. This kind of unconventional detail helped establish the Citz as a bold and innovative ensemble. Using England's most celebrated and canonical playwright to challenge expectations about 'what it might mean to make new work in a Victorian popular repertory theatre located in one of the most deprived areas of Scotland's decaying industrial heartland' (Scullion 2004: 184).

In the event, the critical response to *Hamlet* firmly established the production, and the theatre, as a *cause célèbre*. Writing in the *Scottish Daily Express*, Mamie Crichton, described it as a production of 'unbelievable ineptitude' (Crichton 1970). *The Scotsman's* Allen Wright launched the first of his many attacks on the Citz in a column, rather remarkably, published in full on the front page of the paper:

> Hamlet is presented as the village idiot in Giles Havergal's grotesque production ... the Prince of Denmark is reduced to a jabbering oaf, squealing and prancing like an animal and snorting at the king. It is a hideous spectacle ... Watching this travesty, I wished that someone would have the decency to bring down the curtain before any more wounds were inflicted on a work of art ... Ophelia and Gertrude are played by men — as 'drag queens', howling and sobbing with anguish. Hamlet also seems to luxuriate in grief, as if it were some form of sexual ecstasy ... Perhaps the crudeness of it all is summed up in the fight ... cudgels are used instead of rapiers. (Wright 1970)

Rather than threatening Havergal's position however, the furore in the press and in the City Council, the cancellation of school booking and a general atmosphere of fevered outrage, worked to secure the production's legendary status. In his customary self-deprecatory mode, Havergal later expressed 'regrets that the production was not half as flamboyantly outrageous as the reviews suggested' (Coveney 1990: 41).

What the Citz did not offer was a platform for indigenous new work. With the exception of its house dramatist MacDonald, who was born in Elgin into a well-established Scottish business family, the theatre ignored Scottish writers, a policy which provoked no little resentment. As Hutchison notes, this policy 'angered many Scottish writers, and led to an antagonism between them and the theatre' that took decades to really dissipate (1996a: 61). Once the big idea of an adventure in European classics had taken hold, any new Scottish play of merit submitted for consideration was passed over. Coveney tells us, for instance, that after acknowledging receipt of John Byrne's *The Slab Boys* (1978), Havergal passed it on 'without too much dithering ... to the Traverse in Edinburgh' (Coveney 1990: 63).

Nonetheless, among Scottish theatres, the Citizens was unique and influential not only in its choice of repertoire but also in its approach to that repertoire. MacDonald, who produced more than seventy translations in his time at the theatre and is rightly considered the outstanding translator of his generation, saw his work as contributing only one element:

> In a theatrical climate which regards the writer as the absolute vessel of truth and the text as being the revealed Word of God delivered on Sinai – the writer has got to realize that he is absolutely only an equal part of an enterprise where all parts are equal, with the exception of the actors and audience who must of course be paramount since without them there is no performance. (MacDonald 1990: 60)

As MacDonald points out later in the same interview, the Citz was doing 'auteur theatre' at a time when everyone else was 'doing "author's" theatre' (ibid.). Soon, the radical reworking of texts and the brilliance of Prowse's stage designs were to become the company's signature, and this fact, every bit as much as the choice of repertoire, places the theatre firmly in a European tradition. *Decadence* is perhaps the word most often used to describe the production style in the 1970s and 80s—it features regularly and appreciatively in Coveney's account, for instance, his chapter on the 1970s is subtitled 'divine distractions of decadence'—but this emphasis risks obscuring the fact that what Havergal, MacDonald and Prowse really brought to the fore was a kind of theatrical authorship that was not literature- but performance-oriented (Coveney 1990: v). Such an approach was extremely unusual in the context of post-war British theatre where investment had been focused on theatre buildings rather than companies and where, as Christopher Innes has observed, the growth of Drama in schools, universities and community contexts had led to theatre becoming 'part of the educational establishment' and consequently to an engrained privileging of text over performance (Innes 1997: 382). Thought of in these terms the work of the Citizens triumvirate was a key contributor to the re-theatricalisation of Scottish theatre. It also offered a welcome and necessary counterbalance to the masculinist and realist bias that had dominated Scottish stages in the 1970s.

The privileging of scenic effect that was central to the Citz house style brought it into line with developing postmodern theatre practice in Europe and the US. It offered Glasgow access to a classical European repertoire, then, but also to a daring and iconoclastic approach to theatre. In 2003, Havergal was honoured at the inaugural Critics Awards for Theatre in Scotland (CATS), 'for his immeasurable contribution to theatre in Scotland over the 34 years in which he has been director of the Glasgow Citizens' (Critics Awards for Theatre in Scotland 2003). In the context of post-devolutionary theatre practice, we can note the prevalence of work that owes a debt to high camp tradition of the Citz—this might include for instance David Greig's adaptation of Euripides *The Bacchae* (NTS 2007), which featured Alan Cumming clad in gold lame kilt in the role of Dionysus—and a preference for European stylistics, especially those inspired by Brecht who was a mainstay of the Citz repertoire. During the 1970s and 80s the Citz staged more productions of Brecht than any other UK theatre, culminating 'in 1990 in their production of *Mother Courage*, featuring Glenda Jackson in the title role, which opened in Glasgow in May and transferred to London in July' (Eddershaw 1991: 303).

Traverse 85

Approximately forty-five miles to the east of the Citz, Scotland's pre-eminent new writing theatre, Edinburgh's Traverse, was also busy expanding its vocabulary. This was especially the case in the 1980s as the political situation deteriorated, certainly from a Scottish perspective. Thatcher's government, bolstered by success in the Falkland's Conflict of 1982, was re-elected by a landslide in 1983. In March 1985, the end of the Miner's Strike marked a significant weakening of the Trade Union movement. The Westminster government resisted international pressure to impose sanctions on South Africa's apartheid regime. In light of these events, and others, it seems no coincidence that in a number of major new Scottish plays of the period, the action unfolds against a backdrop of political unrest and war. In the early part of the decade, under the artistic directorship of Peter Lichtenfels, the Traverse had suffered, both from a funding squeeze and also a number of attacks on its reputation and by the end of 1983 'there were explicit indications from Bob Palmer, the Drama Director' that the Scottish Arts Council 'no longer wished to fund the Traverse in its present expensive form' (McMillan 1988: 91). All was not lost, however. In early 1983 the young director Jenny Killick arrived at the Traverse as a trainee. She was twenty-three years old.

Under the mentorship of Lichtenfels, Killick became instrumental in developing relationships with a new generation of Scottish playwrights who shared her vision for an expansive, politically engaged, and theatrically bold repertoire, a theatre that would make a virtue of its liveness and feature 'no sofas and no sinks' (*The Traverse Theatre at 50* 2013). By 1985 Killick was effectively operating in partnership with Lichtenfels as co-artistic director of the theatre. This was to prove a particularly productive year. As Adrienne Scullion observes:

> During the 1985 'Points of Departure' season at the Traverse Theatre a new generation of writers ... burst onto the scene with plays of unexpected eclecticism, robust politics and robust internationalism. (Scullion 2007: 71).

Three of the plays discussed below premiered in this season. Each, as Jan McDonald has noted, went on to be 'performed outside Scotland' providing commentators with welcome evidence that 'Scottish theatre was now gaining an international status' (McDonald 2004: 220). The plays also signalled a shift in the focus of Scottish playwriting. Both Peter Arnott's *White Rose* and Jo Clifford's *Losing Venice* are history plays that deal with events outside Scotland, for instance, and in *Elizabeth Gordon Quinn* Chris Hannan refigures the traditional tenement play for a new generation. All three Traverse playwrights were working against a backdrop of political unrest and from a cultural perspective of ever-increasing marginalisation and disenfranchisement. The trauma of Scotland's political situation found expression in a series of plays that took as their central characters individuals who had lost or developed a false sense of their own identity. Moreover, in these plays, the close focus on the detail of Scottish life, history and language, that had animated the drama in the 1970s and early 80s began to give way to larger political and social themes explored through allegory, parable and satire.

Peter Arnott continues to be a force in Scottish theatre. His 2017 adaptation of Compton Mackenzie's *The Monarch of the Glen* for Pitlochry Festival Theatre won Best New Play at the CATS in 2018, and his short play *The Signalman* (2019), won in the same category in 2020. *White Rose* opened at the Traverse Studio on 22 May 1985, Arnott having been commissioned to write a studio play for three actors. He drew for subject matter on his combined interest in WW2 and female activism. 1985 marked the fiftieth anniversary of the end of the war in Europe, the women's peace camp at Greenham Common was in the news and women had played a prominent role during the Miner's Strike. All of this led Arnott not to a Scottish story, but to Lily Litvak, the White Rose of Stalingrad. The daughter of a Jewish civil servant who fell victim to one of Stalin's notorious purges, Litvak was the first female Red Army pilot to shoot down an enemy plane. She flew as part of a fighter squadron until her death in action in 1943.

White Rose has three principal characters, Litvak, her engineer Ina Pasportnikova and Alexei Salomaten, a fellow pilot with whom Lily becomes romantically involved. Its narrative—a familiar tragic tale of love and loss in wartime Europe—is straightforward enough. Lily and Alexei are both killed in the line of duty. Arnott has objectives beyond those typical of a love story, however, and he employs a number of recognisably Brechtian tropes—newsreel footage, multiple role playing, historical distance—to interrogate what Steve Cramer has described as 'the media's capacity to render narratives of stark, mechanised mass destruction into romanticised human-interest stories' (Cramer 2011: 167). To this end, Arnott follows his central character as she attempts to transcend the apocalyptic tragedy that is the Eastern Front by virtue of a kind of exceptionalism related to her heightened status as a pilot, and more poignantly her love for Alexei, whom she agrees to marry but only when it is too late. Throughout, Arnott also makes effective use of flying in particular, and technological advance in general, as metaphors for disengagement and ideological complacency. Far from enabling them to see the world more clearly, Lily and Alexei's technical expertise allows them to see it from a distance, 'from up there ... where it looks like a map ... with clear directions and targets of opportunity' (Arnott 1985: 49). Growing mistrust in authority and in exceptionalist narratives is primarily figured through the character of Ina, the engineer, whose feet remain literally and figuratively on the ground. Having described the death of Alexei in a training accident and Lily's subsequent depression and disappearance, Ina addresses the audience in the play's final sequence in the manner of a 'propaganda' film: 'Ina Pasportnikova. 586th Division, 73rd Fighter Regiment. Now 67 years old, still living in hope. Never flew, never married, never joined the party' (53). Ina's resistance, in combination with her awareness of her own helplessness in the face of the large political and economic forces that oppress her, strike a note of optimism at the close of Arnott's play. Such clear-sightedness is not shared by the central character of Chris Hannan's *Elizabeth Gordon Quinn* which opened at the Traverse on June 22.

In spite of her narrative unfolding against the backdrop of the 1915 Glasgow rent strikes, with her defiant cry, 'I am not the working class: I am Elizabeth Gordon Quinn. I am an individual', the eponymous anti-heroine of Hannan's play is less an attempt at an accurate portrayal of a tenement dweller in early twentieth-century Glasgow, than a symbol of the fetishisation of the individual in Thatcher's Britain (Hannan 1990: 122). In a reversal of tropes typically found in the most famous tenement plays of the mid-twentieth century—especially Robert McLeish's *The Gorbals Story* (1946) and Ena Lamont Stewart's *Men Should Weep* (1947)—Elizabeth despises solidarity and collective action in all its forms. She refuses to join her neighbours in the rent strike. Disdaining menial work, she prefers to live in squalid conditions and in a fit of patriotic fervour, she goads her son into giving up his job as a post office clerk and enlisting to fight in WW1, only for him later to desert. She drives her long-suffering husband away. The more she sets herself above her neighbours, the clearer it becomes that she shares their background and predicament. Her tragedy, of course, is her failure to recognise that aspiration alone can never be enough to overcome economically determined social realities. You cannot fantasise your way out of poverty.

Elizabeth's powerful if perverse resistance to poverty, to 'living in a tenement where even my toilet is not private', is symbolised in her demented attachment to an upright piano, which she does not play, but which she treasures above all things (127). The dramaturgical significance of the piano cannot be overstated. It represents an intractable barrier to Elizabeth's developing any kind of self-awareness as a mother and wife, and it is the direct cause of her economic undoing. Towards the beginning of the play, it is sequestered by the Sherriff's Officer. The Quinn's have fallen into rent arrears because of Elizabeth's refusal to acknowledge the reality of their reduced circumstances after her husband loses his job. Later she agrees to join her neighbours in withholding rent, not as an act of solidarity, but in order to secure their help in ensuring the piano's return. For Elizabeth the piano is not a source of pleasure as a musical instrument—she cannot play it—but an emblem of resistance, aspiration, superiority and bourgeois respectability. Although Elizabeth's attitudes are as delusional as they are destructive, Hannan's achievement is to invest her with a kind of terrible grandeur. Her final lines, offered by way of explanation, are also the closing lines of the play and exemplify her indomitable spirit: 'I refused to learn how to be poor. That's my whole story. And I still refuse!' (146).

Again, the relevance of this theme to the political culture of 1980s Scotland quite is clear. An important development in public discourse in that decade was the tendency to refer to people as consumers and to attribute authority to individuals on those grounds. To attribute authority in this way, at least in Thatcher's rhetoric, was to undermine or deny that standard or traditional forms of authority were operative, especially those associated with collectivism and working-class life. Like Thatcher, Elizabeth Gordon Quinn has self-belief on her side. However, she does not have access to the material resources necessary to achieve her goals. Her pretensions are therefore ridiculous, although as Hannan makes clear, 'the orotundity of her language is about the energy and imagination required to divert from the actual poverty' (Hannan 1990: 107). In summary, although Elizabeth is an extremist and a fantasist, whose views on the free market would have been cheered at any Conservative Party Conference in the 80s, Hannan does not allow his audience to make easy work of dismissing her. His heroine is as charismatic as she is problematic, especially as played by Eileen Nicolas in Stephen Unwin's original production. Here she left the critics divided. As Alasdair Cameron notes, while some critics wanted to 'knock sense into her' others 'wanted to canonize her' (Cameron 1990: xiii).

Jo Clifford's *Losing Venice* was arguably the most unlikely hit of the 1985 Traverse season. Critics noticed the obvious parallels between Clifford's tale of imperialist opportunism and contemporary political events, in this case the Falkland's War, but in what follows, I want to focus on Clifford's dramaturgical innovations because it is these, I want to suggest, that opened new avenues of exploration in Scottish theatre and extended its vocabulary further towards internationalism. Clifford's sophisticated understanding of Spanish Golden Age drama, which had been the subject of her PhD at St Andrew's in the early 80s, is apparent in the narrative of *Losing Venice*—it tells of a bungled attempt by a seventeenth-century Spanish Duke to invade Venice—but also in the sustained manner in which the play displays a heightened consciousness of the pretence inherent to the maintenance of the social and political status quo, even as it extends to the presentation of the self.

Clifford's Spanish Duchess bemoans the patriarchal system that has prevented her inheriting her father's wealth and forced her into an arranged and unwelcome marriage. She wishes her new husband dead or far away prosecuting some conflict or other, largely so that she is no longer obliged to have sexual relations with him:

> DUCHESS. Where would he go? Somewhere distant. Somewhere impossibly remote. London, for instance.
> MARIA. Where?
> DUCHESS. You're right. Who'd ever want to go there (Clifford 1990: 61).

Cheap jokes at the expense of the metropolitan English elite are not uncommon in Scottish theatre, of course, but Clifford's play is notable for the manner in which the recourses of comedy rub shoulders with those of tragedy. When the Duke's imperial mission misfires—he accidently invades Crete mistaking it for Venice—the suffering inflicted on the innocent population is graphically recounted:

I hid, and they never found me. They were too busy killing. But they found my friend, Marcella. She was pregnant. They split open her belly and took out the baby in front of her eyes. They called it pacification, I saw it. She was still alive. She called for water but I couldn't give her any. Then she died (78).

The focus is thus directed away from the comic machinations of the leading characters towards the inevitable consequences of imperial conflict.

In *Losing Venice* the separation of aristocratic and servant characters and their respective values are also called into question. Pablo and Maria are two Scots-accented servants far smarter than their employers. Conversely, the rulers of Venice—Mr and Mrs Doge—are an unlikely couple that longs for a life of domestic simplicity. Mr Doge confesses his intense dislike of pomp and ceremony and instead wishes he could grow his own beans:

> MR DOGE ... If I could just have a decent patch of ground and a couple of years to work on it.
> MRS DOGE It's no use hankering after what you can't get. We're Doges for life and we'll just have to lump it (89).

This kind of deflationary counterpoint is never far from the surface in Clifford's play. Like that of Calderón de la Barca and Lope de Vega, Clifford's dramaturgy deliberately exceeds formal limitation in a manner designed to please the senses and engage the intellect. 'Audiences' as Alasdair Cameron notes 'both enjoyed the sophisticated wit of the dialogue and warmed to its message about the folly of military posturing and adventuring' (Cameron 1990: xiv). Crucially, in *Losing Venice* the relation between the theme and action of the play has nothing whatever to do with the realism or verisimilitude of the latter. Such confidently decisive breaks from realism were to prove useful to Scottish playwrights in the decades to come.

Of the three plays discussed above only Arnott's *White Rose* failed to have an afterlife in print, a fact that obviously undermines the potential for revival of, and critical engagement with, the play. Arnott's explanation of how *White Rose* receded from view is sanguine:

It's only really since the advent of the National Theatre of Scotland that second productions of plays have really started to happen ... We used to have hits, but they would run for the same length of time as the disasters. *White Rose* transferred to the Almeida in London for two weeks, and that was that ... It wasn't in print in the way a lot of new plays are now, so there was no access to it. It was nearly published in a collection of Scottish plays called *Scot Free*, but in the end there wasn't enough room (cited in Cooper 2013).

Elizabeth Gordon Quinn fared better and was revived in a new version by the NTS in 2006 in acknowledgement of its status as a contemporary Scottish classic. *Losing Venice* was given a new production at the Orange Tree in Richmond, London in 2018. Both were anthologised in Alasdair Cameron's edited collection *Scot Free* (1990). The latter production evidences a renewed interest in Clifford's work to which I will return in later chapters.

OTHER VOICES, OTHER ROOMS

The masculinist and realist dramas of the 1970s, with their focus on Scottish and largely urban identity, in themselves constituted a kind of national style the exhaustion of which derived from a growing awareness of its injustice to the complexity of Scotland's situation in the 1980s. Thought of in these terms, the expansion in vocabulary reflected the country's changing economic landscape, in particular the decline of heavy industry and the attendant extremely high levels of structural unemployment in Scotland's industrial districts. This shaped a narrative of economic change that was highly climactic, even tragic, and in which it was widely believed the employment effects of de-industrialisation were willed rather than the 'accidental' or 'natural' consequence of domestic, regional and international market forces. The historian Tom Devine spoke for many when he described Thatcherism as 'catastrophic for whole sections of Scottish industry' (Devine 2006: 592).

The emphasis on heterogeneity in evidence at the Traverse in the mid-1980s and the determination of the Citizens triumvirate to locate itself 'within international culture' suggests the focus on building a recognisably Scottish tradition apparent in the 1970s, had begun to be recast as interdependence in relation to other cultural formations (Stevenson 1996: 15). The foregrounding of female experience and feminist perspectives in the Traverse plays discussed above is worth noting, in this regard. The building of a theatre tradition that is outward-looking and internationally engaged but remains relevant to national preoccupations and interests is, of course, highly desirable. Nevertheless, in the 1980s as now, the minimal condition for a Scottish theatre tradition remained the supposed validity of the narrative identity of Scotland in the moment and in history. Scullion's observation that plays with more obvious 'Scottish' appeal such Tony Roper's *The Steamie* (1987) and Liz Lochhead's *Mary Queen of Scots Got Her Head Chopped Off* (1987) had a longer and more illustrious career in production and criticism because they 'could be more easily incorporated into a critical orthodoxy and the producing repertoire' remains pertinent (Scullion 2007: 71). Roper's *The Steamie*—set in a Glasgow washhouse on Hogmanay—remains an extremely popular and largely nostalgic evocation of working-class life in the 1950s. It recalls the 'humour in adversity' aesthetic associated with Glasgow Unity in the 1940s and its thirty-fifth anniversary production at Dundee Rep in the late summer of 2022 was warmly received by audiences and critics alike. Originally produced by Wildcat Stage Productions, the company founded in 1978 by three former members of 7:84 Scotland—Dave Anderson, Feri Lean and David MacLennan—*The Steamie* also fitted neatly into the dominant narrative of twentieth-century Scottish theatre studies, characterised by Adrienne Scullion as, 'a critical orthodoxy … that prefers a history of working-class and broadly naturalistic drama and theatre' (Scullion 2002: 215). Roper's play, as Paul Maloney notes, also confirms, 'the sense of shared cultural rootedness that links Scottish music hall of the pre-war period with the working-class drama of the 1940s and the Scottish theatre groups of the 1970s and 80s' (Maloney 2011: 72). *The Steamie* (1987) was a major hit for Wildcat, but its tone was largely nostalgic and sentimental. In this regard it existed in stark contrast to Hannan's *Elizabeth Gordon Quinn*, with its focus on the female outsider and its critique of contemporary Thatcherite values, although both arguably make meaning in relationship to the founding myth of the long-suffering mother, the community spirit of the Glasgow tenement, and the innate socialism of its inhabitants. At any rate the success of *The Steamie* suggests that cultural imperatives drove recurrent patterns of selection and evaluation and had potential to marginalise the contribution made by the Traverse and the Citizens. At the Citz, as Cordelia Oliver has noted, Robert David MacDonald's presence in the company as the most significant and prodigious translator of his generation 'had the effect of opening up the whole spectrum of European drama to Glasgow audiences', but critics nonetheless found it difficult to characterise his work as distinctively Scottish (Oliver 1984: 11).

Elsewhere in the 1980s, translations into Scots—what John Corbett usefully calls 'domesticating translations'—contributed to growing confidence in the medium as an effective stage language, and also to a sense of Scottish theatre as internationally engaged (Corbett 2011: 104). By 1996 Bill Findlay was able to note how far, 'employment of a non-Standard medium has characterized the majority of translators work over the period' (Findlay 1996: 187). Translated authors included Michel Tremblay, Dario Fo, Ernst Jandl, Mario Vargas Llosa, Manfred Karge, Michael Vinaver and Alexander Gelman. Among the most successful was Liz Lochhead's robust Scots version of Molière's *Tartuffe*, which played to packed houses at Edinburgh's Royal Lyceum in January 1986 and was widely admired. This particular translation is significant because it marks the moment when Lochhead discovers a sustained dramatic register in Scots. Randall Stevenson captures much of its energy and appeal in his essay 'Triumphant Tartuffication' (2004: 106–22). Lochhead's expressive mode also had liberatory potential for those coming after her because authenticity did not necessarily drive her language choices. Instead, she developed a kind of invented stage Scots: 'proverbial, slangy, couthy, clichéd, catch-phrasey, and vulgar' based on 'Byron, Burns, Stanley Holloway, Ogden Nash and George Formby, as well as the sharp tongue of my granny' (Lochhead 1985: iv). As Ksenija Horvat has noted Lochhead's work 'does not simply cross the boundary' between drama and poetry, 'it blurs it', and as befits her primary vocation as a poet, Lochhead's main contribution to Scottish drama has been in consolidating and diversifying the use of idiomatic Scots on the stage (Horvat 2011: 181).

Lochhead's commitment to feminism further ensured her influence. In 1987, in collaboration with Communicado, she made a significant contribution to the development of the Scottish history play with her postmodern feminist reworking of the life of Mary Stuart, *Mary Queen of Scots Got Her Head Chopped Off*. In this play, as Randall Stevenson has noted, Lochhead, 'moved beyond' earlier playwrights whose work provided 'little more than historical accounts of historical periods and their people' to create a bawdy Scots drama that drew uncomfortable parallels between the sacrifice of Mary Stuart and the myriad religious, sexual and political tensions and hypocrisies of contemporary Scotland (Stevenson, 1993: 109). Aware of the representational overload that burdened the figure of Mary Stuart, Lochhead set out to consciously disrupt dominant myths about Mary including, for instance, that her gruesome end serves as a warning to lascivious women who are a bit too French for their own good, or that she was a martyr to Protestant/English duplicity.

Lochhead develops her themes by creating a caricature of sixteenth-century Scotland that playfully and subversively mirrors the social prejudices of Thatcher's Britain. Ironic commentary is provided throughout by the semi-detached, folkloric, Franco-Scots figure of La Corbie—corbie is Scots for carrion crow—the narrator, who opens the action alone on stage. After establishing that the subject of the play is Scotland itself, La Corbie, introduces the conflict central to the dramatic action but also the playfully theatrical, popular storytelling mode in which Lochhead's examination of Scotland's persistent problems will be played out. 'Once upon a time' she begins 'there were twa queens on the wan green island, and the wan green island was split intae twa kingdoms' (Lochhead 2009: 6). Thereafter, Lochhead adopts a classic second-wave feminist strategy of retelling well-known historical narratives from a female perspective. She does so via a recognisably feminist, woman-centred and anti-realist dramaturgy which co-opts distinctively Scottish performance traditions—direct address, variety-style, mixing of genres, heightened language—for a radical feminist critique.

In Lochhead's retelling, as Marylin Reizbaum notes, 'Mary and Elizabeth are presented as personally and historically trapped: the former is remembered for her sexual exploits and her infamous death … the latter as a powerful ruler, albeit a sexual curiosity' (Reizbaum 1992: 165). In the event, identity is not a stable construct for Lochhead. In the course of the play Mary and Elizabeth switch roles, and languages, to play each other's maids, for instance, so that a strong affinity between the two women is signalled. Often Mary's biographers have portrayed her as a fated figure, predestined by her historical background to come to a sorry end. By contrast, Lochhead's play suggests that by interrogating Mary's life and her ending, by understanding different choices are available, contemporary women can conjure their own new beginnings. The play was revived in major productions by the NTS in 2009 and again at the Lyceum in Edinburgh in 2011 (Fig. 2.1).

Fig. 2.1 Joyce Falconer as La Corbie in Liz Lochhead's *Mary Queen of Scots Got Her Head Chopped Off* (directed by Alison Peebles, National Theatre of Scotland, 2009) reproduced with kind permission from Peter Dibdin

More recently the NTS revival of her translation of *Medea* (2000), stormed the EIF, in Michael Boyd's superb ensemble production featuring the magnificent Adura Onashile in the title role, and a Chorus of ten canny Scotswomen. Performed on a catwalk stage thrust through the heart of The Hub's main hall and surrounded by a promenade audience, Lochhead's text, as Joyce McMillan observed, 'has never been delivered with more ominous force than in this thrilling new staging' (2022).

Following *Mary Queen of Scots Got Her Head Chopped Off*, Lochhead's next major collaboration with Communicado, *Jock Tamson's Bairns* (1990) was commissioned to celebrate Glasgow's year as European City of Culture. A large-scale promenade production, intended as an exploration of the Scottish psyche, opened at Tramway in January of that year, and featured a 'symbolic Drunk Man descending into hell' where he encounters a motley crew of disreputable Scottish types and eventually becomes 'the haggis at a symbolic Burns supper' (Paterson 1996:

78). The 'ugliness of the story', as Joyce McMillian noted in her review is counterbalanced by the theatricality of the execution which 'is shot through with so much humour and brilliance that the effect is anything but depressing' (McMillan, 1990). The bold and ambitious scope of Communicado's theatrical vision, in this and other projects, was to have a lasting impact on Scottish theatre.

Founded in Edinburgh in 1983 by actors Gerry Mulgrew, Alison Peebles and Rob Pickavance, Communicado created a number of highly praised ensemble productions including *Carmen-The Play* (1984), Georg Büchner's *Danton's Death* (1990) and perhaps most famously Edwin Morgan's Scots translation of Edmond Rostand's *Cyrano de Bergerac* (1992), which was revived by the NTS in 2018. Under Mulgrew's leadership, the company quickly established a distinctive style, actively engaging with an international repertoire, and mingling distinctively Scottish idioms with performance practices associated with influential European figures such as Grotowski and Kantor but perhaps more importantly by John and Sue Fox's radical collective Welfare State International (WSI). Mulgrew founded Communicado after two years of performing with WSI and his techniques were directly influenced by their integration of design, music and performance, not to mention their purposeful engagement with communities. The Communicado aesthetic was emphatically actor-centred and characterised by both robust physicality and pronounced musicality.

Mark Brown has argued that among Communicado's significant achievements in the 1980s was the combining the core aesthetics of two of the 'most influential forces within Scottish theatre … the Citizens and 7:84' (Brown 2019: 95). Certainly, the company's touring practices had much in common with those established by the latter in the 1970s. *Cyrano* premiered in Inverness, for instance, and the company toured extensively in the Highlands and islands. Communicado's commitment to a low-cost aesthetic and its extensive use of music and song is also reminiscent of 7:84 Scotland and its musical off-shoot Wildcat. None of this chimed with the high-art decadence of the Citz, on the other hand, although an emphasis on European repertoire and a commitment to the ensemble certainly did. Mulgrew's achievement nonetheless remains unique because he sought to articulate a European sensibility from and through his subject position as a Scot, and to do so with a company comprised mainly of Scottish actors and musicians. As well as racing across time and location to bring European classics to modern Scottish audiences, Communicado modelled the confident—celebratory even—use of Scottish accents in staging work that was variously Arabian, Bosnian, French, German, Greek, Irish, Russian, South African and Spanish in origin. By contrast Scottish actors were typically underrepresented in the Citz company. The influence of Communicado is everywhere apparent in post-devolutionary Scottish theatre, in the work of performance companies such as Vanishing Point, and in the output of the national company. Previewing the Barbican run of the NTS production of *Peer Gynt* (2009)—in which Mulgrew played a leading role—for the *Sunday Times*, Anna Burnside noted how far 'Mulgrew and Communicado's influence runs through this production's veins. The choice of a supposedly sacred text and its conversion into bold vernacular were the stock in trade of Mulgrew's penniless band of players, traversing the country in a clapped-out van' (Burnside 2009).

OTHER VOICES

As performance vocabularies began to expand in the ways described above, Scottish playwrights also set about systematically troubling, what Kensija Horvat usefully labels 'socially accepted gender clichés' (Horvat 2007: 300). Playwrights such as Iain Heggie and John Binnie productively explored the experience of being gay in a country where heteronormativity and pronounced masculinist bias remained powerful forces. Writing mostly for his own company, Clyde Unity, Binnie created a body of work that explored the felt experience of being Scottish, working class and gay. His first major success was the AIDS play, *Killing me Softly* (1987), which toured in 1990 as part of an HIV-awareness programme, accompanied by post-show discussions and workshops. Heggie's dark city comedy *A Wholly Healthy Glasgow* (1987), lampooned the fitness craze of the late 80s but also revisited some of the tropes of the workplace drama that had been popular in the 70s. Such plays, as Adrienne Scullion has noted, often satirised conventional structure. This is especially the case in *A Wholly Healthy Glasgow* which echoes Roddy McMillan's *The Bevellers* (1973) and John Byrne's *The Slab Boys* (1978), in focusing on 'a new boy' who 'enters a pre-established community of adult men' has his masculinity 'tested, and … is either accepted or expelled from the group' (Scullion 1995: 178). In Heggie's play the new boy is Murdo Caldwell, whose ambition is not to fit in but who is instead on a mission to create a wholly healthy Glasgow:

> ... a city of perfectly proportioned, sinuous but not over-developed physiques ... a city of non-smoking, non-drinking joggers ... a city of reposeful but alert minds. (Heggie 1988: 230).

Murdo is initiated in the ways of the sleazy Spartan Health Club by the distinctly mercenary health instructor Charlie Hood, and the ageing masseur Donald Dick, who is openly gay, dementedly irreverent and unpleasantly predatory. The action unfolds over the course of one day and is delivered in a bold heightened register, in which vernacular Glaswegian is utilised to full comic effect. The presence of women in this male-dominated environment is limited to Alana, the receptionist whose voice is heard over the tannoy system.

While *A Wholly Healthy Glasgow* was busy conforming to unities of time, place and action, Scottish women dramatists were exposing the limitations of realism as a mode for representing their experience, often drawing on mythic and folkloric elements to critique historically determined representations of woman. Sue Glover's *The Seal Wife* (1980), for example, utilised the legend of the selkies—according to tradition, a selkie would transform into human form then marry and bear children, only to return to the sea at some later date—to explore the domestic restrictions placed on women in a coastal village in southern Fife. In Glover's play protagonist Rona is dissatisfied with her culturally assigned role as wife and mother and eventually abandons her family. The legend is thus transformed from a narrative of seduction and deceit to one of resistance and release. In the process cultural pressures that bear upon Scottish women and assign them unproblematically to domestic roles are critiqued.

Female dramatists also took the lead in extending the range of possible settings in theatre, moving beyond the domestic and workplace interiors of urban Scotland. The narrative of Sharman MacDonald's *When I Was a Girl I used to Scream and Shout* (Bush, 1984) unfolds largely on an east coast beach, for instance, as does Glover's *The Seal Wife*. Glover's award-winning history play *Bondagers* (Traverse, 1991) relates a year in the life of a group of female farm labourers in the Borders in the nineteenth century, and consequently has a rural setting, while her *Shetland Saga* (Traverse, 2000) is set in Lerwick. *Bondagers*, was first produced by the Traverse Theatre at Glasgow's Tramway in May 1990, and then subsequently at the Traverse Theatre in Edinburgh's Grassmarket, London's Donmar and the Prairie Theatre Winnipeg in January

1994. As well as expanding the imagined space of contemporary Scotland, these peripheral, and in many instances liminal, settings typically mirror the emotional realities of central characters. In *When I Was a Girl*, MacDonald explores discourses surrounding childbearing, abortion and marriage primarily through the prism of a mother/daughter relationship at the literal edge of the country. Themes of displacements, marginalisation and isolation recur in Scottish women's drama of this period, as does a tendency to explore these issues in personal terms and in specific localities. Questions of belonging are foregrounded in Ann Marie Di Mambro's *Tally's Blood* (Traverse, 1990), which has become a standard text in Scottish schools and shifts location between Scotland and Italy. Covering the period 1936–1955, it tells the story of the Pedreschi family and the racism they encounter as Italian immigrants in Scotland in the run up to and the aftermath of WW2. The possibility, and indeed the desirability, of integration are explored via tensions between Rosinella and Massimo, the husband and wife at the centre of the action. Rosinella's fierce commitment to her Italian identity manifests in a series of racist slurs against her Scottish neighbours and although the tone of the dialogue is largely comic the potentially problematic relationship between nationalist politics and racism is nevertheless spotlighted. It is only after a return visit to Italy that Rosinella is awakened to the potential benefits in embracing the Scottish part of her identity.

Another feature of new writing by women in this period was an atypical use of song, which may, as Peter Zenzinger notes, be seen 'as an extension of the ceilidh formula popularised by John McGrath in *The Cheviot, the Stag, and the Black, Black Oil* (1973)', especially in the way it moves beyond Brechtian modes and sometimes exceeds them (1996: 127). Traditional ballads and folk songs are used in Glover's *Bondagers* and Rona Munro's *The Maiden Stone* (1995), for instance, and Glover uses ecclesiastical chanting in *Sacred Hearts* (1994). The increasing visibility of Scottish women playwrights was, of course, welcome insofar as it contributed to an expansion in the formal and thematic toolkit of Scottish theatre and challenged the pre-existing biases of Scottish culture. However, the picture was not an entirely rosy one. Tom Maguire rightly draws attention to the lack of support within Scotland itself for female dramatists in this period, reminding us, for example, 'that two of the most prolific and widely recognised Scottish women playwrights, Rona Munro and Sharman Macdonald' relied on key relationships with theatres outside Scotland to develop and sustain their work in the 1980s and 90s (Maguire

2011: 156). MacDonald's *When I Was a Girl I Used to Scream and Shout* was rejected by the Traverse and subsequently premiered at London's Bush Theatre. The legacy of these women playwrights can nonetheless be seen, both formally and thematically, in the practices of female performance makers discussed elsewhere in this book. *Move* (2021), for instance, was the inaugural show from Disaster Plan, a new company led by Julia Taudevin and Kieran Hurley. Presented in partnership with epic theatre-makers Slung Low and the Traverse, the show took the form of 'weaving together of stories and songs in a form that is inspired by traditional Celtic keening rituals' and was designed to be performed in the open air on beaches (Taudevin 2021: 2).

Exploiting the liminality referenced above, the audience is located at some distance from the shore and experiences *Move* through headphones, the sound of the sea providing a constant sonic backdrop. Shifting between the first and third person, the women recount tales from across the globe that are 'loosely linked by themes of motherhood, migration and mental health' (Morgan 2021). A refugee woman gives birth and tosses her baby into a stranger's arms. A woman found lost and confused in Glasgow is unable to say where she is and why she is there. A song about sleeping at the bottom of the sea is sung in Swahili. A woman in Queensland in the 1980s speaks at a memorial service for her sister Margaret, who at the end of her life had lost her English, but 'still had the Gaelic, as she would call it' (17). In the end, in a gesture of hope, *Move* takes us back to the Greek island where the stranger sings a lullaby to the rescued baby, 'and the baby sleeps" (Taudevin 2021: 33).

Plays and Playwrighting in the 1990s

The work described above ensured the generation of Scottish playwrights who came to prominence in the 1990s was able to draw on an expanded theatrical vocabulary, both dramaturgically and linguistically. David Greig has been vocal in acknowledging his debt to this earlier generation, especially in relation to their approach to language:

> These writers show you can write in your own poetic idiolect, which is very connected to real language and dialect, but is actually your own synthetic creation. ... When you look at those plays of the 1980s, what they're doing is using language to jump the question of whether you write in

English, Scots or dialect. These writers forge a unique language from all three (Greig 2011: 17).

In the same interview Greig notes that his sense of 'what a Scottish playwright ought to be', with all its attendant freedoms, was directly informed by the achievements and innovations of the playwrights of the 1980s (Greig 2011: 18).

The period also witnessed an expansion in the number of available theatre spaces, so that by the mid-nineties David Hutchison was able to assert with some confidence, that anyone contemplating the Scottish theatre scene 'could not avoid the conclusion that the last twenty years have been a remarkable period of expansion' (1996b: 207). New buildings had been constructed for the repertory theatres in Dundee (1982) and Pitlochry (1981), for example, and for the Traverse in Edinburgh (1992). Elsewhere, new venues had been created in Glasgow at the Tron (1981) and Tramway (1988). The arrival of Philip Howard at the Traverse in Edinburgh as an assistant in 1993 was also to prove enabling. His work there—he was appointed artistic director in 1996 and remained at the helm until 2008—contributed significantly to the upswing in cultural confidence that underpinned the renaissance in Scottish playwriting. During his tenure, Howard established structures—workshops, writers' groups, national and international touring circuits, partnership schemes—that linked pairs of Scottish and international writers and led to a growth in Scotland's reputation as a centre for new writing, especially in Europe. Howard also supported the development of young Scottish playwrights. His notable productions for the Traverse included premieres of David Harrower's *Knives in Hens* (1995) and *Kill the Old Torture Their Young* (1998), for instance, and a string of David Greig plays including *Europe* (1994), *The Architect* (1996), *The Speculator* (1999), *Outlying Islands* (2002) and *Damascus* (2007). Howard played a significant role, then, in the development of a robust playwriting culture in Scotland.

Scotland does not exist in a vacuum, of course, and larger geo-political events were to have significant impact on its playwrighting scene in the 1990s. Most obviously, the reinvention of political Europe in the aftermath of the fall of the Berlin Wall in 1989, fed into an ongoing examination of politics and culture and offered a different perspective than those that had dominated in the 1970s and 80s. This shift in focus and perspective is particularly apparent in David Greig's work, which in the 1990s—as an independent playwright and as part of Suspect Culture, the company he founded with Graham Eatough—established him as a prodigious and precocious talent. His output in the new century has consolidated his position as Scotland's pre-eminent contemporary playwright, while his enthusiasm for Scottish independence as articulated during the 2014 referendum campaign, and his appointment as artistic director of Edinburgh's Royal Lyceum Theatre in 2016 has confirmed his status as a major cultural figure. Greig's work has also received significantly more scholarly attention than that of his peers as accounts of it here and in the following chapters will demonstrate.

Whether writing directly about Scotland, in plays such as *Caledonia Dreaming* (1997) and *Victoria* (2000), or dealing with more cosmopolitan subject matter in *Europe* (1994), *One Way Street* (1995), *The Cosmonauts' Last Message to the Woman He Once Loved in the Former Soviet Union* (1999) or *The Speculator* (1999), Greig's plays in the first decade of his career consistently explored the possibilities inherent in a bold and hopeful approach to the future and the dangers of over-reliance on the assumptions and prejudices of the past. His theatre is determinedly ethical in that it invariably focuses on men and women making choices under pressure, and consequently it privileges context over character. As Steve Cramer observes, 'the precision with which he outlines his characters' circumstances reflects a recurrent thesis throughout his oeuvre about the ways humans are diverted from their organic sociality' (Cramer 2011: 173). *Europe* is exemplary in this regard and, as Clare Wallace reminds us, is also 'a striking piece because it showcases so clearly some of the core qualities of Greig's mature work' (Wallace 2013: 47).

Written against the backdrop of the disintegration of the Soviet Union and the onset of the Balkans war, the action of *Europe* unfolds in a disused railway station in a provincial border town somewhere in the heart of Europe. Trains no longer stop there. Two displaced persons, father and daughter Sava and Katia, take refuge in the station where they initially come into conflict with the stationmaster Fret whose daughter Adele is trapped in an unhappy marriage with a factory worker named Berlin. Berlin spends much of his time at a local bar with co-workers Billy and Horse. Their childhood friend Morocco returns to the town after a long absence. As Anja Müller notes, a 'distinction between residual and migratory characters' shapes both the action and the various hierarchies the characters construct about their identities and sense of belonging (2005: 158). For Jeanne Schaaf, this distinction is concretised through the play's dramaturgy and invariably in its staging, 'where spectators are confronted with dynamics of inclusion and exclusion, connection and isolation, mobility and immobility' (2016: 82). From the opening scene, visual and aural motifs are combined:

Darkness ...

An international express train passes the station. The train makes an incredible noise, building steadily as it approaches. Speed, metal and light dominate the theatre drowning everything for a moment in the train's elemental force. Slowly, as the sound dies, the lights come up.

Morocco arrives in the town square. He is a dark man, unshaven and wearing a dusty suit and sunglasses. He has a heavy suitcase with him. In front of a blue neon sign for the calypso bar he lights a cigarette and puts his suitcase down and considers his situation. (Greig 1996: 1)

Of the play's 20 scenes 15 end with the sound of an express train hurtling through the station, emphasising the town's status as 'left behind'.

Europe is episodic in structure, consciously drawing on European rather than British dramaturgical models. Its 20 scenes are subtitled, each title pointing to the basic attitude that informs the social interaction staged. This foregrounding of the 'gestus' of each scene makes the Brechtian aesthetic of the play explicit and enhances its allusive, parable-like quality. The use of a chorus comprised of the whole cast at the beginning of each of its two acts adds to this impression, partly by producing what Veronica Rodríguez has described as a 'sense of "here", of permanence, of witnessing historical change' (2019: 115). The arrival of Sava and Katia provokes a range of reactions. Fret and Sava initially clash but soon find common ground in their shared love of the railway and nostalgia for what they remember as a more stable and legible Europe of the past. Adele dreams of leaving her husband and the town and travelling to the great cities of Europe. She is drawn to Katia. Meanwhile redundancies at the local light-bulb factory trigger a crisis for Berlin, Horse and Billy. Billy chooses to leave, while Berlin and Horse become increasingly angry and resentful, eventually finding comfort in the certainties of right-wing extremism, and the conviction that outsiders are the source of their problems. Meanwhile, in return for sex, Morocco agrees to use his shady international connections to secure papers that will allow Katia to travel freely, but as a result is badly beaten by his schoolfriends for fraternising with foreigners. In the play's final scene, subtitled 'Europe', Katia and Adele are on a train heading for a new life in some other more famous and beautiful European city, and Berlin—who in the previous scene has fire-bombed the station killing Fret and Sava—reflects on the impact of his actions: 'We were on the television … on the front of magazines. Me and Horse, we were discussed on the radio. Protest songs were written about us' (1996: 84). Optimistic and pessimistic strands thus explicitly overlap and co-exist. The final word is left to the play's least appealing character Berlin who, having boasted that his actions have temporarily put the town back on the map, reminds us:

Berlin … They know that even as they travel to some older …
Adele Salzburg
Berlin Or more beautiful …
Katia Sarajevo
Berlin Or more important place.
Adele Just imagine …
Berlin They know, that in our own way, we're also Europe. (84–85)

Berlin thus rounds off the play by rephrasing the line that closes its opening chorus: 'we are, in our own way, also Europe' (1996: 2).

Greig's conjuring of Europe as both a spatial and a conceptual entity—at the precise moment when both are contested—and his use of the railway as a central metaphor, provide rich thematic terrain for an exploration of belonging and identity as they are shaped by the impacts of global capitalism and its attendant conflicts. Perhaps unsurprisingly, the play has attracted a good deal of scholarly attention, much of which is effectively summarised by Clare Wallace in *The Theatre of David Greig* (2013: 47–48). More recently, Mark Robson's 2016 essay 'David Greig's Other Heading' explores the 'motif of movement' in the play in some detail, unpacking the significance of the ways it means different things to different characters, and indeed to different readers and audience members (2016: 43). Veronica Rodríguez, in *David Greig's Holed Theatre* (2019), devotes a chapter to discussion of the play which she reads as exploring 'two extreme visions that tear across any static, homogeneous understanding of Europe' and as prophetic insofar as it offers 'a glimpse of what the pain-ridden continent that goes by that name might become' (2019: 124). This last remark speaks to *Europe's* prescience and is echoed in responses to recent revivals. Reviewing Michael Longhust's 2019 production, with which he launched his tenure as artistic director of London's Donmar Warehouse, Michael Billington described *Europe* as 'richly resonant' and as 'a play that not only reveals a deeply European sensibility' but 'also addresses the vital question of whether the continent can ever live up to its visionary ideals' (2019). For Jay Nuttal, James Brining's revival at Leeds Playhouse in the previous year demonstrated that Greig's play was 'timeless' and 'could be a snapshot of history from almost at any time in twentieth-century Europe or, unfortunately, twenty-first century Europe also' (2018).

The indeterminacy of the setting and the international scope of Greig's imagination in *Europe* stands in contrast to an emphasis on the narrative identity of Scotland that had characterised—if not exclusively—major Scottish plays in earlier decades. This shift might, as Janelle Reinelt notes, have the effect of submerging Greig's 'connection to Scotland', however, as she also observes 'underplaying this aspect of his work would be a mistake' (2011: 204). One impetus for the play—which Greig has mentioned in a number of interviews—is the decimation of the industrial towns of central Scotland as a consequence of the decline of heavy industries such as steel, rail, shipbuilding and coal from the 1950s onwards. This left a significant number of communities isolated, impoverished and marginalised, facing a complex set of problems relating to loss of status and its associated identity crises. Reflecting on this context in an interview with Paul Taylor of the *Independent* in 1999, Greig insisted, 'if I had my time again, I would call the play Scotland. That border town could just as easily be Motherwell' (1999: 27). Alongside Greig, David Harrower and Anthony Neilson were the most lauded Scottish playwrights to emerge in the 1990s, although Stephen Greenhorn's *Passing Places* (1997) made a considerable impact as did Harry Gibson's stage adaptation of Irvine Welsh's *Trainspotting* (1994).

Harrower's debut, *Knives in Hens,* opened at the Traverse on 2 June 1995, and immediately established him as an important new voice in Scottish and European theatre. The German premiere, directed by Thomas Ostermeier at the Baracke am Deutschen Theater in Berlin in 1997, won the Theater Heute award for Best Foreign Play, and was instrumental in establishing the play's reputation in Europe where it has been widely produced in numerous translations. In October 1999, it opened at the Kamra, the studio stage of the Katona József Theatre in Budapest, and was an instant success, remaining in the repertoire until 2006 with more than 120 performances. Doubtless, the indeterminacy of the play's location—the stage direction read 'Rural place'—in combination with its archetypal narrative about an adulterous wife murdering her husband, contributed to its effective translation across borders and theatre traditions (Harrower 2015: 19). *Knives in Hens* is, according to the National Library of Scotland website, 'the most performed Scottish plays of all time' apart from *Peter Pan* (2010).

Set in an ill-defined pre-industrial past and in no identifiable country, in 24 scenes *Knives in Hens* follows its central character, Young Woman, as she escapes the clutches of her oppressive husband Pony William, by joining forces with her lover, the local miller Gilbert Horn, to murder him. This short synopsis of the plot does little to convey the play's peculiar power, however. As the relationship between the miller and the Young Woman develops, and he teaches her to read, Harrower utilises a stark, heightened and lyrical mode to reveal the shifts in self-awareness that accompany the acquisition of literacy, and the radical social change such shifts can engender. Reading and writing, Young Woman discovers, shape language in ways that influence her understanding of reality and change it, distancing her from the intuitively experienced material world. On one level *Knives in Hens* is a compelling exploration of how patriarchal power relations are enforced through language then, but Young Woman's awakening also serves as a metaphor for modernisation. It is significant in this regard that her lover and teacher, the miller, is the object of resentment and suspicion in the village. In his introduction to the published text Mark Fisher links this trope to a specifically Scottish context, noting that the miller 'was seen as someone who profited unfairly from the labour of others' in pre-industrial Scotland and was thus typically a hate figure in folk culture (2015: 4). Gilbert Horn lives free from the oppressiveness of subsistence labour and is the only literate lay person in the village. He represents both an escape route and a shift towards more alienated forms of labour, therefore, and *Knives in Hens* is shot through with this kind of ambivalence. While her newly acquired command of language allows Young Woman increased agency, for example, it also signals the end of her innocence. Most obviously, it teaches her how to lie: 'He's left me. He's gone for a better wife. He walked away in the night. I sit alone by the fire. Look at my tear puddles. I'm the broken-hearted wife' (2015: 54).

Mark Fisher observes that a preoccupation with the 'changing nature of land use' links *Knives in Hens* with Sue Glover's *Bondagers* (1991),

Alasdair Cording's stage adaptation of *Sunset Song* (EIF 1993), even John McGrath's *The Cheviot, the Stag, and the Black, Black Oil* (2015: 2–3) but its elegiac and luminous qualities also gesture towards Chris Hannan's *Shining Souls* (1996), although the latter has an ostensibly more concrete contemporary urban setting. Hannan's play, set in Glasgow's east end in and around the famous Barras market, is a shimmering city comedy that recasts its variously desperate working-class Glaswegian characters as poets, prophets and philosophers cut adrift in a post-industrial postmodern world in which once stable notions of collective identity have been shattered. They are seeking forms of absolution and redemption no longer available to them. 'Society', one character notes, has 'no more structure than a pile of burst binbags' (Hannan 1996a: 25).

First performed at the Traverse in August 1996, *Shining Souls* was revived by the Old Vic in 1997, and again at the Tron in Glasgow in 2003, where it was directed by Communicado's Alison Peebles who played its central character Ann in Ian Brown's inaugural production. Ann, as Joyce McMillan observes, is 'one hell of a woman, a kind of Mother Courage cum Marilyn Monroe of the post-industrial wastelands' who has lost two sons to suicide but whose life-force nonetheless burns bright (2003). The action unfolds on her wedding day, the smooth running of which is complicated by the fact that she cannot quite decide which of her two lovers—both called Billy—to marry, and is even tempted by a third possibility, a charming down-on-his-luck chancer named Charlie. Charlie, by Hannan's own account is 'fragile, broken and desperate. But quite handsome' (Hannan 1996b). In the play's second scene Charlie, who is sleeping rough and has blown his giro on the horses, invents a story about his mother's imminent demise as a means of extorting money from the wife he has abandoned, only to immediately receive news from his elder brother that his mother has actually been rushed to hospital. Tarot cards are read, psychics are consulted, prayers are said, unwelcome insights are provided by the local Prophet John.

Hannan's characters are all seeking something outside their lived experience, something that will give their lives purpose and direction. They cannot make decisions, or rather they cannot commit to the decisions they have made but they are all 'are all desperately testing themselves to find out who they are – if they deserve to have love – if they are allowed to feel love for someone else' (Hannan 1996b). The play is also shot through with religious poetry drawn from Hannan's Catholic upbringing. Ann spends much of the play wandering the streets of Glasgow's east end 'looking for a signal' that will show her how to move forward (1996a: 39). Charlie is also *'waiting on a sign from God'* (1996a: 32). He is an astonishingly erudite creation who, according to Hanna's note to the actors in the published text *'is often ambushed mid-flow by some fresh thought jumping out of his brain-infested head'* but who also believes himself to be speaking in *'lucid and magisterial Augustan prose'* (1996a: 4). Charlie is a fantasist who rejects his own fantasies, a figure to be both pitied and admired as he lurches between self-deluding waster and romantic poet. He is a woefully absent father, whose wife resorts to telling their toddler that his father is in prison, but he is also a man who can reduce himself to tears with the power of his own rhetoric. Hannan skilfully navigates a fault line in his drawing of this character between pathetic chancer and tragic enigma, and in so doing he conjures a post-industrial working-class Glasgow that is at once tragic and beautiful. Despite the abjection of its characters, a pronounced sense of anarchic Glaswegian vitality pervades *Shining Souls*. Hannan's characters are depicted as not so much in tune with the supernatural, as desperately dependant on it as an unlikely means of escape from present realities, but he does offer them something beyond the reification of gritty realism. In taking them out of the workplace and out of any concrete political context, he gives a metaphysical resonance to the everyday lives of working-class characters in search of meaning, and imbues them with the grandeur and significance they deserve. In this way, Hannan stages something akin to the exhaustion of daily life under late capitalism. David Greig's *The Architect*, which had opened at the Traverse in February of that year, was revived as part of the same festival season, demonstrating that Scottish playwrighting was in good health. *The Architect*, like *Europe* and *Knives in Hens*, was directed by Philip Howard who took over as the Traverse Theatre's Artistic Director in October 1996.

Conclusion

The account of *Shining Souls* with which I have closed this chapter suggests that specifically Scottish subject matter, and indeed peculiarly Glaswegian modes of linguistic expression, remained potent as a means of exploring larger political and societal shifts. As the opening section of the chapter also demonstrates, with the exception of its family Christmas shows, the Citz disdained this approach and instead, enriched Scottish theatre by looking determinedly outwards, towards Europe and European traditions. In 1985 Hannan's *Elizabeth Gordon Quinn* had made its own contribution to this enrichment, of course, by revisioning the traditional Glaswegian tenement play for a new age, an age of neoliberal hegemony and rampant individualism, again showing the potential of local subject matter for interrogating global issues. In the same Traverse season, Arnott's *White Rose* and Clifford's *Losing Venice* had broken decisively with realism in ways that opened new ground, while the emergence of women playwrights in the 1980s, and their bold experiments with setting and form, further supplemented the toolkit available to Scottish playwrights. Lochhead's *Mary Queen of Scots Got Her Head Chopped Off* all but reinvented the Scottish history play, just as her work in translation, along with that of Bill Findlay, reinvigorated Scots as theatrical idiom.

As this discussion has revealed the impact of the generation of Scottish playwrights who came to prominence in the 1990s—especially David Greig and David Harrower—has also been significant, and their international success would doubtless be the envy of earlier generations. Of course, the account of Scottish theatre in the 1980s and 90s offered in this chapter has covered a relatively small number of plays, playwrights, theatres and theatre companies. It would be wrong to suggest it offers a comprehensive or complete picture and there will be omissions that are more obvious and significant to some readers than others. Nonetheless, the work has been selected because a consensus of sorts has emerged around the value of its engagement with the challenges facing Scotland and Europe as the new millennium approached. The artists discussed unquestionably made substantial contributions to the growing reputation of Scottish theatre. Perhaps most importantly, they evidenced a cultural determination—shared by other key institutions and individuals—to develop a sustainable theatre culture in which the careers of theatre practitioners could develop beyond the first flush of success. This determination found its most concrete expression in the establishment of the NTS in 2004. Before turning my attention to the national company in Chapter 4, I want to spend some time tracing the history and impact of more experimental forms of performance in Scotland, partly because this history has been under-researched and thus under-represented, but also because it feeds directly into the national company in ways that are tangible and impactful.

References

Arnott, Peter (1985) *White Rose*. Unpublished Rehearsal Script.
Arts Council of Great Britain (1988) *43rd Annual Report and Accounts*. London, Arts Council of Great Britain.
Aston, Elaine (1999) *Feminist Theatre Practice: A Handbook*. London, Routledge.
Billington, Michael (2019) 'Europe Review: Refugees Shelter in Train Station as a Continent Frays'. *Guardian*, 28 June.
Brown, Ian (2007) 'Alternative Sensibilities: Devolutionary Comedy and Scottish Camp', in Berthold Schoene (ed.) *The Edinburgh Companion to Contemporary Scottish Literature*. Edinburgh, Edinburgh University Press, pp. 319–327.
Brown, Mark (2019) *Modernism and Scottish Theatre Since 1969*. London, Palgrave Macmillan.
Burnside, Anna (2009) 'Theatre with a Scottish Accent'. *Sunday Times*, 10 May.
Cameron, Alasdair (1990) (ed.) *Scot-Free: New Scottish Plays*. London, Nick Hern Books.
Clifford, Jo (1990) *Losing Venice*, in Alasdair Cameron (ed.) *Scot-Free: New Scottish Plays*. London, Nick Hern Books, pp. 41–98.
Cooper, Neil (2013) 'White Rose, Tron Theatre Glasgow'. *Herald*, 28 February.
Corbett, John (2011) 'Translated Drama in Scotland', in I. Brown (ed.) *The Edinburgh Companion to Scottish Drama*. Edinburgh, Edinburgh University Press, pp. 95–106.
Coveney, Michael (1990) *The Citz: 21 Years of the Glasgow Citizens Theatre*. London, Nick Hern Books.
Craig, Cairns (1989) 'Scotland Ten Years On: The Changes That Took Place While Rip MacWinkle Slept', *Radical Scotland*, pp. 8–10, p. 5.
Cramer, Steve (2011) 'The Traverse, 1985–97', in Ian Brown (ed.) *The Edinburgh Companion to Scottish Drama*. Edinburgh, Edinburgh University Press, pp. 165–176.
Crichton, Mamie (1970) 'Hamlet Proves Tragedy for Citizens', *Scottish Daily Express*, 5 September.
Critics Awards for Theatre in Scotland (2003). 'Special Honour'. Available at: https://criticsawards.theatrescotland.com/2003-winners/
Devine, Tom (2006) *The Scottish Nation: 1700–2007*. London, Penguin.
Eddershaw, Margaret (1991) '"Echt Brecht?" Mother Courage at the Citizens, 1990', *New Theatre Quarterly*, 28:7, pp. 303–314.
Findlay, Bill (1996) 'Talking in Tongues: Scottish Translations 1970–1995', in Stevenson and Wallace (eds.) *Scottish Theatre Since the Seventies*. Edinburgh, Edinburgh University Press, pp. 186–197.
Gifford, Douglas (1996) 'Imagining Scotlands: The Return to Mythology in Modern Scottish Fiction', in S. Hagemann (ed.) *Studies in Scottish Fiction: 1945 to the Present*. Frankfurt, Peter Lang, pp. 17–49.

Greig, David (1996) *Europe & The Architect [Two Plays]*. London, Methuen.
Greig, David (2011) 'Interview: Mark Fisher & David Greig, Suspect Cultures and Home Truths', in Anja Muller and Clare Wallace (eds.) *Cosmotopia: Transnational Identities in David Greig's Theatre*. Prague, Univerzita Karlova v Praze, pp. 14–31.
Hannan, Chris (1990) 'Elizabeth Gordon Quinn', in Alasdair Cameron (ed.) *Scot-Free: New Scottish Plays*. London, Nick Hern Books, pp. 105–146.
Hannan, Chris (1996a) *Shining Souls*. London, Nick Hern Books.
Hannan, Chris (1996b) 'Fragile Broken and Desperate: Playwright and Actor Simon Donald Interviews Chris Hannan'. Typescript. National Library of Scotland. Acc.11865/2b
Harrower, David (2015) *Knives in Hens*. London, Methuen.
Heggie, Iain (1988) *A Wholly Healthy Glasgow*. London, Methuen.
Horvat, Ksenija (2007) 'Varieties of Gender Politics, Sexuality and Thematic Innovation in Late Twentieth-Century Drama', in Brown, I. (ed.) *The Edinburgh History of Scottish Literature: Volume 3*. Edinburgh, Edinburgh University Press, pp. 295–303.
Horvat, Ksenija (2011) 'Liz Lochhead', in Ian Brown (ed.) *The Edinburgh Companion to Scottish Drama*. Edinburgh, Edinburgh University Press, pp. 177–187.
Hutchinson, David (1996a) 'Glasgow and its Citizens', in Randall Stevenson and Gavin Wallace (eds.) *Scottish Theatre Since the Seventies*. Edinburgh, Edinburgh University Press, pp. 57–64.
Hutchinson, David (1996b) 'Economics, Culture and Playwriting', in Stevenson and Wallace (eds.) *Scottish Theatre Since the Seventies*. Edinburgh, Edinburgh University Press, pp. 206–214.
Innes, Christopher (1997) 'Theatre After Two World Wars', in Russel Brown, John (ed.) *The Oxford Illustrated History of Theatre*. Oxford, Oxford University Press, pp. 380–435.
Kershaw, Baz (1994) 'Framing the Audience for Theatre', in R. Keat, N. Whiteley and Nigel Abercrombie (2004) *The Authority of the Consumer*. London, Routledge, pp. 154–173.
Lochhead, Liz (1985) *Tartuffe: A Translation into Scots from the Original by Molière*. Edinburgh, Polygon and Third Eye Centre.
Lochhead, Liz (2009) *Mary Queen of Scots Got Her Head Chopped Off*. London, Nick Hern Books.
MacDonald, Robert David (trans.) (1990) *Pirandello, Enrico Four*. London, Oberon Books.
Maguire, Tom (2011) 'Women Playwrights', in Ian Brown (ed.) *The Edinburgh Companion to Scottish Drama*. Edinburgh, Edinburgh University Press, pp. 154–164.

Maloney, Paul (2011) 'Twentieth-Century Popular Theatre', in Brown (ed.) *The Edinburgh Companion to Scottish Drama*. Edinburgh, Edinburgh University Press, pp. 60–72.
McDonald, Jan (2004) 'Theatre in Scotland', in Baz Kershaw (ed.) *The Cambridge History of British Theatre: Volume 3, Since 1895*. Cambridge, Cambridge University Press, pp. 195–227.
McGrath, John (1981) *The Cheviot the Stag and the Black, Black Oil*. London, Methuen.
McMillan, Joyce (1988) *The Traverse Theatre Story*. London, Methuen.
McMillan, Joyce (1990) 'Jock Tamson's Bairns'. *Guardian*, 28 January.
McMillan, Joyce (2003) 'Shining Souls'. *Scotsman*, 2 March.
McMillan, Joyce (2022) 'Medea Review'. *Scotsman*, 14 August.
Milling, Jane (2012) *Modern British Playwriting: The 1980s*. London, Methuen.
Morgan, Fergus (2021) 'Move: The Setting Is the Star'. *Stage*, 9 August.
Müller, Anja (2005) 'We are also Europe: Reviewing Displacement in David Greig's Plays', in Houswitschka and Müller (eds.) *Staging Displacement, Exile and Diaspora*. Trier: Wissenschaftlicher Verlag Trier, pp. 151–168.
National Library of Scotland (2010) 'Twelve Key Scottish Plays 1970–2010: Knives in Hens'. Available at: https://digital.nls.uk/scottish-theatre/knives-in-hens/index.html
Nuttal, Jay (2018) 'Europe-Leeds Playhouse'. *THEREVIEWSHUB*, 16 October. Available at: https://www.thereviewshub.com/europe-leeds-playhouse/
Oliver, Cordelia (1984) *Glasgow Citizens' Theatre, Robert David MacDonald and German Drama*. Glasgow, Third Eye Centre.
Paterson, Lindsay (1996) 'Language and Identity on the Stage', in Stevenson and Wallace (eds.) *Scottish Theatre Since the Seventies*. Edinburgh, Edinburgh University Press, pp. 76–83.
Reinelt, Janelle (2011) 'David Greig', in Middeke, Martin, Peter Paul Schnierer and Aleks Sierz (eds.) *The Methuen Drama Guide to Contemporary British Playwrights*. London, Bloomsbury, pp. 203–222.
Reizbaum, Marilyn (1992) 'Canonical Double-Cross: Scottish and Irish Women's Writing', in Karen R. Lawrence (ed.) *Decolonizing Tradition: New Views of Twentieth-Century 'British' Literature Canons*. Urbana, University of Illinois Press, pp. 165–190.
Rodríguez, Verónica (2019) *David Greig's Holed Theatre: Globalization, Ethics and the Spectator*. Cham, Switzerland, Palgrave Macmillan.
Robson, Mark (2016) 'David Greig's Other Heading'. *Contemporary Theatre Review* 26:1, pp. 39–48.
Schaaf, Jeanne (2016) 'Non-Places" and u-topos in The Cosmonaut's Last message to the Woman he Once Loved in the Former Soviet Union and Europe by David Greig', in Peraldo (ed.) *Literature and Geography:*

The Writing of Space Throughout History. Newcastle, Cambridge Scholars Publishing, pp. 81–98.
Scullion, Adrienne (1995), 'Feminine Pleasures and Masculine Indignities', in Christopher Whyte (ed.) *Gendering the Nation: Studies in Modern Scottish Literature.* Edinburgh, Edinburgh University Press, pp. 169–204.
Smith, Donald (1998) '1950–1995'. Bill Findlay (ed.) *A History of Scottish Theatre.* Edinburgh, Edinburgh University Press, pp. 253–308.
Scullion, Adrienne (2004) 'Citz Scotland where it Did? Shakespeare in Production at the Citizens' Theatre, Glasgow, 1970–1974', in Willy Maley and Andrew Murphy (eds.) *Shakespeare and Scotland.* Manchester, Manchester University Press, pp. 172–186.
Scullion, Adrienne (2007) 'Devolution and Drama', in B. Schoene (ed.) *The Edinburgh Companion to Contemporary Scottish Literature.* Edinburgh, Edinburgh University Press, pp. 68–77.
Stevenson, Randall (1993) 'Re-enter Houghmagandie: Language as Performance in Liz Lochhead's Tartuffe', in Crawford and Varty (eds.) *Liz Lochhead's Voices.* Edinburgh, Edinburgh University Press, pp. 109–123.
Stevenson, Randall (1996) 'Charting Scottish Theatre', in Randall Stevenson and Gavin Wallace (eds.) *Scottish Theatre Since the Seventies.* Edinburgh, Edinburgh University Press, pp. 1–20.
Stevenson, Randall (2004) 'Triumphant Tartuffication: Liz Lochhead's Translation of Molière's *Tartuffe*', in Bill Findlay (ed.) *Frae Ither Tongues: Essays on Modern Translations into Scots.* Clevedon, Multilingual Matters, pp. 106–122.
Taudevin, Julia (2021) *Move.* London, Bloomsbury.
Taylor, Paul (1999) 'There's No Place Like Home', *Independent*, 28 April.
Todd, Richard (1996) *Consuming Fictions: The Booker Prize and Fiction in Britain Today.* London, Bloomsbury.
The Traverse Theatre at 50 (2013) BBC Radio 3, 17 March.
Wallace, Clare (2013) *The Theatre of David Greig.* London, Bloomsbury.
Weight, Richard (2002) *Patriots: National Identity in Britain, 1940–2000.* Basingstoke, Palgrave MacMillan.
Wright, Allen (1970) 'Hamlet Depicted as a Gibbering Oaf'. *Scotsman*, 7 September.
Zenzinger, Peter (1996) 'The New Wave', in Stevenson and Wallace (eds.) *Scottish Theatre Since the Seventies.* Edinburgh, Edinburgh University Press, pp. 125–137.

CHAPTER 3

Other Stages

It is Saturday 26 October 2013 and an audience of around sixty has entered the café at Edinburgh's Summerhall to be welcomed by an usher and led down a flight of stairs to the basement. A number of people—myself included—have noticed that the widely celebrated scenographer, artist, playwright and screenwriter John Byrne is present, a detail that adds a little glamour to the proceedings. Byrne, as ever, cuts a dashing figure. In the basement we encounter a detailed exhibition spread over four adjacent rooms, which concerns the young experimental Scottish theatre-maker Paul Bright, and his attempt in the late 1980s to stage an adaptation of James Hogg's cult gothic novel *The Private Memoirs and Confessions of a Justified Sinner* (1824). After browsing the various artifacts on display,—programmes, posters, photographs, newspaper reviews, sketches, video clips, props, letters from the Scottish Arts Council and several annotated copies of Hogg's novel—we are escorted upstairs to the main performance space. Here we find a lone actor, George Anton, who for the next ninety minutes or so reflects, in a kind of lecture demonstration, on his own involvement in Bright's ambitious and ill-fated venture.

Anton describes the various theatrical happenings and avant-garde performances that made up Bright's project, which was conceived in six episodes, and performed in various locations including a Celtic pub in Glasgow and the summit of Arthur's Seat in Edinburgh. With the

© The Author(s), under exclusive license to Springer Nature Switzerland AG 2024
T. Reid, *Theatre and Performance in Contemporary Scotland*, https://doi.org/10.1007/978-3-031-61191-9_3

Fig. 3.1 George Anton as George Anton in Untitled Projects' *Paul Bright's Confessions of a Justified Sinner*, 2013. Reproduced with kind permission from Tommy Ga-Ken Wan

help of a young computer operative, he illustrates his account with film clips drawn from original archive footage but also several interviews with contemporary theatre-makers including Tim Crouch, Giles Havergal, Katie Mitchell and Alison Peebles, who each share their own recollections of Bright. Bright we learn, left Scotland in 1989 before completing his final chapter and died a forgotten man in a Brussels hospital in 2010. After his death a housemate came across a box of memorabilia among his effects, which contained much of the material used in the exhibition and also a letter addressed to Anton. The evening's performance, we are told, is a response to that letter, in part an attempt to rescue an important and inspirational figure from obscurity, but additionally an opportunity for Anton to ruminate with some regret on the deterioration of his personal relationship with Bright, especially their final parting. The show, *Paul Bright's Confessions of a Justified Sinner*, is a co-production between Glasgow's Untitled Productions and the National Theatre of Scotland (NTS) (Fig. 3.1).

What are we to make of this show? The autobiographical testimony of the actor, the recorded interviews, the presentation of material evidence in the form of an exhibition, each element references strategies employed by documentary theatre-makers. The performance is presented as a reliable, authentic and meaningful witness to history. However, as the evening unfolds, and audience members old enough to be familiar with the Scottish theatre scene in the 1980s struggle to remember Bright, they begin to suspect that this documentary is an elaborate hoax, a fiction, a lie even. There was, and is, no such person as Paul Bright. What we are witnessing is simultaneously a contemplation on the toolkit currently employed to establish theatrical 'truth', and a multi-layered homage to Hogg's classic novel, which itself features an unreliable editor, a visionary fanatic and Scottish literature's original doppelganger. There is quite a lot going on in this show.

Paul Bright is a show that sets out deliberately to deconstruct representational practice. Director Stewart Laing and writer Pamela Carter seem at least partly intent on exposing the mechanics of the strand of theatre that eschews fiction in favour of something supposedly more authentic or real. In this sense the piece is a timely intervention. As Stephen Bottoms has noted in the aftermath of 9/11 and the war on terror, mere 'dramatic fiction' was 'seen as an inadequate response to the current global situation' and this feeling led to an explosion in documentary and verbatim theatre (2006: 57). Beyond employing a number of strategies typically associated with documentary theatre, however, *Paul Bright* foregrounds a number of other concerns including a powerful mistrust of metanarratives and a deliberate troubling of the ground on which notions of dramatic character are constructed. These last two preoccupations place it firmly in a tradition of experimental performance although the show was co-produced by the national company and consequently positioned quite centrally in the mainstream of theatre practice. The question of how such work comes to be situated in this way is one that concerns me in this chapter because, I want to suggest, the answer reveals a significant expansion in Scotland's theatre and performance culture which has not been fully reflected in scholarship. With few exceptions, existing accounts of theatre in contemporary Scotland have tended to focus on plays and playwrights or theatres and theatre companies and have not sought to locate experimental performance within the national performance archive. In his essay 'History in Contemporary Scottish Theatre' David Archibald notes in passing that 'the use of historical settings is notable by its relative absence' in the work of performance companies such as Suspect Culture and Vanishing Point, for example, but *The Edinburgh Companion to Scottish Drama* in which Archibald's essay is included, contains no chapter dedicated to experimental work (2011: 90). Similarly, in his book *Scottish Theatre: Diversity, Language, Continuity*, Ian Brown dedicates a couple of pages to the work of performance companies, in this case Untitled Projects and Grid Iron, acknowledging that through their contribution 'the possibilities of Scottish theatre have expanded', but again his discussion of the work is limited (2013: 231). In *Modernism and Scottish Theatre Since 1969* (2019), Mark Brown includes an interview with Stewart Laing much of which is devoted to discussion of the Glasgow Citizens where early in his career Laing was assistant to Philip Prowse.

In this context, Alasdair Cameron's 1994 essay 'Experimental Theatre in Scotland' is an unusual piece of writing. Its choice of topic is clearly in tension with what Adrienne Scullion has identified as 'the preferences and priorities that shape[d] the evolution of Scottish theatre studies in the period from the late 1970s' which favoured establishing a visible text-based tradition (Scullion 2002: 216). By focusing on experimental work Cameron, identified a lacuna in what was at that time still a relatively young discipline. Perhaps he would have continued to explore this territory, but his early death in June of 1994 left a gap in scholarship which has only recently begun to be filled. The chapter takes Cameron's work as its starting point to consider the ways in which experimental work has fed into and shaped Scotland's contemporary performance culture. It is also indebted to Steve Greer's Arts and Humanities Research Council funded project *Live Art in Scotland* (2022) which is explicitly designed to fill this gap in scholarship. Greer explains:

> Though Scotland has been home to some of Live Art's most (in)famous events, existing histories of theatre and performance emphasise a literary dramatic tradition of plays and playwrights, and rarely address Live Art as a significant field of practice. At the same time, studies of Live Art tend to focus on practice in England and London – with Scotland either ignored or only included at the margins. (Greer 2022)

In what follows, I adopt a fairly loose definition of the experimental, to encompass the work of companies, such as Untitled Projects with whom I opened this chapter, but also individual artists, festivals, venues and funding streams. My aim is to give prominence to the experimental, as a distinct strand of contemporary Scottish performance practice, to trace some of its history, and to tease out some of the ways in which its manifestation might be considered distinctively Scottish, and consequently as contributing to the national conversation. To this end, I want to return to that evening at Summerhall in the autumn of 2013.

It is significant that the makers of *Paul Bright* should turn to a famous Scottish historical novel for inspiration. Hogg's book is a study of the seductive power of evil and the excesses of Calvinism, but it is also a contemplation on the respective values of the intellect and the imagination, of the rational and irrational. Set in early eighteenth-century Scotland, around the time of the Treaty of Union (1707), it tells of the corruption of Robert Wringhim, a young man of strict Calvinist upbringing, by a mysterious stranger named Gil-Martin under whose influence Wringham commits a series of murders including that of his brother George. By applying remorseless Calvinist logic, Gil-Martin convinces Wringhim that no sin can affect his salvation. Because Robert is one of the 'elect', chosen by god and pre-ordained to enter the kingdom of heaven, he can commit any act without fear of consequence, he is thus the 'justified sinner' of the book's title and according to Gil-Martin his duty 'as one of God's consecrated is to cut off' sinners (Hogg 2008: 152). As Hogg's narrative progresses Robert's state of mind deteriorates and he finds himself unable to shake off Gil-Martin, whose menacing presence harasses him at every turn. He begins to experience blackouts during which he apparently commits the vilest of atrocities. Finally, partly in order to escape his tormentor, Robert kills himself.

The Confessions is a kind of satire on religious fanaticism then, and clearly at some level, Hogg wants us to recognise Gil-Martin as the devil incarnate, as alluring as he is dangerous. However, the structure of the novel never quite allows us to dismiss the idea that Gil-Martin is simply a figment of Robert's diseased imagination. The 'confessions' of the title take the form of a memoir written by Robert before his suicide in 1712 which forms the heart of the book. It is, however, bracketed by an 'Editor's Narrative' dated 1824, which gives details of Robert's origins and upbringing, and various other versions of his story drawn from folklore and rumour. The novel ends with the editor's discovery of the memoir in a grave containing Robert's un-naturally preserved corpse. The *Confessions* thus stages its meditation on fanaticism from the inside and the outside and in terms of an opposition between metalanguage and performance, surface and depth, conviction and ambiguity, historical distance, and proximity. Many of its key events are narrated twice from radically different perspectives. Hogg even disrupts his own authorial power by appearing as himself towards the end of the novel in his authentic folk persona as the Etterick Shepherd to whom the baffled editor applies for information about the whereabouts of Wringhim's grave. In this interlude, Hogg refuses to have anything to do with the unseemly business of ransacking a grave for antiquarian trophies. Thus, as Scot Brewster observes, at 'every level, Hogg's text is riven by questions concerning legitimacy, coherence, and the distinctions between the "inside" and "outside" of the self' (Brewster 2005: 80).

Like Hogg's novel *Paul Bright* involves dissimulation, and it deliberately foregrounds the instability of signs, in this case theatrical signs. Just as the unreliable voice of the editor is crucial to the overall effect of the novel—he is ostensibly rational and pragmatic but also self-serving and judgemental—in Carter's text these characteristics are reproduced in the figure of George Anton, the actor narrator. Early in his lecture demonstration, Anton explains how he came to abandon Bright's project:

> I left Scotland because I got one of those offers you can't turn down ... a TV series about pilots in world war two ... a massive budget and a great cast with the likes of Jeremy Northam, and Neil Dudgeon (Carter 2015: 23).

Although his testimony is unreliable, in the sense that Paul Bright never existed, the actor playing George Anton in the show is the actor George Anton who appeared in *Piece of Cake*, a six-part television series produced by London Weekend Television in 1988, which also featured Northam and Dudgeon. Similarly, the fabricated testimonies of Mitchell, Crouch, Havergal and Peebles are delivered in video clips featuring Mitchell, Crouch, Havergal and Peebles. Among other things, this troubling of the fundamental premise of testimonial theatre exposes what Cormac Power describes as 'the stage as a site of representation and citation rather than "presence" and "immediacy"' (Power 2008: 118). Throughout the piece, like the editor in Hogg's novel, Anton attempts to rationalise uncanny events retrospectively. The fictional Paul Bright is conjured as an Artaudian figure, a man of mysterious and disastrous passions, whose mission is to create a mystical and spiritual theatre. Like Wringhim he is a decidedly gothic creation who rejects the illusion of surface realities in favour of something more authentic, in this case, more authentically Scottish. It is significant in this context that the historical backdrop to Bright's fictional attempts is the 1980s, the decade when the divergences in political aspiration that sowed the seeds of devolution, and the growth of the independence movement became readily apparent.

In his influential essay 'Heartlands: Contemporary Scottish Gothic' David Punter identifies a preoccupation with history as the defining characteristic of Scottish Gothic, especially 'the issues and problems which accompany the depiction of past and present national history' and 'a certain dealing with the necessary distortions of history' (1999: 101–102). Ian Duncan takes up this theme:

> The thematic core of Scottish Gothic consists of an association between the national and the *uncanny* or *supernatural*. To put it schematically: Scottish Gothic represents (with greater historical and anthropological specificity than in England) the uncanny recursion of an ancestral identity alienated from modern life (2012: 123).

This alienation has its roots in Scotland's condition as a stateless nation and consequently, in this way of thinking, Scottish Gothic represents the re-resurgence of a native or ancestral power that has been alienated from Scottish life by the Act of Union, by modernisation, by the defeat of the Jacobite Clans, by the Enlightenment and by increasing divisions between an educated urban professional class and the rural population. Hogg understood himself as emerging from a pre-modern, largely pre-literate rural folk culture—somewhat akin to the one conjured by Harrower in *Knives in Hens*—and he understood this culture's authentic primitivism as something distinct from both the discourses of the Enlightenment and the politically aware rural working-class culture of south-west Scotland which we now associate with Robert Burns. It is no coincidence that Scottish Gothic emerges in the aftermath of Enlightenment and the consolidation of Unionist hegemony, therefore, and it can, as Murray Pittock argues, be understood as 'the aesthetic sign of the political defeat of opposition to the British state' (Pittock 2008: 26). On the other hand, we might read the recurring trope that combines isolation and conviction, particularly when mediated through madness, criminality and the sociopathic, as evidence of the impossibility of Union, either in an individual or collective sense. The connections that Punter makes between the Gothic and Scotland—the former about states of crisis, the latter a state in crisis, the former haunted by the past, the latter haunted by history—proves especially pertinent to *Paul Bright*, in which the historian, the unreliable narrator, is clearly identifiable, to borrow Liz Tomlin's phrase, as 'a constructed representation or strategic illusion of unmediated presence' and in which the slippage between past and present, fact and fiction, evidence and imagination increases as the performance progresses (Tomlin 2013: 80).

To return to my original observation, then, *Paul Bright's Confessions of a Justified Sinner* is simultaneously a contemplation on the strategies employed to establish theatrical 'truth', and also a multi-layered reworking of Hogg's classic gothic novel. Like the novel that inspired it, it is something more than fiction. It is a lie, a deliberate, elaborate lie, which nonetheless carries a vital charge of explanatory power. Consequently, it raises interesting questions about the relationship between performance and truth, performance and the past, and the unstable character of history in the construction of national narratives. The show opened in June 2013 at Glasgow's Tramway a venue that has facilitated the kind of experimental performance *Paul Bright* exemplifies.

Tramway

In the second half of the twentieth century, experimental theatre in the UK had largely, if not exclusively, been produced in London. However, in the 1980s the threat of interference from a government whose outlook was dominated by conservative social values became a reality. The abolition of the Greater London Council (GLC) in 1986 made London the only Western capital without a single unitary elected local government and was, as Michael Jacobs noted at the time, 'specifically designed to defeat an example of successful, popular and socialist public administration' (1986: 1306). The GLC was a major supporter of the Arts, and one consequence of its dissolution was the disappearance of over one million pounds a year in grants. Subsequently, a hike in property prices, the persistence of a 'value for money' rhetoric, and a rise in the cost of living made the prospect of creating experimental work in London increasingly less attractive. Meanwhile, four hundred miles north, Glasgow District Council began to take the view that a thriving Arts sector would bring economic benefits to the city. It then invested accordingly, creating a favourable environment for a variety of forms of performance. The Council had been persuaded by evidence collated in John Myerscough's report *The Economic Importance of the Arts in Britain*

(1988), in which he understood the Arts as a small but important part of Glasgow's economy, which also had the additional benefit of generating growth in retailing and hospitality. In the wider context they had the potential to offset the decline in heavy industry and manufacturing that marked the period. In 1987, the Council's commitment paid off when Glasgow was named European City of Culture for 1990, joining Amsterdam (1987), Berlin (1988) and Paris (1989). Preparations began at pace.

A Festivals Unit, led by Robert Palmer and Neil Wallace, was established in 1987 to coordinate the cultural programme of the City of Culture year and their first production, in 1988, was Peter Brook's *Mahabharata*. Brook's acclaimed eight-hour-long epic had a significant impact, partly because it was not staged in any other location in the UK, but also because a new venue was built to house it. A Victorian tram shed located south of the Clyde, which had served from 1964 to 1986 as the city's Museum of Transport, was converted into a large performance venue: Tramway. The building's monumental scale, its relatively peripheral location, and its industrial past also drew comparison with other major European performance venues including Cartoucherie in Paris, which had formerly been a munitions factory, and Mercat del Flors in Barcelona, which had also been established in the 1980s in an old warehouse of the Palace of Agriculture. The arrival of Tramway brought a couple of distinct benefits. In the first place, its cavernous main space encouraged established Scottish companies to experiment with approaches to staging not easily accommodated in black box or conventional proscenium arch theatres. Wildcat's ambitious promenade production of John McGrath's *Border Warfare* (1989), which used free-floating platforms, was one example, as was its production of *John Brown's Body* (1990), for which the designer Pamela Howard built a fairground railway around the perimeter of the space and used gigantic puppets of the kind usually associated with outdoor European performance. Communicado's *Jock Tamson's Bairns*, which initiated the 1990 theatre programme, was similarly ambitious. The venue had the additional benefit of attracting high-profile international companies to the city.

Outside of August at the EIF Scotland had struggled to establish itself as a regular destination for large-scale international work. Tramway changed that, and as well as delighting audiences the international work staged there inspired current and future Scottish theatre-makers. In 1989 the venue hosted Brith Gof's *Gododdin*, which as Cameron notes 'brought a taste of dangerous theatre to the Tramway with … the seemingly indiscriminate hurling of trees' and 'the unleashing of huge quantities of water' (1994: 128). In demonstrating the potentials of large-scale site-responsive work made without reference to London *Goddodin's* proved inspirational. Its focus on national identity, post-industrial space and grand scale were echoed by the music/theatre collective Test Department in their 1990 multi-media extravaganza *The Second Coming*, for example. Organised around a text by the Scottish journalist Neal Ascherson, the show was performed at the St. Rollox Engineering Works, a working locomotive yard in the northeast of the city and, as Cameron recalls, 'combined the smell of oil, multi-screen projection and heavy machinery with a startling exploitation of the unusual perspectives afforded by the forest of columns which supported the glass roof' (1994: 128). The idea of a 'ghost that haunts the site' is 'recurrent in site-specific performance' as Cathy Turner has noted, but the question of 'whether the site haunts the work or vice versa often seems intriguingly unclear' (Turner 2004: 374). Involving around fifty performers against a backdrop of industrial detritus in a space the size of two and a half football pitches, *The Second Coming*, was an explicitly political interrogation of Thatcherism's policy of de-industrialisation and the resulting heritage industry, which Ascherson viewed as deeply problematic in its uncomplicated nostalgia for a time when workers knew their place. It was pretty clear that the site was intended to haunt the work. The show also made extensive use of local people both as performers and as technical support, again making the connection with location explicit. Similar spectacular forays into Glasgow's industrial past were staged by Bill Bryden at the Harland & Wolff Shed in Govan, in *The Ship* (1990) and *The Big Picnic* (1994). The former involved the construction and launching of a ship, in apparent celebration of the importance of the industry to Glasgow's identity, and the latter followed a group of Glaswegian men as they experienced the horrors of WW1. As Olga Taxidou argues, the 'unreconstructed glamourisation of labour presented in *The Ship*' and the presentation of war 'as a set of personal journeys from innocence to experience' in The Big Picnic appeared ahistorical and uncritical, and while strong on affect, both now look like sentimental studies in Glaswegian masculinity (1996: 173). Nonetheless, their staging gestured towards new possibilities for large-scale Scottish theatre.

Elsewhere, the City of Culture programme at Tramway also included Robert Lepage's *Tectonic Plates*, the sophistication and pronounced playfulness of which made a strong impression on the director John Tiffany who saw it while still a science student at Glasgow University. 'It made me want to be a director', Tiffany recalls, 'I want to create magic for people and for them to see how it is done' (Tiffany 2010). Similarly, when Suspect Culture—the company founded by David Greig and Graham Eatough in the early 1990s—began making work, they did so under the influence of 'European and North American work they'd been exposed to during the early days of Glasgow's Tramway … Eatough cites The Wooster Group and Pina Bausch as his own biggest influences at that time' (Cooper 2009). The Wooster Group, with its distinctive brand of experimental theatre and its deliberate disturbing of representational norms, bought three shows to Tramway in 1990, *L.S.D (… Just the High Points …)*, *Frank Dell's the Temptation of St Anthony*, and a work in progress of *Brace Up!* These shows were a great success with Glasgow audiences, which had already begun to develop a taste for interrogations of representational norms.

As the twentieth century drew to a close, the EIF, the Fringe and Glasgow's Mayfest, all curated programmes that included experimental performance, although none was principally dedicated to its production. During Mayfest 1990, for example, Glasgow audiences were treated to performances from Spalding Gray, with his monologue *Monster in a Box*, the burlesque drag company La Gran Scena from New York, and the Belgian choreographer Wim Vandekeybus' *The Bearer of Bad News* (*Les Porteuses de Mauvaises Nouvelles*). This last piece went on to win a Bessie—New York Dance and Performance Award—for ground-breaking choreography. Seeds were sown in this period then, and in subsequent decades Glasgow was to become a centre for experimental performance, particularly the 'unruly, divergent and extensive practice(s) of live art' (Heddon and Klein 2012: 1).

NRLA, Behaviour, Take Me Somewhere

In March 2010, the National Review of Live Art (NRLA), 'the longest running international festival of performance art in the world' celebrated its thirtieth anniversary as part of the larger *New Territories* performance festival in venues across Glasgow: The Arches, Tramway, the Centre for Contemporary Arts (CCA) and the Glasgow Film Theatre (Klein 2010:

55). This 2010 NRLA was to be the last, and in form and function it had the flavour of a memorial celebration, offering as it did a condensed snapshot of work performed at the NRLA over its thirty-year history. Its artistic director, Nikki Millican, who had relocated with the festival to Glasgow in 1988, and whose company New Moves International (NMI) was responsible for both *New Territories* and NRLA, invited artists and collectives who had been associated with the latter since its early years at Nottingham's Midland Group Arts Centre, 1979–1986. These included Alastair Snow, Anne Seagrave, Anne Bean, Robert Ayers, Forkbeard Fantasy, Forced Entertainment and Neil Bartlett, who had been MC for the festival in 1986, and reprised that role in 2010. Younger artists, such as Sam Rose, Richard Dedomenici, Kate Stannard, Francesca Steele and Kira O'Reilly, who had been promoted via the NRLA's Platform initiative for emerging talent, also performed as did international artists including Stelarc, Guillermo Gómez-Peña, Ron Athey, Jamie MacMurray, Lee Wen, Yann Marussich and Silke Mansholt. In the years between 1988 and 2010—apart from a brief sojourn at London's ICA in 1993—the NRLA remained in Glasgow.

The CCA, which was a key venue throughout the period, had begun life in Glasgow's Blythswood Square in 1973, as an initiative intended by the SAC to counterbalance the art gallery it supported in its Edinburgh Charlotte Square offices. The playwright Tom McGrath successfully applied for the job of Director, and on appointment changed its name to The Third Eye Centre. In 1975 he moved the Centre to its current more central location in part of the listed Alexander 'Greek' Thompson building at 350 Sauchiehall Street, where it could expect higher foot fall. The venue occupied and thus centrally located was the site of several very significant performance events, before changing its name and relaunching as the CCA in 1992. The first NRLA in Scotland was hosted at The Third Eye Centre, and for it Millican commissioned DV8 Physical Theatre's *Dead Dreams of Monochrome Men,* which was to become among the company's most renowned productions. Inspired by Brian Masters' book, *Killing for Company* (1985), about the mass-murderer Dennis Nilsen, *Dead Dreams* offered a sustained and visceral critique of the alienation and homophobia suffered by gay men in the 1980s, living as they did in the shadow of AIDS, and an acute dissection of male violence as a response to fear both of vulnerability and genuine male intimacy. In 1996 Millican commissioned Forced Entertainment, who had premiered their durational piece *Speak Bitterness* at NRLA 1994, to produce *Quizoola!*

another durational performance in which 'one member of a pair of performers in clown makeup chooses from a list of some two thousand questions, ranging from the mundane to the personal to the metaphysical' while the other improvises answers (Buckley 2016: 35). *Quizoola!* has remained in the company's repertoire, and was performed as recently as May 2023, in Maribor, Slovenia. The list goes on. For NRLA 2002, Third Angel's ten-minute performance for a single audience member, *Where Have They Hidden All The Answers?* was Millican's key commission, and in 2005 Franko B was artist in residence with *Still Life* and *Why are You Here?*

The activity described above can be credited substantially to Millican's tenacity and her inspired commissioning and curatorial policy, which purposefully encouraged risk taking and experimentation. Over the course of its lifetime the NRLA showcased dozens of artists, established and emerging, national and international, as well as becoming 'the occasion for the meeting of the international coalition of live art programmers and organizers' (Klein 2010: 55). As part of *New Territories* it also provided training opportunities. The NMI Winter School, 2003–2011, was as Stephen Greer explains:

> ... the direct evolution of the organisation's earlier Choreographic Core scheme developed in the mid-1990s to support artists working in contemporary dance and running parallel to the Platform and later Elevator strands of the NRLA programme for emergent and early-career artists. (Greer 2020: 215)

Contributing artists, Greer notes, included 'many of the major figures of Live Art active before and since the turn of the millennium' and the Winter School thus offered Scottish artists, and artists living and working in Scotland, the opportunity to benefit from engagement with Live Art pedagogies which, like the work itself, tended to exist outside the mainstream (2020: 214). Conservatoire training, which in Scotland largely took place at the Royal Scottish Academy of Music and Drama (RSAMD)—from 2011 the Royal Conservatoire of Scotland—was almost exclusively industry and skills-based in focus. By contrast, the Winter School offered training opportunities free from the usual pressures of professional practice, and in which experimental and experiential processes took centre stage.

The impact of initiatives like the Winter School, and the vibrant Live Art scene from which it emerged, on the ecology of Scottish theatre is not easy to quantify, but insofar as both moved consciously and purposefully beyond conventional approaches to performance making, they opened new possibilities. Greer records the impact on Tashi Gore, artistic director of the multi-award-winning Glass Performance, of attending the Goat Island workshop in 2003, for instance, and the transformation in playwright Jenna Watt's approach to her work as a result of attending Ron Athey's Winter School course in 2009 (2020: 222, 225). Moreover, the close relationship between the Winter School and RSAMD, where classes were rescheduled to allow students on contemporary performance programmes to attend workshops, ensured emerging artists were able to experiment with new approaches to subject matter and new kinds of agency.

The Arches, which was situated under Central Station and the West Coast mainline, had been a venue for the NRLA from 1994, and was well placed to pick up some of its activity after Millican retired from the festival in 2010. Jackie Wylie, who took over as artistic director in 2008, after its founding director Andy Arnold became artistic director at the Tron, was particularly instrumental in promoting and supporting new work and in inviting international artists to the venue. Wylie had joined the Arches as a fundraising officer in 2004, and been arts programmer from 2005 to 8. She credits Arnold with establishing the venue's 'commitment to the uncovering of newness' and 'taking a chance on people' (in Bratchpiece and Innes 2021: 125). In 2009, the Arches launched its Behaviour Festival which brought international artists including Gob Squad, Peggy Shaw and Lois Weaver, Tim Crouch, Ann Liv Young, Ontroerend Goed and Brooklyn-based ensemble The TEAM to Glasgow and staged it alongside the work of emerging Scottish artists. Robert Softley Gale, later artistic director of Scottish disability-led performance company Birds of Paradise, premiered his solo piece *If These Spasms Could Speak*, at Behaviour 2012, for instance, and Peter McMaster's *27* in 2015. The recent publication *Brickwork: A Biography of the Arches* (2021) captures something of the energy and creativity of the venue under Wylie's leadership. Alongside Behaviour, the Arches Live festival supported emerging talent and a new generation of Scottish performance makers benefited. The work produced by Rosana Cade, Rob Drummond, Nic Green, Kieran Hurley, Gary McNair, Julia Taudevin and Jenna Watt has been widely admired, and it has also productively challenged existing category boundaries between theatre and performance. Hurley, Drummond and McNair have gone on to produce more conventional plays, for example, while their solo work, continues to trouble the hierarchies of conventional text-based theatre.

As a performance venue the Arches was always reliant for income on its famous nightclub. In 2015 it was forced into administration following the decision, taken in response to Police Scotland concerns about disorder at the venue including illegal drug use, of the city's licencing authorities to force it to close at midnight. Artists and arts commentators were appalled at what appeared to be a deliberate act of cultural vandalism. It also seemed hugely ironic, as Lyn Gardner observed, that at a time when governments were calling on arts organisations to be more entrepreneurial, it was 'the Arches' commercial business model—in which the club side of the business supported the art—that … resulted in this disaster' (2015). Wylie was on maternity leave at the time of the closure, but by her own account refocused her energy 'on finding resources for the arts programme to carry on … outwith the building, because that was the only option' (in Bratchpiece and Innes 2021: 184). Subsequently, using a grant from Creative Scotland and Glasgow Life and working with her collaborator LJ Findlay-Walsh, who had been her senior arts programmer at the Arches, Wylie founded Take Me Somewhere (TMS), a biennial festival and support organisation that since 2017 has worked to maintain Scotland's position as a centre for radical performance making.

TMS's development work continues the traditions of NMI and Arches Live Its Initiative Studio Somewhere which provides affordable rehearsal space and supports a series of residencies for artists based in Scotland. The eclecticism of its output is encouraging. Katy Dye's *Climate Grief Karaoke* (2022) encourages audience members to use rock standards—including Bon Jovi's *Living on a Prayer* the night I attended—to support each other through climate anxiety. Kirstin Halliday used her 2022 residency to develop a dance/drama piece about whiptail lizards, an all-female species that reproduces without fertilisation, but nevertheless engages in behaviour designed to stimulate ovulation. Halliday is interested in the labelling in natural history documentaries of this behaviour as 'lesbian'. She explains:

> Humoured by this cis-heteronormative description of queer sex, this performance work will draw parallels between the narration of Whiptail

Lizards' sex and depictions of lesbian sex in mainstream pornography. Embodying references from pop culture, cinema and porn, we will imagine the Whiptail Lizard population as an all-lesbian fantasy world, in which the male gaze and the fetishization of lesbians can be purposefully enacted and reconfigured as a kink dynamic within queer sex (TMS 2022).

In a further echo of the Winter School, Studio Somewhere Invites is an artist-led initiative that brings international artists to Glasgow to give workshops and also offers Graduate Residencies in partnership with the Contemporary Performance Practice course at the Royal Conservatoire of Scotland. These are designed to include free rehearsal space and mentorship.

The TMS festival itself has continued to platform international artists alongside homegrown talent. The inaugural 2017 event featured Kieran Hurley's solo piece *Head's Up* (2016) for instance, and AJ Taudevin's *Blow Off* (2016) alongside works by Barcelona-based El Conde De Torrfiel, Manchester's Quarantine and the Nigerian performance artist and poet Jaamil Olawale Kosoko. TMS 2023, ran at venues across Glasgow during 13–28 October and included work from Armenia, Belgium, Brazil, Cameroon, Italy, Finland, Scotland and South Africa.

Performance Companies

On 30 April 2008, the Scottish Arts Council (SAC) announced its annual round of flexible funding grants. As usual, there was not enough money to go round and among the more eyebrow-raising decisions, was the discontinuation of funding for the Glasgow-based performance Suspect Culture, which had been a leading innovator on the Scottish theatre scene since its establishment in the early 1990s. On the day of the SAC announcement, the company's show *Static* was in the middle of a successful run at Soho Theatre, London, where it was hailed by the *Time Out* critic Lucy Powell as 'a triumph of haunting drama', so the decision was more than usually perplexing (2008). It was, of course, neither the first nor—as the philistine closure of The Arches demonstrates—the last time choices made by Scottish funding bodies were to cause consternation and alarm, but Scotland, to borrow Neil Cooper's phrase had 'been waiting for Suspect Culture for a very long time' (2013: 49). The withdrawal of funding meant it ceased to make work much sooner than many would have wished, therefore, but its legacy and impact were none the less vital.

The company—whose core artistic team comprised the actor and director Graham Eatough, the playwright David Greig, the composer/musician Nick Powell and the designer Ian Scott—enriched Scotland's performance culture in several significant ways. Firstly, Suspect Culture was a determinedly collaborative creative venture, a fact which, as Clare Wallace notes, has tended to be 'subordinated to considerations of Greig's work as a playwright', but is worth considering because it modelled ways of working that connected Scotland with European and global trends in aesthetic experimentation (2015: 202). Secondly, its thematic focus on the existential yearnings of a twenty-something generation adrift in an age of inexorable neoliberal expansion set it apart from the mainstream Scottish tradition of direct political engagement, exemplified by 7:84 Scotland which incidentally also lost its funding in the same SAC round. Thirdly, and equally importantly, the work was marked by a consistent commitment to formal innovation. A brief account of some of its major projects will illustrate this last point.

Mainstream (1999) is a meditation on a sexual encounter between a record company executive and a personnel consultant, an anonymous 'hotel near the sea' (Greig 2013: 189). Its two central characters are played by four actors who appear and re-appear in all available combinations, including in same-sex combinations, in fifty-six short scenes, revising, re-voicing and echoing conversations so that it becomes difficult to recall who said what to whom. The actors lose their attachment to character and the encounter becomes universalised. 'If I put out my hand to touch you', one of the personnel consultants says to one of the record company executives:

> You would disappear.
> The room would disappear.
> And I'd be standing on a beach.
> In the dark.
> In the wind.
> And this maybe never happened (205)

There is yearning in the proposed gesture of reaching out a hand, that carries a utopian impulse, the impulse towards meaningful connection.

Like *Mainstream*, *Lament* (2002), makes use of verbal and gestural repetition. It begins on a highly personal level, with projections of video footage of interviews with the performers. Each recalls childhood memories, favourite outfits, present-day problems and fantasies about the future.

This material is then transcribed into the fabric of the remainder of the show with performers appearing in the clothes previously described, and recycling phrases used by their on-screen selves. Repetition intermittently acts as a suturing device. A discussion of apricots moves from their use as a staple in a primitive community, to a diet food in a book called *The Apricot Way*, to an object of bitter nostalgia in a war-ravaged country, for instance. The theme of loss, which as its title suggests, pervades the whole piece, and recurring motifs of endangered communities, species and languages as well as exploitative Western tourism and internecine conflict, suggest a critique of neoliberalism, and are interwoven with 'intensely personal experiences of alienation, longing and grief' (Wallace 2015: 197). These are accompanied by Nick Powell's rich score, which mirrors the construction of the text and actions' supporting characters who are 'only ever half in the world, trying but never succeeding to connect with it and each other' (Powell 2013: 70). Characters were still trying to connect with the world in *8000 m* (2004) when design took centre stage in a drama about the obsessive pull of mountaineering. Ian Scott covered Tramway's famous Peter Brook wall in layers of gauze and projections conjuring up the icy face of a Himalayan peak which the performers proceeded to climb.

The innovation and formal variety that marked Suspect Culture's work was accompanied by a commitment to collective creation which did not go unnoticed. After commenting on its 'superbly slick production' values, for instance, Sarah Jones described *The Escapologist* (2006) as 'all very Suspect Culture, born of their method of creating work in which words, design and music contribute equally from the moment of inception' (2006). This kind of practice is not without risk, of course, and its end results are sometimes uneven, and typically not to everyone's taste. For Elisabeth Mahoney *Lament* was 'another example of Suspect Culture's ability to discard many dramatic clichés to access a raw emotional landscape we rarely see in contemporary theatre' (Mahoney 2002). For Rebecca Caldwell, on the other hand, while 'terrifically ambitious' it was ultimately 'a triumph of style over substance' (Caldwell 2003). In the end, relatively poor critical response to the company's global revue *Futurology* (2007) were given disproportionate weight by SAC assessors who raised concerns regarding the company's ability to achieve its fundraising targets, despite its existing track record in attracting creative partners.

Although something of a forerunner, Suspect Culture was not the only influential and highly successful performance company to emerge in Scotland over the period covered by this study, nor was it alone in making a significant contribution to extending and enhancing the vocabulary of Scottish theatre by bringing it into conversation with theatre practice in Europe and beyond. Dan Rebellato's evaluation of its impact does, however, capture something of the capacity of small-scale companies to respond to the cultural zeitgeist with inventiveness and immediacy:

> Over twenty years, the theatre company Suspect Culture created one of the most ambitious and complex bodies of work in British theatre. Based in Scotland, but with international reach and reputation, their work was widely acclaimed for its originality, range, and restless formal inventiveness that sought to capture, interrogate and transcend the contemporary world. (Rebellato 2013: 299)

Thinking about the place of small-scale theatre companies from a Scottish perspective raises questions particular to national contexts. Funding mechanisms in Scotland differ from elsewhere in the UK, for instance, and the Scottish sector is small which necessarily affects conceptions of scale. Nonetheless, in so far as they remain outward-looking, experimental and internationally engaged, companies like Grid Iron, Vanishing Point and Untitled Projects have, like Suspect Culture, made valuable and sophisticated contributions to conversations in and about Scotland, during a time of political and constitutional transformation, as my account of *Paul Bright* earlier in this chapter shows.

Liz Tomlin notes that the expansion in activity in the independent theatre sector that marked the end of the twentieth century and the beginning of the twenty-first, was substantially enabled by National Lottery funding which was rolled out in 1995 (2013: 55). In 1997/8 there were five regularly funded independent companies in Scotland, and by 2007/8 there were fifteen. Building on the experiments of Test Department and Bill Bryden, the Edinburgh-based company Grid Iron has been well placed to engage with the possibilities of site-specific theatre. Although not the only Scottish company engaged in site-related work, it has certainly been the most prominent, and consequently provides a useful case study. As Fiona Wilkie observes the decision to move away from traditional theatre space is often motivated by a desire to foreground 'ideas of place and community' and because such ideas have taken centre stage in Scotland in recent decades, site-related practice has proved increasingly popular (Wilkie 2002: 144).

Originally conceived as a new writing company when founded in 1995 by co-artistic directors Judith Doherty and Ben Harrison, Grid Iron quickly became associated with award-winning site-related work. Although it has produced more than thirty shows this section will touch on a small selection, each of which engages with the possibilities of site-related performance differently. Within the context of a developing field Grid Iron has tended not to work on a monumental scale, nor has it systematically adopted a directly political agenda. It has instead created a number of promenade performances in which audiences are led or enticed through cleverly chosen interiors—and sometimes exteriors—and encouraged to explore their own response to the environment and its effect on their reading of the performance. Such practices work to throw spectators into awareness of themselves as interpreting subjects, and often lead to particularly vivid experiences. The company's breakthrough production, *The Bloody Chamber* (1997), involved staging an adaptation of Angela Carter's retelling of the Bluebeard myth, in Mary King's Close, one of many seventeenth-century streets built over during the modernisation of Edinburgh's Old Town. The small audience was led by a lantern-bearing woman—in Keith Lodwick's adaptation an older version of the young bride narrating her own tale—through a dark labyrinth of passages to the threshold of the room in which the heroine makes her grisly discovery. The show toured successfully in 1998 to among other places the London Dungeon and the concrete chambers under Belfast's Lagan Weir, but never quite recaptured the atmosphere supplied by Edinburgh's gothic past. *The Bloody Chamber* nevertheless established the company's reputation, winning a prestigious Herald Angel Award. Unearthing performance spaces in Scotland's capital was to become a habit. In the summer of 1998 their next show, *Gargantua,* was performed in the vaults beneath the Central Library on George IV Bridge, a venue christened the Underbelly by the company.

Grid Iron's next significant piece of work, its production of Douglas Maxwell's *Decky Does a Bronco* (2000), provides a more complex example of the potentials of this relationship. Staged outdoors using specialist equipment but in existing swing parks, *Decky* tells the tale, narrated by the grown-up David, of a group of nine-year-old boys in Girvan on Scotland's west coast in the summer of 1983. Capturing the excitement and danger of school holidays, at a time when these were spent relatively free of adult supervision, the adult cast's death-defying displays of playground gymnastics centred around the 'bronco' of the title, the ultimate swing trick which the boys use to vie for status. As the smallest and least confident of the group, Decky's inability to perform this trick leads to constant teasing and ultimately to the play's grim dénouement. In Harrison's production adult actors played the boys and their grown-up selves, these older selves constantly circling their younger ones. In combination with the outdoor setting, this doubling created a kind of palimpsest of memory and nostalgia. Adult performers were employed not as a gimmick, but to suggest that vivid experiences in childhood are inevitably carried into adulthood. At the Edinburgh Fringe in August 2000, *Decky Does a Bronco* was premiered in the Scotland Yard Playground in the New Town. Here as elsewhere, the sounds of real children playing in the distance added atmosphere and poignancy. In addition, and in common with other performances in genuinely public spaces, the site carried the threat of possible disruption, however accidental. Occasionally such interventions proved entirely fortuitous, as Susannah Clapp acknowledged in her review for *The Observer*:

> ... as the hero reflected on the persistence of things after childhood tragedy, a real - proper-size - child burst out of the bushes surrounding the stage and gamboled towards it, carefree and callous - as if to prove his point. (Clapp 2000)

Decky Does a Bronco won a Scotsman Fringe First award for innovation in theatre and outstanding new production, and a Stage award for Best Ensemble. It toured extensively in Britain and Ireland and was successfully revived by Grid Iron in 2010. In 2012 the Wales Millennium Centre, in collaboration with Theatr na n'Óg, toured a Welsh language version of the play retitled *Ma Bili'n Bwrw'r Bronco*.

2005 saw Grid Iron expand its international reach with a new work commissioned as part of Cork's European Capital of Culture celebrations. *The Devil's Larder*, adapted by Harrison from the novel by Jim Grace, premiered at the Old City Morgue as part of a larger project, entitled *Relocation*, which brought together four of Europe's more established site-specific companies, Teatr Buiro Podrozy (Poland), Jo Bithume (France), Corcadorca (Ireland) and Grid Iron. By the middle of the first decade of the new millennium the company was therefore very well placed to contribute to and benefit from any expansion in opportunity provided. By 2005 Grid Iron was Scotland's pre-eminent site-specific performance company. Its practices, alongside those of other companies such as Suspect Culture and Vanishing Point had been key in establishing Scottish theatre's reputation as eclectic, internationally engaged and formally inventive. It was from this lively sector that the NTS was born, and it is unsurprising that the new national company commissioned a major work from Grid Iron in its first year.

In an age of heightened airport security, it seems remarkable that BAA Edinburgh International Airport ever agreed to host *Roam* (2006). Performed as the final flights of the day left the runway, Harrison's show utilised four airport check-in desks, several TV monitors, a baggage carousel and a section of the departure lounge. Audience members, who were bussed in from Edinburgh city centre, were told to bring passports to guarantee admission. The show worked in range of modes, some comic, some serious, to expose the institutional conditions in which the site habitually worked, drawing attention to borders within borders and the hierarchies that allow some people free passage where others are denied it. On boarding the bus, for instance, audience members were welcomed by a young woman standing by a box of confiscated knives holding up a tomato and asking them to identify it. In this way, discourses of identity—in this instance citizenship tests, which invariably require applicants to answer questions about the country's society, history and culture—were problematised from the outset. In the airport itself, two immigration officers, positioned next to a sign requesting the removal of all beards, quizzed a Palestinian traveller who claimed to be Scottish on the precise nature of his national identity. In its self-conscious appropriation of this highly controlled space, therefore, *Roam* emphasised the constructed nature of identity and its relationship to place, while in the process engaging with contentious questions about international terrorism and political refugees in the post-9/11 world. Harrison, who was writer and director of this project, clearly intended his audience to identify imaginatively with the degradation suffered by many—particularly those from the Arab world—in their attempt to negotiate international borders. As the narrative of piece developed, TV monitors announced that a civil war had prompted an exodus from Scotland to the safe havens of Sarajevo, Beirut and Kigali, cities synonymous with the war-torn histories of Bosnia, Lebanon and Rwanda. As desperate refugees began to arrive the audience was obliged to line up under 'them' and 'us' signs.

Moreover, *Roam* moved its audience around in a way that echoed the institutional practices of the airport itself.

In *Roam*, more clearly than in the other projects discussed above, Grid Iron's choice of site recalls what the anthropologist Marc Augé has termed 'non-place'. For Augé such places are constitutive of supermodernity and are thus emblematic of the contemporary moment, and of the process usually referred to as globalisation. His definition of non-place relies on a distinction in anthropological terms between substantive and transitive sites:

> If a place can be defined as relational, historical and concerned with identity, then a space which cannot be defined as relational, or historical, or concerned with identity will be a non-place. (Augé 1995: 63)

Non-place implies two separate but related meanings: 'spaces formed in relation to certain ends (transport, transit, commerce, leisure) and the relations that individuals have with these spaces' (Augé 1995: 76) The airport, like the hotel room used in Suspect Culture's *Mainstream*, is an archetypal non-place. In *Roam* Grid Iron attempted to explore its significance from perspectives that called into question, or at least were not constrained by, fixed regional or national boundaries. That is not to say, of course, that *Roam* failed to acknowledge the extent to which advances in communications and exchanges between cultures are conditioned by economic or political factors. On the contrary, the show worked precisely to uncover these inequities and was informed throughout by an awareness of the tensions between the local and the global, tensions that provide the backdrop to current discussions about the future of Scotland.

Some of Grid Iron's work has been located in more quotidian spaces. *Muster Station* (2022), commissioned for the EIF to mark the end of its four-year outreach residency at the school, was an indoor promenade staged at Leith Academy. The audience is cast in the role of climate refugees, and we receive a short video in advance of attending urging us not to attempt our own 'exit transport' because the 'seas around the UK are treacherous and unpredictable' and 'there have been more than three thousand fatalities in the last few weeks (McCartney et al 2022). On arrival at the Muster Station, we queue before being ushered into the school hall, now a processing centre for the Department for Evacuation. Water levels are rising, and scientists predict we are six days away from a devastating tidal wave. It is 45 degrees in Fife and 'our white skins no longer work'. We are questioned by security guards with varying degrees of warmth, separated into four groups, instructed to turn off our phones and made to wait. There is a lot of waiting in this show which adds, I think, to our sense of lack of agency. A woman from middle-class Corstorphine has paid for a 'Climate Gentrification Pass', establishing economic inequality as a theme. 'You are all doomed' yells the janitor who wanders around taunting us for having shown up in the first place, as if we are fools for having placed our confidence in the authorities. Eventually each group is herded from the holding-pen to different parts of the school—the library, the gym, the pool and the common room—where we are witness to a number of vignettes in which performers test their ability to cope. We are with the young people on a pool holiday in Malaga when their dingy capsises and a helicopter pilot asks them to choose who will be winched to safety, and with a woman in meltdown as she screams for her daughter, and with an asylum seeker, already refused sanctuary, who nevertheless offers to share his food.

Muster Station is written by Harrison with the playwrights Nicola McCartney and Uma Nada-Rajah, and the storyteller Tawona Sitholé. Using multiple perspectives and a range of performance registers to make connections between social class, colonialism and the climate crisis, it works to expose the inequalities that underwrite the emergency as well as those that will inevitably shape its outcomes in terms of who gets to survive. There are obvious resonances with the current asylum system, particularly when the show satirises the absurdity of notions of cultural competency as they are applied to exclude people. Arbroath? Have you been to Arbroath? was one of the questions barked by processing officers as we arrived. Our survival is contingent on fluency in the language and culture of Finland, the only country willing to accept us and we are being processed to board—or not board—the Arcs, built in Leith Docks, which promise safe passage. David Paul Jones' foreboding soundtrack, which includes radio interviews with politicians and experts discussing the impending disaster, as well as the ticking of a large countdown clock, stalks our progress.

The kind of promenade work described above is clearly facilitated by developments in audio technology, as well as an interest in the potentials of non-traditional sites for performance. The impulse to expand performance vocabularies via a more particular emphasis on the visual, however, is perhaps best exemplified in the work of Vanishing Point, the company formed in Glasgow in 1999 by Matthew Lenton. In contrast to Grid

Iron, as David Archbold notes 'the absence of geographical or temporal specificity is a recurring feature in their work' which is typically visually stunning forms (2011: 90). Lenton, who has directed almost all the company's output, has shown a particular interest in European texts and aesthetics, creating *Little Otik* (2009), inspired by the film of the same name by cult surrealist Czech animator Jan Švankmajer, for example, and adapting Maurice Maeterlinck's late nineteenth-century symbolist dramas *Les Aveugles* and *Intérieur*, as *The Sightless* (1999) and *Interiors* (2009). His recent adaptation of Franz Kafka's 1915 novella *The Metamorphosis* (2021) continues in this vein and Vanishing Point also produced a celebrated production of *The Beggar's Opera* in 2009. As these examples suggest, the turn to the visual that defines the company's work, should not be read straightforwardly as a rejection of text. The adaptation of classic texts has in fact been a recurrent strategy for Vanishing Point, and while the language is often discarded or repurposed the original text still underpins the theatrical vocabularies chosen to respond to its challenges. On the other hand, the company's emphasis on the visual does, to borrow Dominic Johnson's phrase, 'challenge the supposed primacy of textual production over other forms of representation' (2012: 40). This is plainly the case with *Interiors*, which has been among the company's most successful and critically acclaimed shows. In Maeterlinck's original, a family is sitting quietly of an evening unaware that one of its daughters has drowned. An old man and a stranger peer through the window from the darkness outside, reluctant to be the bearers of terrible news. Maeterlinck's play, like much of his work in the 1890s, deploys the potent symbolism of darkness, utilising it as a dramatic device. Vanishing Point picks up on this theme. I last saw the show at the Barbican in London in early 2022 and the following account is based on my recollection of that event.

Somewhere in the far north, on the longest night of the year, we are looking through a large glass window into a dining room. Inside, an annual dinner party held by an older man and his granddaughter is being prepared in celebration of the winter solstice, and the promise of returning light. We know this because a young woman dressed in white is acting as a narrator. She is positioned with us outside the illuminated room. The designer Kai Fischer uses this darkness to frame, focus our attention on and accentuate the lit space that occupies the centre of the stage. Onto this dark frame Finn Ross' projections of the moon and stars, various wintery weather effects and occasionally the faces of the room's occupants, accentuates the scale of the darkness that surrounds the social gathering. This extremely 'selective use of "active" light allows the surrounding dimly lit stage to bleed into our world in the darkened auditorium' and also imbues the outside world of the show with an atmosphere of menace and danger (Palmer 2017: 53). Guests arrive carrying rifles, presumably out of fear of wild animals. They proceed to behave as guests do, eating, flirting, dancing, joking and bickering, until it is time to disappear back into the night.

Interiors moves away from its source material towards a more comprehensive focus on the visual by not allowing us to hear anything of the interactions taking place in the dining room. The window, which is essentially a huge glass wall, acts as a soundproofing device, and the action is seen but not heard, with only the wry commentary of the ghostly young woman, and Alasdair Macrae's plaintive piano-led score as aural accompaniment. The action is by turns comic and sad, often turning on familiar moments of social embarrassment: an unwelcome teenage crush, a badly timed nosebleed, an ill-fated marriage proposal. The visual elements of Lenton's production produce deeply pleasurable effects. The audience moves between visual investment in the exquisite stage craft and the heightened technique of the performers—which is extremely carefully choreographed—to vicarious identification with the characters, as the staging allows for the passionate articulation of seemingly ordinary social relations and invites the audience to take pleasure in looking.

This theme of looking is a constant in the company's work but moves more explicitly towards fetishisation in *The Destroyed Room* (2016). Inspired by Jeff Wall's 1978 photograph of the same name, which famously shows a room that has been thoroughly ransacked, leaving the viewer to ponder how such destruction has come about. The Vanishing Point show explores our fascination with voyeurism in an increasingly mediatised world. Three middle-class characters, two females and one male, take the stage for what seems to be a kind of late-night discussion show. Two cameras project their interactions in close-up onto a screen above. Beginning with what seems to be harmless enough banter among friends, the trio embarks on a part-improvised wine-fuelled discussion that grows increasingly darker and combative in tone, as they ponder the unremitting display of global suffering they consume daily on television and smart-phone screens. A man committing suicide, a drowned asylum seeker, a captive set on fire, these images are understood as 'repeating endlessly and returning insistently in the visual fabric of the contemporary' (Kear 2015: 52). As relations become more fractious, the low rumble of Mark Melville's score gradually intrudes until the room itself begins to fill with water and the walls disintegrate. This can be understood at its simplest as a visual metaphor for the danger of continually recycling images of suffering in a way that diminishes their moral and ethical significance. The political dynamics of passive spectatorship are brought to the fore and because the show offers no easy answers, the results are extremely uncomfortable from an audience point of view.

Vanishing Point exemplifies the internationalisation of Scottish theatre discussed elsewhere in this book. Originally a co-production with Napoli Teatro Festival, Mercadante Teatro Stabile di Napoli, the Traverse and the Tron, *Interiors* won awards for Best production, Best Director and Best Ensemble at the CATS awards in 2009, and has since toured widely, including to Paris (2010), Rome (2011), Brussels (2012), Buenos Aires (2013), Santiago (2013), the EIF (2016), Shanghai (2018), Seoul (2019) and London (2022). As this chapter illustrates, experimental modes of performance and small-scale performance companies have played a significant role in the development of contemporary Scottish theatre. They have enriched its vocabulary and perhaps more than any other part of the sector, embodied its newfound confidence. Their impact is evident in the range of experimental work produced and co-produced by the NTS since 2006, which is discussed more fully in the next chapter. Not only did the NTS's inaugural project *Home* (2006) include work by Vanishing Point, Stewart Laing and Graham Eatough, the company commissioned Grid Iron's *Roam* in its first year, and from the Angus-based site-specific company Poor Boy, *Falling*, a nightly promenade performance through Glasgow city centre. In 2017, Jackie Wylie became the third artistic director of the NTS following the resignation of Laurie Sansom. Her appointment very clearly signals the importance of experimental and artist-led performance practices to the ecology of Scottish theatre. The journey of these practices from the margins to the mainstream has been one of the great successes of Scottish theatre in the post-devolutionary period. In November 2023 Vanishing Point announced the establishment of a new creative hub, 'Our Space', at Cadogan Square in the centre of Glasgow, which will make free meeting and rehearsal space available for the development of new projects.

Festival City

It is impossible to fully account for theatre in Scotland without considering the impact and influence of Edinburgh's summer festivals. The NTS has had a consistently high profile there since it began producing work in 2006. Its first season included *Black Watch* on the Fringe and Anthony Neilson's *Realism* as part of the EIF. The relationship between the festivals and wider Scottish theatre community has historically been more vexed, however, and is worth commenting on because the summer festivals represent a window through which Scotland has viewed international performance cultures and vice versa, at least until the arrival of Tramway. Along with Avignon, Edinburgh was one of the founding performance festivals of Europe. Established in 1947, it initially 'served to shore up Western civilisation and (high) culture in the wake of the devastation of the Second World War' (Knowles 2020: 2). It was accompanied from its inception by the Fringe—although this term was not applied until 1948—and by the Film Festival. In 1950 the Military Tattoo was established, and other annual festivals continued to emerge, including the Jazz Festival in 1978, the Book Festival in 1983 and the Art Festival in 2004, making the combined Edinburgh summer festivals the largest arts event in the world.

From many perspectives the Festivals have been a remarkable success, not least in terms of ticket sales. In *Banquo on Thursdays: The Inside Story of 50 Years of the Edinburgh Festival* (1997), Iain Crawford gives a figure of 180 000 for the inaugural festival (1997: 14) By 2004, the summer festivals were recording combined ticket sales of just over 2.5 million, and in 2022 that figure rose to 3.2 million. According to a BOP consulting report published in June 2023, the overall economic impact of the festivals on the city increased 'from £280 m in 2015 to £407 m in 2022, and in Scotland from £313 m to £367 m' (2023: 2). These figures are important for a number of reasons, not least because the decline of industry in the post-war period has meant the festivals have acquired increasing importance to the service economy of the city, and the country as a whole. In 2017, the Edinburgh Festival Fringe (EFF) reported hosting 3,398 shows and 53,232 performances over its three week duration in August (Edinburgh Festival Fringe Society 2017: 6). The report also notes that 62 countries participated in the Fringe and that its website 'received visits from every country in the world, with the predictable exception of North Korea' (16). The more distinctive and imitated aspects of the Fringe—round the clock programming, inexorable expansion, internationalisation, open policy as regards companies applying to perform—are explored by Jen Harvie who notes that while these features are precisely what makes the Fringe a success for many commentators, they in fact constitute an 'almost entirely unregulated ... model neo-liberal capitalist market, with all the collateral social damages that entails' (2020: 103). Competition takes precedence over collaboration. Artists are allowed to sink or swim at their own expense. Marginalised and economically challenged artists are most likely to be excluded. The EIF is a different animal, of course, not least because it is curated by a festival director.

In an earlier article 'The Cultural Effects of the Edinburgh International Festival' (2003) Harvie stresses how far the celebrated EIF production of David Lyndsay's *Thrie Estaites* in 1948—and its revivals 1949, 1951, 1959, 1973, 1984, 1985 and 1991—'testified to the EIF's commitment to Scottish culture' and further observes 'that Scottish drama and theatre have been increasingly well represented as the Festival has continued' (2003: 17–18). This has increasingly been the case in the post-devolutionary period when a significant amount of new Scottish work has been commissioned by the EIF. To David Greig's *The Speculator* (1999) and *San Diego* (2003), can be added Douglas Maxwell's *Variety* (2002), David Harrower's *Blackbird* (2005), Anthony Neilson's *Realism* (2006), Rona Munro's *The Last Witch* (2009), Vanishing Point's *Wonderland* (2012), Grid Iron's *Leaving Planet Earth* (2013), Rona Munro's *The James Plays* (2014), a double bill of Vanishing Point's *The Destroyed Room* and *Interiors* in 2016. 2022 saw the revival of Liz Lochhead's *Medea* at the Hub and the premiere of Alan Cumming and Stephen Hogget's *Burn,* both produced by the NTS. In 2015 alone David Greig's *Lanark,* Untitled Projects' *Paul Bright's Confessions of a Justified Sinner*, and the NTS and Vox Motus show *Dragon,* were all part of the EIF (2015). The EIF thus appears more engaged at a national level than it did in its early decades and has become a key platform for the internationalisation of Scottish theatre. In 2023 the EIF premiered the NTS production of Nat McCleary's debut play *Thrown,* about five socially and ethnically diverse women living in contemporary Scotland, each drawn, for her own reasons, to the old Celtic sport of backhold wrestling, which is practised each summer on Scotland's Highland Games circuit. For Joyce McMillan, *Thrown* is an 'impressively brave and vivid Scottish play about the fraught politics of identity in our time' and its inclusion in an EIF programme curated by violinist and arts educator Nicola Benedetti, the first woman and the first Scot to perform the role of Festival Director, illustrates an increasingly visible commitment to Scottish culture (2023).

References

Archibald, David (2011) 'History in Contemporary Scottish Theatre', in Ian Brown (ed.) *The Edinburgh Companion to Scottish Theatre*. Edinburgh, Edinburgh University Press, pp. 85–94.

Augé, Marc (1995) *Non-Places: Introduction to an Anthropology of Supermodernity*. Translated by John Howe. London, Verso.

BOP Consulting (2023) *Economic Impact of the Edinburgh Festivals*. Available at: https://www.edinburghfestivalcity.com/assets/old/Edinburgh_Festivals_Impact_Study__digital__original.pdf?1687855168.

Bottoms, Stephen, J. (2006) 'Putting the Document into Documentary: An Unwelcome Corrective?' *The Drama Review*, 50:3, pp. 56–68.

Bratchpiece, David and Kirstin Innes (2021) *Brickwork: A Biography of the Arches*. London, Salamander Street.

Brewster, Scott (2005) 'Madness, Mimicry and Scottish Gothic'. *Gothic Studies*, 7:1, pp. 79–86.

Brown, Ian (2013) *Scottish Theatre: Diversity, Language, Continuity*. Amsterdam, Rodopi.

Brown, Mark (2019) *Modernism and Scottish Theatre Since 1969*. London, Palgrave Macmillan.

Buckley, Jennifer (2016) 'Long 'Live" Theater: Feeling Time and Togetherness in Forced Entertainment's Livestreamed Durationals'. *Theater*, 46:2, pp. 35–53.

Caldwell, Rebecca (2003) 'Sum of *Lament* Less than its Parts'. *The Globe and Mail*. 30 January.

Cameron, Alasdair (1994) 'Experimental Theatre in Scotland', in Theodore Shank (ed.) *Contemporary British Theatre*. Basingstoke, Macmillan Press, pp. 123–138.

Carter, Pamela (2015) *Paul Bright's Confessions of a Justified Sinner: Reconstructed by Untitled Projects*. London, Oberon Books.

Clapp, Susanna. (2000) 'Decky Does a Brono review'. *Observer*, 13 August.

Cooper, Neil (2009) 'Suspect Culture Make and Exhibition of Themselves'. *Herald*, 24 March.

Cooper, Neil (2013) 'Still Timeless After All These Years', in Graham Eatough and Dan Rebellato (eds.) *The Suspect Culture Book*. London, Oberon Books, pp. 49–52.

Crawford, Iain (1997) *Banquo on Thursdays: The Inside Story of 50 Years of the Edinburgh Festival*. Edinburgh, Goblinshead.

Duncan, Ian (2012) 'Walter Scott, James Hogg and Scottish Gothic', in David Punter (ed.) *A New Companion to the Gothic*. Oxford, Blackwell, pp. 123–134.
Edinburgh Festival Fringe Society (2017) *The Annual Review 2017*. Available at: https://edfringe.s3-eu-west-1.amazonaws.com/docs/2017-Annual-Review.pdf
Gardner, Lyn (2015) 'The Closure of the Arches in Glasgow Will be Felt Around the World'. *Guardian*, 10 June.
Greer, Stephen (2020) 'Training for Live Art: Process Pedagogies and New Moves International's Winter Schools'. *Theatre, Dance and Performance Training*, 11:2, pp. 214–228.
Greer, Steve (2022) *Live Art in Scotland*: https://liveartscotland.org/
Greig, David (2013) *Mainstream* in Graham Eatough and Dan Rebellato (eds.) *The Suspect Culture Book*. London, Oberon, pp. 188–246.
Harvie, Jen (2003) 'Cultural Effects of the Edinburgh International Festival: Elitism, Identities, Industries', *Contemporary Theatre Review*, 13:4, pp. 12–26.
Harvie, Jen (2020) 'International Theatre Festivals in the UK: The Edinburgh Festival Fringe as a Model Neo-Liberal Market', in Ric Knowles (ed.) *The Cambridge Companion to International Theatre Festivals*. Cambridge, Cambridge University Press, pp. 101–117.
Heddon, Deirdre & Jennie Klein (2012) (eds.) *Histories & Practices of Live Art*. Basingstoke, Palgrave Macmillan.
Hogg, James (2008 [1824]) *The Private Memoirs and Confessions of a Justified Sinner*. Edinburgh, Canongate.
Jacobs, Michael (1986) 'Farewell to Greater London Council'. *Economic and Political Weekly*, 21:30, pp. 1306–1308.
Johnson, Dominic (2012) *Theatre & the Visual*. Basingstoke, Palgrave Macmillan.
Jones, Sarah (2006) 'The Escapologist, Tramway, Glasgow'. *Independent*, 24 January.
Kear, Adrian (2015) 'Restaging the Anxiety of the Image'. *Performance Research*, 20:5, pp. 51–62.
Klein, J. (2010) 'Live Art in the UK'. *Performing Arts Journal*, 96, pp. 55–62.
Knowles, Ric (2020) 'Introduction', in Knowles, Ric (ed.) *The Cambridge Companion to International Theatre Festivals*. Cambridge, Cambridge University Press, pp. 1–11.
Mahoney, Elisabeth (2002) 'Lament review'. *Guardian*, 9 April.
McCartney, Nicola, Uma Nada-Rajah, Tawona Sitholé and Ben Harrison (2022) *Muster Station*. Unpublished rehearsal script.
McMillan, Joyce (2023) 'Thrown review'. *Scotsman*, 7 July.

Myerscough, John (1988) *The Economic Importance of the Arts in Britain.* London, Policy Studies Institute.

Palmer, Scott (2017) 'Harnessing Shadows: A Historical perspective on the Role of Darkness in the Theatre', in Alston, Adam and Martin Welton (eds.) *Theatre in the Dark: Shadow, Gloom and Blackout in Contemporary Theatre.* London, Bloomsbury, pp. 37–63.

Pittock, Murray (2008) *Scottish and Irish Romanticism.* Oxford, Oxford University Press.

Powell, Lucy (2008) 'Static review'. *Time Out*, 29 April.

Powell, Nick (2013) 'Something in its Place: Misremembering Suspect Culture', in Graham Eatough and Dan Rebellato (eds.) *The Suspect Culture Book*, London, Oberon, pp. 66–70.

Power, Cormac (2008) *Presence in Play: A Critique of Theories of Presence in the Theatre.* Amsterdam, Rodopi.

Punter, David (1999) 'Heartlands: Contemporary Scottish Gothic'. *Gothic Studies*, 1:1, pp. 101–118.

Rebellato, Dan (2013) 'Suspect Culture: Reaching Out', in Graham Eatough and Dan Rebellato (eds.) *The Suspect Culture Book.* London, Oberon, pp. 299–329.

Scullion, Adrienne (2002) 'Glasgow Unity Theatre: the Necessary Contradictions of Scottish Political Theatre'. *Twentieth Century British History*, 13:3, pp. 215–252.

Take Me Somewhere (TMS) (2022) 'Studio Somewhere Residencies'. Available at: https://takemesomewhere.co.uk/studio-somewhere-residencies

Taxidou, Olga (1996) 'Epic Theatre in Scotland', in Randall Stevenson and Gavin Wallace (eds.) *Scottish Theatre Since the Seventies.* Edinburgh, Edinburgh University Press, pp.164–175.

Tiffany, John (2010) 'The Best Performance I've Ever Seen'. *Guardian*, 11 April.

Tomlin, Liz (2013) *Acts and Apparitions: Discourses on the Real in Performance Practice and Theory.* Manchester, Manchester University Press.

Turner, Cathy (2004) 'Palimpsest or Potential Space? Finding a Vocabulary for Site-Specific Performance'. *New Theatre Quarterly*, 20:4, pp. 373–388.

Wallace, Clare (2015) 'Suspect Culture', in Liz Tomlin (ed.) *British Theatre Companies 1995–2014.* London, Bloomsbury, pp. 179–206.

Wilkie, Fiona (2002) 'Mapping the Terrain: A Survey of Site-specific Performance in Britain'. *New Theatre Quarterly*, 18:2, pp.140–160.

CHAPTER 4

A New Model for a New Nation

Early in 2022 the National Theatre of Scotland (NTS) announced its programme for the year. The status of visual and physical theatres was evidenced in *Burn*, a collaboration between the well-known Scottish actor Alan Cumming and the choreographers Stephen Hogget and Vicki Manderson exploring the troubled life of the country's national poet, Robert Burns. On a bleak monochrome set containing only a single desk, and piles of discarded paper, Cummings performed solo accompanied by Andrzej Goulding's sombre video, displaying dates, locations and the ghost of a galloping horse. An NTS, EIF and Joyce Theater co-production, *Burn* opened in Edinburgh in August to extremely positive reviews, before touring Scotland and then transferring to New York, where Cumming is an established star, having won a Tony for his performance of the MC in *Cabaret* in 1998. Liz Lochhead's Scots translation of Euripides' *Medea* was revived in a new staging by Michael Boyd, again in partnership with the EIF, and May Sumbwanyambe's *Enough of Him*, a new play about Scotland's involvement in the slave trade, was co-produced with Pitlochry Festival Theatre. *Enough of Him* proved to be the critical success of the year, winning three CATS awards in 2023 for Best Director, Orla O'Loughlin, Best Production and Best New Play. Elsewhere, Cora Bisset directed *Orphans*, a musical based on the 1998 Peter Mullan film of the same name, and Rona Munro added to her output of Scottish history plays with *James IV: Queen of the Fight*. Nic

Green directed *Like Flying*, a promenade performance for schools, which trained its cast of 12–14 year olds drawn from five local authorities in aerial performance methods. NTS screen projects were presented internationally. Hannah Lavery's *Lament for Sheku Bayoh*, about the death of a young black man in police custody in Fife in 2015, was presented at the Auckland Festival, a film version of Frances Poet's *Adam*, originally staged at the Edinburgh Fringe in 2017, was streamed as part of the Arts Emerson, Boston 2021/2022 Season and Sydney Opera House's UK/AU Digital festival, and *Carry Me Home*, a short digital artwork celebrating Scotland's coastal and island communities was screened at the Berlin Short Film Festival.

The range of work produced by the NTS in this snapshot is impressive, but in terms of its formal and thematic preoccupations, not especially out of kilter with work produced across the UK as a whole. The popularity of immersive and participatory practices is evidenced in *Like Flying*, for instance, and the vogue for testimonial performance in *Adam*, in which Adam Kashmiry plays himself in a performance that deals directly with his lived experience as a trans man. Renewed interest in adaptation and translation, which can be seen elsewhere in British theatre in recent years, is evident in *Medea* and *Orphans*, and the 'interrogation and gradual problematization of a supposed antagonism between "New Writing" and "New Work"', identified by Andrew Haydon as evidence of twenty-first-century theatre's increased plurality, is apparent in *Burn* and also *Lament for Sheku Bayoh* (2013: 40). The latter uses a mixture of live music, verbatim and spoken word, to reflect on and interrogate responses to the events surrounding Bayoh's death from the perspective of Scottish people of colour.

The work described above exists across, and sometimes in between, documentary theatre, physical theatre, theatre for young audiences, new writing, revival, translation, community and popular theatre frameworks. Questions of distinctions and commonalities between these fields remain pertinent, of course, but they are not the focus of this chapter. My aim has been simply to demonstrate, as I have written elsewhere, 'that contemporary Scottish theatre shares many of its aesthetic preoccupations and formal innovations with theatre elsewhere in the UK' (Reid 2016: 192). Beyond that it operates in an unusually culturally charged environment and the NTS, as the national company, is central to its operation. The aim of this chapter is to trace something of the company's origins, reflect on its innovative working model, and review some of its major highlights.

Given the company works across a wide range of scales and performance modes, it may seem unrepresentative to isolate specific productions, but as a state-funded and state-sponsored institution the NTS performs the role of cultural ambassador. The kinds of shows it chooses to tour therefore, and that are deemed attractive by foreign programmers, tell us something about residual and dominant conceptions of Scottish cultural identity active in the twenty-first century. The impact of the NTS has been significant, and aspects of it will be considered in the following chapters not least because, as will become clear, its geographical reach has been extensive and has enabled it to create innovative and ground-breaking work, to expand audiences and engage meaningfully with local communities.

It is not my purpose in this chapter to consider why Scotland delayed for so long in establishing its own national company, or to detail the longer history of the campaign. Robert Leach's article 'The Short, astonishing history of the National theatre of Scotland' (2007) and my own 'From Scenes Like These Old Scotia's Grandeur Springs' (2007) can provide details for interested readers. The key thing to note is that since its acclaimed inaugural season in 2006 the company has achieved sustained cultural prominence, attracting praise for its extensive work in Scotland and for bringing the work of Scottish theatre-makers to international attention. Moreover, it has provided an inclusive framework, geographically and aesthetically, through which national debates, trends and preoccupations can be articulated. Its innovative and flexible co-producing model meant its success was predicated on collaboration with existing theatre artists, companies and venues and the NTS was therefore, from the outset, by virtue of its structure, plugged in. Its dispersed model immediately attracted positive attention from theatre scholars interested in its potentials for diversity and inclusion. Writing before its inaugural season Jen Harvie was optimistic, for example, about the company's potential to create 'confidently heterogeneous, authoritative, socially purposeful and independent' imaginings of Scottish identity (2005: 34). Sometime later, Nadine Holdsworth praised the way the NTS's programming encapsulates 'the multiple communities that constitute the Scottish nation in a way that is outward looking, forward thinking and internationally significant' (2010: 37). Elsewhere, Joanne Tompkins notes that the company 'engages with its constituents very successfully by choosing not to have a fixed venue', and Ariel Watson acknowledges the company 'has been acclaimed for its radical decentering, even explosion, of the standing model of theatrical nationalism and national theatre' (Tompkins 2014: 122; Watson 2014: 229). Finally, Rebecca Robinson concludes that 'as a non-building-based, commissioning and producing cultural institution, the NTS appears to be particularly well placed to accommodate and reflect diverse imaginings of identity and respond to contemporary expressions of belonging' (2012b: 399). It is worth reflecting briefly on how this innovative national company came into existence.

During the 1980s and 1990s the idea of a national theatre resurfaced in various consultation documents, but no solid plan emerged, although the SAC continued 'to fund reports that deferred provision' throughout the 1990s (Agnew 2000: 225). The situation changed with the election of a Labour government in 1997 and its delivery of a manifesto pledge to hold a devolution referendum. It was the establishment of a new Scottish Parliament in 1999 that made concrete action a viable prospect. In 2000 the recently elected Scottish Executive approved funding for a national theatre company but stopped short of specifying what form it should take. The following year, an SAC working group recommended the new company be buildingless and to all intents and purposes nomadic. Importantly, a 2000 report by the Federation for Scottish Theatre (FST), under the chairmanship of Hamish Glen, then artistic director of Dundee Rep, had already outlined this model, and its recommendations had directly influenced the thinking of the SAC working group. In this way the idea of a national theatre without a building emerged from the Scottish theatre community itself in a moment of consensus that meant among other things that the new company was born in an atmosphere of goodwill. The NTS thus conceived would act as a 'creative producer ... working with and through the existing Scottish theatre community to achieve its objectives' (Scottish Arts Council 2001: 6). This flexible model offered a specifically Scottish solution to problems of geographical inclusivity and participation, in a country where the population, although concentrated in the central belt, is widely distributed elsewhere. It was also an explicit rejection of existing models for national theatres which involve monolithic civic buildings located in national capitals. It is noticeable, if we reflect on the 2022 season discussed briefly at the beginning of this chapter, that with the exception of Michael Boyd's production of *Medea*, all of the NTS productions toured: *Burn* to Inverness, Aberdeen, Perth and New York; *James IV* to Glasgow, Dundee, Inverness and Stirling; *Orphans* to Glasgow, Edinburgh and Inverness; *Enough of Him* to Pitlochry, Cumbernauld, Musselburgh and Perth and *Like Flying* to schools across the country, including Auchinleck Academy, Craigmount High School Edinburgh, Bellahouston Academy, Ardrossan Academy, St Thomas Aquinas Glasgow and Rossie School, Angus.

The 2001 SAC report remained largely silent on the question of repertoire, but an earlier one produced by the Advisory Council for the Arts in Scotland (AdCAS)—a lobbying group formed in 1981—was explicit in its privileging of text-based theatre and the desirability of constructing a national canon. AdCAS had organised a conference on the question of a national theatre in 1987 and set out its main priorities in the following terms:

> (a) To establish a theatre company in Scotland aiming at the very highest standards and concentrating on the best Scottish plays of all periods. (b) To encourage the writing and production of new plays in Scotland. (c) To produce also outstanding plays from other countries and, when this is appropriate, in Scottish adaptations and translations. (d) To provide an outlet for Scottish talent in all aspects of theatre, writing, acting, direction and design, and to cultivate the distinctive Scottish style in all of these matters. (e) To work in close collaboration with other theatre companies in Scotland. (f) To tour productions in Scotland and abroad. (g) To bring the theatre to the service of education by co-operation with the schools, colleges and universities. (AdCAS 1987)

The expansion in repertoire outlined in the earlier part of this book produced a more multifarious and nuanced understanding of the potentials of a national company, but most of the voices raised in criticism of the NTS since its establishment have echoed the priorities laid out above. I will return to these a little later in this chapter.

Having approved funding, the Executive proceeded to drag its feet in delivering and the first announcement was not made until September 2003. The broadcaster Richard Findlay was appointed Chair in December of the same year, and the appointment in July 2004 of Vicky Featherstone as inaugural artistic director was particularly well-received. Formerly of Paines Plough, and later of the Royal Court, Featherstone, a young female director with an established reputation for producing new work, was seen by many as a part of 'a generation of UK theatre professionals ... used to seeing Scotland as one of Europe's leading centres of great playwriting and innovative theatre work' (McMillan 2005). Featherstone proceeded to assemble an impressive creative team. The NTS's first chief executive, Neil Murray, had worked in Scottish theatre for twenty years and been instrumental in making Glasgow's Tron Theatre a leading force. In early 2005, John Tiffany was appointed director of new work. Tiffany had been based at the Traverse for 1997–2001 where he was considered 'one of the most brilliant literary directors the ... theatre ever had' (McMillan 2005) The addition of David Greig as the company's first dramaturg, raised expectations further. The new team thus assembled, spent most of 2005 planning its first season, conscious that it was about to break new ground nationally and internationally, for no such model for a national theatre had ever been tested. Undeniably, the establishment of a buildingless national company represented a bold and independent cultural initiative on behalf of Scottish policy makers. I now want to spend some time discussing the company's first season because it was key in establishing its reputation and thus in demonstrating the efficacy of the new model.

2006

On the weekend of 25–26 February 2006, the NTS launched its programme with ten more or less simultaneous site-related events. In the disused Caithness glass factory on the outskirts of Wick in the far north, an old woman talked to her television and her television talked back. In an abandoned tenement in Aberdeen a fisherman mourned the devastation of the cod stocks that had once been central to his existence. Elsewhere, busloads of families were taken to a forest near Musselburgh to peer inside a gingerbread house, three black-clad figures abseiled down the side of a high-rise in Glasgow's east end, and the car deck of the Hjaltland ferry in Lerwick harbour vibrated to the sound of a hundred Shetland fiddles. These scenes were parts of performances that were themselves part of NTS's evocatively entitled *Home* project. On the same night, in five other locations Scotland's theatre artists performed under the banner of a national company for the first time.

There were a number of possible answers to the question of what kind of event would be suitable for the launch of the new company, but most produced potentially troublesome answers. The production might, for instance, have featured a star actor in a classic role—the National Theatre of Great Britain had launched in October 1963 with a production of *Hamlet* starring Peter O'Toole—but voices in support of new writing and the wider Scottish acting community would have undoubtedly been raised against it. One of Scotland's more luxuriously appointed theatres in Glasgow, say, or Dundee might have been chosen as the venue for the launch, but dissenters in Edinburgh or Aberdeen would inevitably have grumbled their dissatisfaction. In this context, as Fiona Wilkie rightly suggests, the NTS found in site-specificity 'a convenient marker of a set of ideas with which' it wanted 'to be associated' including 'experiment, accessibility' and 'a shift away from the primacy of the metropolitan theatre building' (Wilkie 2008: 88). In late 2005 Featherstone commissioned ten of the most prominent directors working in Scotland to create entirely new performances for the launch of the NTS. Broadly inspired by the idea of 'home', they would run simultaneously in non-traditional spaces across the country and would be devised in collaboration with local companies, communities, and artists. In February 2006 the NTS launched with not one but ten productions: *Home Aberdeen, Home Caithness, Home Dumfries, Home Dundee, Home East Lothian, Home Edinburgh, Home Glasgow, Home Inverness, Home Shetland, Home Stornoway*. Featherstone's choice of directors also evidenced a commitment to a diversity of practices and forms. They included, for example, Vanishing Point's Matthew Lenton, *Home Caithness*; Communicado's Alison Peebles, *Home Aberdeen*; Untitled Project's Stewart Laing's, *Home Stornoway*; Suspect Culture's Graham Eatough, *Home Dumfries* and the leading children's theatre company, Catherine Wheels, *Home East Lothian*.

Home represented a confident and imaginative response to pressure on the new company to assert its authority as a national company and its flexibility as a buildingless one. The absence of building overheads, after all, 'ensured that a comparatively significant percentage of the £4 million annual grant could go directly into artistic costs' (Tomlin 2015: 31). With *Home* the new company not only brought expertise and money to the table, but also fulfilled its remit of engaging creatively with local communities in a diverse range of Scottish settings. The geographical scope of the project demonstrated the NTS's commitment to exploring Scottish identities in the communities in which those identities are made. This was crucial in establishing its reputation as a truly national company. Locations ranged from Lerwick in the far north to Dumfries in the south, and from Stornoway in the Outer Hebrides to Edinburgh and East Lothian in the east. The new company satisfied its objective 'to serve and reflect the whole range of Scottish life, social, geographic and cultural' by invading the material spaces of contemporary Scotland: the tenement; the factory; the high-rise; the drill hall; the ferry; the forest (McMillan 2006). A number of *Home* performances were able to evoke local memories in ways not usually associated with mainstream theatre practice because they took place in sites that triggered particular memories for their audiences and that had specific non-theatrical material and spatial histories of their own. Two such performances were Matthew Lenton's *Home Caithness* and Wils Wilson's *Home Shetland* which I will discuss in slightly more detail, in order to give a more vivid sense of the ambition and impact of the work.

The site for *Home Caithness* was the disused Caithness Glass factory on the outskirts of Wick, about 100 miles north of Inverness. The glass factory, which had been a major source of prestige for the town, closed in 2004 with significant job losses. The site had since been earmarked for redevelopment, but a pause before its commencement allowed the NTS access. The disused factory thus resonated with discourses of cultural, economic, and regional decline as well as cultural regeneration and change. Lenton's promenade production led the audience through the factory's formerly productive spaces, and told the story of Elsie, an old woman confined to a care home after the death of her husband. One night she is inspired by a visit from characters in Sergio Leone's *Once Upon a Time in the West* to make a break for home to find her husband again. She abandons the security of her bedroom—built on a raised platform—for the enormous factory space where she encounters a number of characters, some drawn from her own past. Lenton's visuals are in keeping with the vivid imaginative inner life of the central character. The production ends with her death.

Elsie's objective is to return to a place she recognises as home and the person she associates most strongly with that place. The sense of loss that permeates the production is intensified by the choice of a site that once promised security and permanency. Equally the possibility of a new and productive future for the building chimes with our sense of Elsie having lived a full and imaginatively rich life which is now drawing to a natural close. While *Home Caithness* certainly 'triggered its audience's living memory of times of greater economic security followed by times of economic decline' in order to highlight the vulnerability of ordinary women and men in the face of larger economic imperatives, it also exploited the transitional nature of the site to emphasise the inevitability of change, the passing away of all things (Harvie 2005: 49). The spectacle of the diminutive figure of Elsie, in her final act of resistance, was thus made doubly moving because of the material history of its setting.

Home Shetland, the most northerly *Home* production, was directed by Wils Wilson, at that time one half of the Halifax-based company wilson + wilson specialised in site-specific performance and installation art. Wilson has since established herself as a significant figure in Scottish theatre, particularly through her work as associate director at the Lyceum in Edinburgh where she has directed award-winning productions, most recently *Life is a Dream* (2021) which won her the Best Director award at the 2022 CATS. *Home Shetland* was performed on the Northlink Ferry while it berthed in Lerwick harbour between journeys and Wilson chose a more direct engagement with her site than Lenton. The sea is a constant presence on Shetland. It is impossible to be more than three miles away from it, and the Lerwick–Aberdeen ferry is the main artery connecting the archipelago to the mainland and the world beyond. It is, consequently, as one critic observed, 'the repository of the countless stories, dreams, hopes, and crises that take people away from Shetland or bring them home' (Haswell 2006). Wilson's production explored the ferry's centrality to both leaving and returning and conflated these meanings to produce a meditation on a Shetland identity significantly defined by partings and reunions.

The performance began in the ferry terminal where each member of the audience was furnished with a personal headset, from which they received directions and instructions, before being ushered onto the ferry. From then on *Home Shetland* took the form of an audiovisual tour through the ferry's public spaces. The poet and playwright Jackie Kay and Jacqueline Clark, a young Shetlander, provided much of the text and Wilson enlisted forty local volunteers who, alongside professional performers, became the ferry's passengers and crew. Wandering through the ferry, audience members encountered 'fellow travellers, catching snippets of … inner monologues', which coalesced in a 'poignant patchwork of lives weathered by family quarrels, fleeting liaisons, old age [and] bereavement' (Burnett 2006). Wilson's production produced a tangible sense of how far, for Shetlanders at least, 'home' is an ephemeral notion often tinged by nostalgia and separation. *Home Shetland* reached its climax on the ferry's car deck where one hundred suspended boiler suits playing fiddle music from their hearts were surrounded by projected images from the islands' past. The movement of this melancholic finale was choreographed by the natural swell of the sea. The ferry timetable ensured that *Home Shetland* was the first ever performance by the NTS.

With its emphasis on local identity *Home Shetland* was typical of the pervasive regionalism that characterised the *Home* project. In *Home Aberdeen*, director Alison Peebles with the help of the playwright Rona Munro, injected new life into a derelict council block in the city's run-down Middlefield district. As the audience, who had been bussed to the site from the city centre, moved from flat to flat, it encountered teenagers squabbling, a fisherman reflecting on his life at sea, an oil widow deciding she preferred life with her husband away, and a lonely old woman surrounded by photographs of her family, long since dispersed. As the audience departed, 'a country and western rendition of *Wherever I Lay My Hat (That's My Home)* segued into a rapturous a cappella finale, the cast giving rich voice to the lives once lived in the disused tenement' (McMillan 2006). Elsewhere, Graham Eatough's *Home Dumfries* used the Loreburn Drill Hall, originally built in 1890 for the Dumfries and Galloway Territorials, as the site of a mixed-media installation that incorporated the memories of local elderly people. Anthony Neilson's *Home Edinburgh* was a verbatim performance devised in collaboration with a group of local schoolchildren. The show, performed by professional actors, was based on the children's sense of what First Minister's questions at the Scottish Parliament might involve. In *Home East Lothian*, Gill Robertson of the acclaimed children's theatre company Catherine Wheels took her audience on a journey that began outside the Brunton Theatre in Musselburgh and involved them peering into a specially constructed gingerbread house at the Prestongrange Industrial Heritage site, for a version of *Hansel and Gretel*. *Home Glasgow*, created and directed by John Tiffany, was a largely outdoor event performed at a tower block in the city's east end. Frantic Assembly's Scott Graham produced an animated photograph album at the Arts in Motion Creation Centre in Evanton for *Home Inverness* and the director and designer Stewart Laing led a team of model makers in the creation of *Home Stornoway*, which took the form of a miniature theatrical installation in a shop on the town's Church Street. The sound track of *Home Stornoway* was delivered in English and Gaelic.

As noted in the last chapter, the NTS also commissioned a major site-specific work from Grid Iron for its first season and *Roam* was subsequently performed by an international cast at Edinburgh International Airport in April 2006. In combination *Home* and *Roam* had the effect both of emphasising the efficacy of site-specific and small-scale work in the exploration of identities at local and national levels, and also of positioning the NTS as forward-looking and contemporary. These programming choices also seemed to indicate the new company would not necessarily be privileging 'the play' as a vehicle for actioning its manifesto commitments. On the other hand, in April, the NTS's schools and community work was launched with a co-production with TAG theatre company of Arthur Miller's *The Crucible*. Guy Holland's production of Miller's classic play toured community venues with a core cast of nine professional actors supplemented by community casts picked up on the way. In April a new adaptation of Neil Gaiman and Dave McKean's celebrated children's book *The Wolves in the Walls* (2003), directed by Featherstone in partnership with Julian Crouch of Improbable Theatre, became the first NTS show to be staged outside Scotland at the Lyric Theatre Hammersmith. A substantially reworked revival of Chris Hannan's *Elizabeth Gordon Quinn* (1985) toured Scotland's major stages from later that month until mid-June enjoying healthy audiences and positive reviews, and in October, Featherstone directed Friedrich Schiller's *Mary Stuart* (1800) in a new version by David Harrower. The NTS did not appear to be looking to make major revivals of classic Scottish plays central to its producing model. Alison Peebles directed a revival of Liz Lochhead's *Mary Queen of Scots Got Her Head Chopped Off* (1987) in 2009, and Graham McLaren revived Ena Lamont Stewart's Glasgow Unity classic *Men Should Weep* (1947) in 2011, and the following year Joe Corrie's *In Time o' Strife* (1927), but these examples did not entirely satisfy commentators who wanted to see the company support a repertoire that balanced the old with the new, and that worked more purposefully to uncover a continuous Scottish tradition in playwrighting. Writing in 2013, for instance, Ian Brown notices that the NTS had 'still never presented a Scottish play written before the twentieth century' (Brown 2013: 240). 'What is very odd' he continues 'is the creative amnesia that has sometimes occluded from the mind of theatre artists and the public the rich, diverse, linguistically varied and continuous traditions of Scottish drama and theatre' (2013: 241). Similarly, but more recently, Alan Riach, who holds the Chair in Scottish Literature at the University of Glasgow, has reiterated the uncontroversial view that one of the five key functions of a national theatre should be 'to review, reappraise and perform new productions of plays from the entire history of Scottish literature' (2021). These tensions between the old and the new, canon formation and innovation, have never been fully resolved, and the company has continued to experiment.

Nevertheless, in 2011, the NTS responded to its critics by launching the Staging the Nation programme, a series of events running throughout its fifth year, which explicitly addressed questions relating to Scotland's theatre history and its legacy. Promoted as 'a conversation about theatre in Scotland' Staging the Nation involved rehearsed readings, panel discussions, lectures and related activities. The first event, 'The Traverse, New Writing and How It Changed the World', centred on a discussion hosted by playwright Chris Hannan of the impact of John Byrne's *The Slab Boys* (1978) which reunited the original creative team, including writer John Byrne, director David Hayman and actor Robbie Coltrane. Staging the Nation continued with a series of rehearsed readings titled Favourite Plays, each selected by a prominent theatre-maker. On 31 March Glasgow Citizens hosted a reading of Joe Corrie's *In Time o' Strife* (1927) chosen by playwright Peter Arnott, and readings of Tony Roper's *The Steamie* (1987), John McGrath's *The Cheviot, the Stag and the Black, Black Oil* (1973) and Mike Cullen's *The Cut* (1995) followed, selected by Johnny McKnight, Graham McLaren and Gregory Burke respectively. The scope of Staging the Nation's engagement was not limited to discussion of particular plays. On September 30 the playwright Nicola McCartney hosted a discussion about the impact and legacy of Glasgow's Tramway Theatre, for instance, and Alan Cumming devised a 90-minute front-of-curtain entertainment on the influence of pantomime, variety and the Music Hall on Scottish performance styles. In December, in the member's restaurant in the Scottish Parliament McLaren and David McLennan, curated Nursing the Thistle, a series of three-minute interventions from current theatre artists. These included Liz MacLennan, widow and partner of John McGrath, reflecting on how busy her husband would be in the age of Occupy had he lived long enough, Peter Arnott engaging in a testy conversation with his idol Bertolt Brecht, and Kieran Hurley expounding on the radical inheritance of Gil Scott Heron. For Joyce McMillan, the event achieved 'a rare balance between paying tribute to a remarkable past and celebrating the new wave of radical thought and energy now pulsing through Scottish theatre, often driven by artists well under 30' (2011).

Back in 2006, Featherstone did commission a new Scottish play for the NTS's first season, but not one that paid homage to existing traditions in Scottish playwriting, at least not in any obvious way. Focusing on decidedly ordinary behaviour and misbehaviour within the private sphere, Anthony Neilson's *Realism* (2006), in a co-production with the

EIF, concerned itself with the rich texture of everyday life. Its scenario is deceptively simple. For reasons of laziness, mild depression and romantic melancholy Stuart, played by the Scottish actor Stuart McQuarrie, has decided not to leave his flat and to spend a Saturday at home. The play opens in the morning with a dishevelled Stuart, slouched on the sofa and still in his nightclothes, being visited (or perhaps receiving a phone call) from his friend Paul who wants him to come and play football. The possibility that Paul is not actually present during this conversation is hinted at via the stage direction '*at no point in the following scene do the actors make eye contact*' and also by Paul's opening line, which is strongly reminiscent of the beginning of a telephone conversation: 'Did I wake you?' (2008: 293). Stuart declines Paul's invitation, insisting he just wants to do nothing. He puts out some food for his cat and decides to go back to bed. As he does so, in what may be the echo of a dream, his mother appears asking if he has noticed that the sky is 'full of bombers' (297). His father enters carrying a newspaper and his parents sit at the dining table reading. The action continues much in this way. Stuart recalls fragments of dreams, past relationships and childhood games. He has real time interactions and fantasies about sex and death all of which intrude in a seemingly random fashion as he carries out mundane domestic tasks such as making a cup of tea or loading the washing machine. He becomes extremely irate over an unpaid utility bill. He watches television and listens to the radio. He waits for a phone call from Angie with whom he has recently broken up. He reminisces about Laura, his first love, and fantasises about a sexual encounter between the two women. He is insulted by a telesales cold call and reacts with disproportionate fury. He is chastised by his parents. He has something to eat, falls asleep in front of the television, fantasises his own death and finally, as night falls, decides to go to bed. A little later, he is awakened by a call from Angie, and they share a sad conversation, of the kind that occurs towards the end of a failed love affair. During this last exchange the lights fade to black.

Neilson explores Stuart's inner life by means of a playful and confusing cocktail of fantasy, memory and reality and provides no stable perspective from which the audience can distinguish these elements. John Bull describes the effect as 'hilarious and engrossing' (2011: 359). Although *Realism* ostensibly conforms to Aristotelian unities of time and place—it unfolds over the morning, afternoon and evening of a single day inside a single room—for the most part characters, interactions and conversations occur in ways that contribute to the theatrical presentation of

Stuart's mood rather than any sense of developing plot. There is little in the way of exposition or resolution, and certainly no recognisable climax. Apart from the central character, members of the ensemble play multiple roles, including those of Stuart's family, friends, lovers, politicians, television pundits and even his cat, Galloway. They come and go in no discernible pattern and questions of whether they actually exist in the real time of Stuart's Saturday at home are never fully resolved. Indeed, for the audience, this pronounced and sustained lack of clarity in relation to the 'realism' of what is presented, works to produce a sense of disorder, confusion, and sometimes pleasurable disorientation analogous with Stuart's muddled and melancholic state of mind. For Janine Hauthal, '*Realism* not only erodes the very project its title proclaims, but eventually questions the accessibility of reality as such' (2013: 147). This indeterminacy is central to the play's effects. In suggesting, to borrow Lyn Gardner's phrase, 'that it is only by tapping into our unconscious that we can most fully and completely be ourselves', *Realism* challenges the notion that a realist aesthetic is best suited for the accurate representation of human experience (Gardner 2006b). In a gesture towards expressionist and absurdist scenography, Miriam Buether's set design was recognisable as the interior of Stuart's flat but no longer as a detailed realist interior. Instead, the space was scattered with isolated domestic objects—washing machine, sofa, standard lamp, toilet—set on a severely raked stage, at odd angles and half buried in sand. The set was an appropriate home for a character similarly confused and off kilter, and Anna Harpin has noted that 'play quietly demonstrates how reality is a house built (quite literally in the original production) on sand' (2017: 175). Buether's set was also very expensively achieved, signalling that the new company had both the willingness and the resources to invest in high production values.

As John Bull notes, the 'fact that Stuart is presented as an unremarkable man' is what gives *Realism* its wide appeal because the character's very ordinariness serves as a 'testament to the untapped—if often embarrassing—resources of each member of the audience' (Bull 2011: 359). The play ends with an optional coda in which the usually invisible relationship between interior and exterior realities is emphasised. In the original production, a glass box was flown in—another impressive coup de théâtre—containing a hyper-realistic kitchen with furniture exactly the same as that dotted around the original set. This time, all domestic appliances are in their correct place and everything '*looks very real*' (Neilson 2008:355). In this hyper-realist setting, objects are restored to their status as signs of observable reality. Stuart enters wearing his dressing gown and proceeds to make '*in real time and with little fuss, a cup of tea*' (355). While he sits drinking at the kitchen table, Angie enters similarly attired, empties the washing machine and leaves. Stuart then continues to drink his tea until the audience realises it is '*expected to leave*' (355).

Realism was admired for its dramaturgical daring and formal ingenuity, but the standout smash hit of the NTS's first season was John Tiffany's production of Gregory Burke's *Black Watch* (2006), which created a sensation and 'quickly became', to borrow David Pattie's phrase, 'as iconic a production for the NTS as John McGrath's *The Cheviot, the Stag and the Black, Black Oil* was for 7:84 in the 1970s' (Pattie 2011: 31). Originally conceived as a site-responsive event, *Black Watch* opened at the University Drill Hall, Forest Hill, on the night of 5 August 2006. Based on first-hand accounts by members of the regiment of their experiences in Iraq, it quickly became the must-see production of the summer. The Drill Hall setting, and Tiffany's traverse staging, undoubtedly resonated as intended with the annual Edinburgh Military Tattoo and the generations of soldiers who had used the hall, but the key measures of the production's subsequent success were the number of overseas venues to which it subsequently travelled, the number of critics it wowed, and the number of awards it received. These last amounted to 22 and included a Fringe First, a Herald Angel, four Olivier's and a New York Drama Circle award for Best Foreign Play. *Black Watch* has since been recast and re-launched on five occasions, most recently in 2012/13 when it was performed in Korea for the first time. In the interim it has visited Australia, Canada, Ireland, New Zealand and the US, in the process showcasing some of Scotland's emerging acting talent, including Richard Rankin and Jack Lowden.

Black Watch was the iconic Scottish production of the 2000s and its success contributed significantly to establishing the NTS's reputation and raising its public profile. The company may have included international visibility in its original objectives, but it can hardly have expected to achieve such success in its early years. For Joanne Zerdy the show effectively performed 'as an advancing scout ... stimulating international (particularly American) interest in the artistic institution and Scottish theatre at large' (Zerdy 2013: 182). Reviewing the first decade of the new century in *The Scotsman* on 17 December 2009, Joyce McMillan echoed a popular consensus in observing that among the many events worth celebrating in Scottish theatre, the most notable was 'the NTS's 2006 launch and subsequent success' (2009). *Black Watch*, she stresses was 'the greatest of all the 25 productions and projects staged by Scotland's National Theatre during its now legendary first year of operation' and as the highlight of the theatrical decade (2009). Lyn Gardner's review of the original production captures something of its impact:

> John Tiffany's storming, heart-stopping production is all disorienting blood, guts and thunder, threaded through with the history and songs of the regiment and intercut with lyrical moments of physical movement. (2006a)

Oliver Letts praised the 2008 revival in similar, if less eloquent, terms: 'This pulsating epic of a night swirls with bagpipe music. Its emotions boomerang from boredom to bravado, jitters to jocularity' (2008). Both commentaries give some sense of the way the production moves between different performance registers and modes in making and managing the feelings of its audience. They also demonstrate, coming as they do from *The Guardian* and *The Daily Mail*, *Black Watch*'s appeal across the political spectrum. Tiffany's expert management of affect is, I would argue, the production's most striking aspect.

Broadly speaking *Black Watch* is comprised of three different types of scenes. Those set in a pub in Fife in which the character of the 'writer' interviews former members of the regiment about their experiences in Iraq which are interspersed with scenes set in Iraq during the regiment's final tour of duty. Although largely fictional, the latter are more emotionally charged because, while they often affect boredom, the soldiers are presented as in imminent physical danger. Television and radio news footage is used to anchor these scenes in reality. In addition, the audience is aware from quite an early stage that some kind of tragic dénouement is inevitable: Burke's play tells of the death of three Black Watch soldiers in a suicide bombing. Finally, Tiffany, his movement director Steven Hoggett and musical director Davey Anderson create a number of sequences that exist outside the temporal logic of either of the former. These are particularly affecting because they marshal the full array of theatrical vocabulary—music, communal singing, movement, scenic effect—to act upon the sensate bodies of the audience. The production's final scene is a case in point. A parade drill, accompanied by the raucous sound of pipes and drums, literalises the affiliation of each individual soldier to the group and the regiment. One of the actors is actually playing the highland bagpipes. 'The music intensifies as the parade becomes harder' and a super-imposed pattern of movement in which individuals stumble and fall and are 'helped back to their feet by the others', further emphasising comradeship while adding a significant dimension of tenderness (Burke 2007: 73). This coming together of pronounced masculinity and feeling, which Lyn Gardner describes as a 'great dirty ballet of pulsating machismo and terrible tenderness', is central to *Black Watch's* appeal (2006). It is worth noting also that in each iteration of the show, the cast purposefully does not include star actors and the majority of characters are working-class infantrymen. Another section in which each soldier creates an abstracted movement sequence, to music, in response to a letter from home has a similarly cumulative emotional impact. Throughout the production's musical sequences are varied in tone, producing a variety of affective responses ranging from exhilaration to melancholy. Davey Anderson's arrangement of the traditional song 'Twa Recruiting Sergeants' is markedly melancholy and plaintive, for example, and in his arrangement this typically upbeat song is given the quality of lament, an effect heightened by the fact the two characters singing it are later killed in the suicide bombing.

The above account is necessarily a snapshot, but the overall impact of *Black Watch* is evidenced in the universally ecstatic reviews it received. The *New York Times* critic Ben Brantley echoed the sentiments of many when he described it as 'a necessary reminder of the transporting power that is unique to theatre' and reflected that it arrived 'like a blazing redeemer in the grayness of the current New York theater season' (2007). With its shifts in register, its privileging of demotic speech patterns and its self-conscious populism, *Black Watch* rightly earned widespread praise for embodying and reinvigorating Scotland's eclectic and populist theatre traditions. However, my interest in the affective power of Tiffany's production, in the way it manages its audience's emotional response, proceeds partly from admiration and partly from the conviction that the ambivalence of its politics is problematic when considered on a purely cognitive level. Although it contains extended sequences based on interviews with veterans, and thus opens up a space in which ordinary soldiers are given an opportunity to represent themselves in something like their own terms, in *Black Watch* these individual histories are given real context only within the history of the regiment itself. This is most obvious in Steven Hoggett's expertly choreographed central section, in which this history—The Golden Thread—is narrated by Cammy, the character who functions as a spokesperson for the group throughout the show:

Music. A red carpet rolls out, and as Cammy narrates the following history of the Black Watch the other soldiers manoeuvre him around the stage dressing him into and out of significant and distinct uniform from the regiment's history. (Burke 2007: 30)

This history begins in 1715 in Scotland and encompasses Culloden, The American War of Independence, France, Egypt, Portugal, Spain, Flanders, The Crimean War, The Boer War, The First World War, The Second World War, Burma, Korea, Africa, Palestine, Syria and Mesopotamia. The entire sequence has something of the celebratory flavour and chutzpah of a fashion show. In spite of its spectacular impact, however, Cammy's chronology, as David Archibald observes in one of the few pieces of contemporary writing critical of the production's politics, 'has no explanatory power, containing, as it does, only a few passing references to *why* the Black Watch ventured abroad' (Archibald 2007).

Because of the way the material is selected and organised in Tiffany's production, key discontinuities and disturbing events in the regiment's history—especially its involvement in Ireland and Africa—are omitted or skimmed over in favour of a totalising narrative of continuity through heroism. Thus, the discursive reproduction of nationhood the production offers is marked by a certain kind of silence, a deliberate failure to directly address Scotland's involvement in the crimes that enabled the colonial project. While the idea of 'lions led by donkeys' is given some prominence, particularly to absolve individual soldiers from responsibility for political decisions made by successive governments, especially the recent conflict in Iraq, it is this notion of continuity that the production privileges and celebrates. Moreover, this layering of the martial tradition onto notions of nation, class and gender is at the heart of *Black Watch's* appeal. In his introduction to the published text, Burke describes soldiering as 'arguably the only indigenous industry to have lasted into the twenty-first century', contrasting its fate favourably with that of fishing, shipbuilding and mining (2007: viii). Moreover, he stresses the benefits of pronounced regionalism to the regiment—its members have traditionally been drawn from Fife, Tayside and Perthshire—arguing that 'fighting units tend to be more at home with homogeneity' (viii). In *Black Watch* the idealisation of community, and by implication the national community, thus carries a conservative charge that is both exclusionary and exclusive.

The ambivalence of the show's treatment of militarism provoked disagreement among scholars. For Ariel Watson *Black Watch* 'manages to ennoble fraternal loyalty and unity without glorifying war, which is largely portrayed as dull, exploitative, and tawdry in its everyday minutiae', for instance (2014: 245). On the other hand, Aleks Sierz suggests that by 'excluding the families of the men, especially their wives', *Black Watch* 'presented war as a delirious festival of masculinity' (2011: 203). In addition, the absence of any significant or sustained attempt to address the regiment's role in British colonial violence is problematic by any measure. In spite of a supposed focus on the regiment's history, no mention is made of the way definitive symbols of Scottish identity mobilised in the production—the kilt, the tartan, the bagpipes—were mobilised in the eighteenth and nineteenth centuries by political elites to rally Scots, the mainstay of the British army, behind the project of Empire. This is a significant omission because, in the re-imaging of Scottish identity that devolution has precipitated, the imperative to acknowledge Scotland's role in British imperialism has remained urgent. 'Collective memory', as Michael Morris notes, 'is a key feature which shapes behaviour and beliefs in the present' and consequently enables certain kinds of future while disabling others (Morris 2015: 3). Communal amnesia about the country's role in the colonial project enables the devolved nation to avoid the critical reappraisal of national history that any credible postcolonial project demands. *Black Watch* avoids the legacy of this history by failing to address it directly. Its chauvinism in this regard was greatly enabled by reviewers who either determinedly turned a blind eye to its omissions, or simply did not notice them, preferring instead to celebrate its peculiarly affective theatrical power. Perhaps, as Sierz observes, 'because it felt like a triumph for Scottish manhood, Scottish theatre and Scottish national pride, few were brave enough to raise an eyebrow about its implicitly militarist ideology' (2011: 203).

The published play text is titled *The National Theatre of Scotland's Black Watch*, which gives weight to Sierz's argument insofar as it centres the national company while slightly side-lining the playwright. Thought of in these terms, *Black Watch's* extraordinary success raises uncomfortable questions about the uses and misuses of history in contemporary Scottish culture and about the robustness of heterogeneous conceptions of Scottish identity in the face of totalising heroic national narratives. In contrast to *Home* and *Roam*, which are notable for their pronounced ephemerality, *Black Watch* was repackaged and purposefully deployed to raise the company's profile. The assumption that productions that showcase iconic aspects of Scottish culture and history are appropriate adverts for the NTS in ways that small-scale, experimental or site-specific ones do not persist, as we will see in the next section.

SINCE 2006

In 2007, the newly elected SNP government under Alex Salmond mounted two Gala productions of *Black Watch* to mark the opening of the new parliamentary session although Salmond had not previously seen the show. The extent to which *Black Watch* had already begun to acquire its own burden of representation—it appeared to have been appropriated for the nationalist cause—is worth noting. Not everyone was happy with this turn of events. *The Herald's* Keith Bruce 'worried that rank had been pulled to compel' the NTS to stage the show at the parliament, a charge Featherstone refuted, and which is not supported in evidence. Although at the time of its establishment the NTS had been funded by the SAC, since April 2007 it—along with Scottish Ballet, Scottish Opera, Royal Scottish National Orchestra and the Scottish Chamber Orchestra—has received core funding directly from the Scottish Government. The national companies as a group had lobbied for this outcome before the existence of *Black Watch*, insisting that the scale of their operations made them a special case. Although the SAC argued against this shift, on the grounds that each artform should be considered as a whole, the national companies won the argument. All other theatre companies remained under SAC purview until they came under the strategic remit of a new organisation, Creative Scotland, which replaced both the SAC and Scottish Screen in 2010. Nonetheless, as Rebecca Robinson notes, removal of 'the arbitration offered by funding through the arm's length of the Scottish Arts Council' as 'leaves the NTS vulnerable to, as well as potentially gainful of, the exigencies and capriciousness of political decision-making' (2012a: 54). In the event, while the new arrangement freed the company from the vicissitudes of applying for funding, it has not been immune to budget cuts. It saw a cumulative cut of £900,000 to its core funding between 2011 and 2015, for instance, as austerity policies took effect across the UK.

Nevertheless, from the outset, the absence of the running costs associated with a large building meant the NTS could put almost all its resources into the creation of performance work. Consequently, it immediately appeared prolific, and has more or less continued to do so. In the two-year period after its official launch, for instance, the NTS created

59 productions in 101 locations. In February 2011 when the company celebrated five years of operation it was now firmly established as a major feature of the Scottish cultural landscape. Over the five years the NTS had created 161 productions, reached an audience of 730,000 people, and delivered 5736 workshops involving 129,000 participants. The Scottish Governments *National Performing Companies Annual Report of Activity* (2012) which provides comparative data on the activities of the five centrally funded companies, shows that the period from April 2011 to April 2012 the NTS staged 501 performances—around four times as many as its nearest rival, the Royal Scottish National Orchestra—and hosted 2,422 education and outreach events, more than four times that of any other national company. In that year *Black Watch* toured in the US, to Washington DC, North Carolina, Texas and Illinois. Subsequently, the company has continued its impressive and eclectic output. The government's *Report for the Five National Performing Companies, 2016–18,* shows that in the year 2016–2017, 733 performances were staged and 155 outreach and education activities hosted, reaching an audience of 212,625 people. The NTS performed just under six times more frequently than any of the other centrally funded companies, although the country's orchestras engaged in a very extensive outreach programme.

In terms of international touring, David Greig's adaptation of Euripides *The Bacchae* (2007), featuring Alan Cumming clad in gold lame kilt in the role of Dionysus, owed much to the high camp tradition of the Citz. In John Tiffany's production it made a splash at the Lincoln Center Festival where the *New York Times* critic praised its 'full-blooded theatricality' and 'desire to harness all the elements of theatre, dance, music, comedy and drama to cast a potent spell' (Isherwood 2008). Cumming has been an NTS regular, and he returned to the Lincoln Center Festival in 2013, this time in a radical reworking of Shakespeare's *Macbeth*, again directed by Tiffany with Andrew Goldberg, which began life at Glasgow's Tramway where I saw it in July 2012. As the show opens, a clearly disturbed man is being examined by a doctor in a room lined with sickly green institutional tiles. His bloodied street clothes are removed, he is dressed in drab hospital pyjamas and an orderly leads him to a bed. Just as the doctor and the orderly move towards the security-coded door, the man finally speaks: 'When shall we three meet again / In thunder, lightning or in rain?'. In what follows, Cumming plays an unnamed psychiatric patient whose only dialogue consists in his compulsive channelling of the text of Shakespeare's tragedy. Accompanied by a number of surveillance cameras which project the actions onto screens, he channels Shakespeare's eponymous anti-hero as well as Lady Macbeth, Banquo, McDuff, Malcolm, the witches and around eight other characters. In one sequence we see Cummings face livestreamed from three different angles as he embodies the witches. Lady Macbeth's famous sleepwalking scene is played as the psychiatric patient scrubs himself in a bathtub with a brush that releases blood, so we are positioned with the hallucinating subject as he wonders whether his hands will ever be clean. The adaptation, focusing as it does on the theme of insanity, is clearly inspired by Freud's reading of the play as 'a tale told by an idiot', and the programme tells us the designer Merle Hensel found inspiration for her set in images of abandoned insane asylums. It is impossible not to admire Cumming's versatility, stamina and memory as well as his excellent technique. He is a performer of prodigious skill.

Shakespeare's original is often referred to as the Scottish Play, of course, and is generally thought to have premiered sometime in late 1606 in the aftermath of the Scottish king James VI having succeeded Elizabeth 1. James had imagined an integration of the two countries that far exceeded that brought about by the Union of Crowns in 1603, but this vision was not fulfilled. Instead, as Sharon Alker and Holly Faith Nelson remind us, 'the renegotiation of the nation that took place in Parliament over the next four years was marked by dissension culminating in the failure of the Union project in the summer of 1607' (2007: 380). *Macbeth* emerged at this key juncture, when various contradictory proposals for a new shared identity were in play, including the notion that Scotland should be subsumed and English institutions and practices should dominate. In one reading—although as usual Shakespeare facilitates several—the ultimate defeat of the murderous Scottish usurper by Malcolm, who is complicit in English hegemony, suggests that Scotland's barbaric instincts need to be tempered by England's civilising power. This theme of the perceived barbarity, and thus inferiority, of the Scots and its corollary, the compulsion to demonstrate English superiority, is picked up by David Greig in *Dunsinane* (2010), which was to become another of the NTS's flagship touring shows.

Like *Black Watch*, *Dunsinane* became an ambassador for the NTS abroad. Commissioned by the RSC in 2010 and premiered at London's Hampstead Theatre, it was revived the following year in a co-production with the NTS, in a move which demonstrated the company's agility in picking up shows that began life elsewhere, and later toured to China, Hong Kong, Taiwan, Russia and the US, as well as to various locations across the UK. The production obviously had a different genesis from *Black Watch,* then, having been commissioned outside Scotland. Ariel Watson notes that 'although much of the workshopping took place in Scotland, the production itself was an English one, spearheaded by no less canonical an institution than the Royal Shakespeare Company' (2014: 243). That said, *Dunsinane* is the work of a major Scottish playwright and was commissioned by Michael Boyd, who was at that time artistic director at the RSC but had been a key figure in Scottish theatre while running Glasgow's Tron theatre from 1986 to1996. Additionally, *Dunsinane* was directed by Roxanna Silbert, who had been Literary Director at the Traverse from 2001 to 2004. The show's Scottish connections were relatively deep therefore, if not immediately obvious. Greig approached the commission with his customary intelligence and sophistication and, as Victoria Price suggests, 'in reclaiming the Macbeth story and shifting the focus of Shakespeare's play away from the corrupt ruler to English intervention in Scotland', he appears 'to call for a renegotiation' of the relationship between the two countries (2012: 19).

Perhaps best described as a revisionist sequel to *Macbeth,* Greig's play looks both inward, towards Scotland's past and British theatre traditions, and outward to comment on twenty-first-century identity politics and international conflict. *Dunsinane* begins in the middle of the battle that signals the final defeat of Shakespeare's tyrant, and follows the fortunes of the English army, and particularly their commander Siward, as they attempt to facilitate Malcolm's restoration. It is a play of four scenes, which borrows its temporal and thematic structure from the changing seasons: Spring, Summer, Autumn, Winter. Each opens with a chorus of English soldiers, who provide exposition and narration, and who invariably comment negatively on the otherness of the Scottish landscape:

> In time the fleet found the soft waters
> Of the river Forth and we landed in a place called Fife –
> Which is a wild place compared to Kent. (Greig 2010: 10)

In common with many invading and occupying forces, the English in *Dunsinane* fail to understand Scotland, its people, its customs, its landscape or its language. Instead, they long for home, for 'lovely oak woods where everything is sun-dappled, and the forests are full of wild boar and deer' (51). The medieval Scotland evoked by Greig is a harsh and mythical place, a country, it is strongly implied, too subtle, multifaceted and geographically hostile ever to be understood or conquered by the English.

Greig's Scotland is not the one described by Shakespeare in the closing scenes of *Macbeth*. In his retelling, the country remains divided by shifting tribal allegiances, Malcolm's return is not universally welcomed, and the Scots remain stubbornly hostile to the English interlopers who accompany him. Most notably, Macbeth's widow—her historical name, Gruach, restored—has survived, along with her fifteen-year-old son. Siward has been misled. He has marched north intent on restoring Malcolm to his rightful place on the Scottish throne and securing England's northern border, but has not been welcomed as a liberator; he has instead been wilfully deceived. 'You told me the tyrant had lost the support of the chiefs and he had no son and his queen had died of madness', he complains to Malcolm (2010: 27). Gruach has not taken her own life but instead lives on to become initially a focal point for Scottish resistance to the occupying army, then Siward's seducer, and finally a guerrilla leader bent on wearing the English invaders out. 'You'll go home in the end' she tells the English commander in the play's final scene:

> And when you are back in your empty castle, Siward and one of mine is on the throne again in Dunsinane, I'll send parties of men raiding into your beloved Northumberland to take cattle and women and burn villages and kill your knights. For as long as I reign, I'll torment you and when I die I'll leave instructions in my will to every Scottish Queen that comes after me to tell her King to take up arms and torment England again and again and again until the end of time. (136)

As this short synopsis indicates, Greig makes a number of corrections to the historical record in *Dunsinane*. It is not clear this is his main purpose, however, or the main source of the audience's enjoyment of the play. Like *Macbeth* before it, *Dunsinane* is not a play that strives for historical accuracy. It is strikingly contemporary in resonance, and to borrow Clare Wallace's 'replete with metaphors of ontological dislocation set within the cultural frameworks of postmodernity and globalisation' (2011: 196).

Greig's title deliberately conjures Shakespeare's *Macbeth* and *Dunsinane's* meanings are therefore partly inter-textual, relying as they do on familiarity with the older text. As most school children in the UK are taught, Shakespeare's *Macbeth* is itself a revisionist history play written to appeal to the prejudices of the Stuart King James VI/I. However, although it is significantly more faithful to the actual historical record, insofar as it figures 'tyranny' as a product of propaganda rather than deeds—Greig's Macbeth has been 'a good king' who 'lasted fifteen years'—and attacks the politics of benevolent imperialist intervention, *Dunsinane* also functions as a powerful contemporary political allegory (Greig 2010: 32). 'Imagine', observed one critic, 'an inhospitable terrain full of powerful warlords and an occupying army aching to get home' (Billington 2010). Greig's concern with the folly of attempting to establish peace through war is succinctly exposed both in the play's action and in Malcolm's observation to Siward: 'You can no more force peace into existence than you can wander across the surface of the sea stamping the waves flat' (Greig 2010: 126).

Even as he contradicts Shakespeare's version of Scottish history Greig borrows something of his thematic focus. Both *Macbeth* and *Dunsinane* might be accurately described as plays about good soldiers who lose their way. Greig is careful to present Siward as a highly principled man, one whose morality is based on the Aristotelian notion that ethics rests in the character of the individual. Siward thinks only of how he should act in response to particular circumstances and is unable to comprehend an ethics in any way oriented towards the other. Inevitably, his inflexibility leads him to acts of barbarism until he is, like Shakespeare's protagonist, steeped in blood too far. Greig is not a didactic playwright, however, and if Siward and his actions are presented partly as emblematic of English arrogance, they are counterbalanced by the pragmatism and wry humour of Egham, his second in command. On learning that Siward has ordered the immolation of a group of men because of their refusal to give up Gruach's son, Egham describes his commander's action as 'a bit Scandinavian', for example, insisting that to burn people alive is a dubious military tactic because 'it makes them dead' (94). As the action progresses and the political situation worsens, questions of disengagement take precedence and, in the end, the only question for Egham is how to get out. When he suggests they should leave a garrison to protect their border and go home Siward responds:

>**Siward** You sound like you would prefer us to be defeated

> **Egham** Who said 'defeated'? I didn't say 'defeated'. Did you say 'defeated'? I didn't say 'defeated'. I said 'leave'.
> **Siward** 'Defeated—'leave'—what's the difference?
> **Egham** All the difference (95).

Siward is increasingly out of place and out of his depth, his failure to understand the host culture evident both in his inability to comprehend, or learn, the indigenous language and his failure to appreciate the complexity of Scotland's political discourse. Eventually his resolve begins to erode and his character to disintegrate. He hands power to his deputy and in the play's final image walks off aimlessly into a blizzard.

Dunsinane proposes a way of perceiving a contemporary ethical and political impasse, the War on Terror, by means of a semi-familiar quasi-historical Scottish narrative. If he invites his audience to reconsider Shakespeare's play through inter-textual reference, Greig equally invites them to recognise correspondences with Western interventions in Iraq and Afghanistan, the effects of which appear increasingly disastrous with the passage of time. In *Dunsinane's* opaque ending Greig provides no straightforward solution. As he walks into the snow Siward, now in a state of obvious existential despair, in answer to the question of where he is going repeats the line, 'We walk … we walk … we walk', echoing Macbeth's famous, 'tomorrow and tomorrow and tomorrow' (138).

Mark Fisher describes *Dunsinane* as 'an irresolvable drama about an irresolvable conflict' and this insight draws our attention to its focus on immutable cultural differences, and thus to the politics of language and place (Fisher 2011). 'I have no interest in England' Gruach insists, and English political concerns certainly remain peripheral in the play, relevant only insofar as they impinge on Scotland (Greig 2010: 63). The Scottish queen is also particularly scornful of Siward's language, noting that to 'seduce a man in English' is 'like dancing wearing wooden shoes' (69). When Siward complains that Gaelic is 'hard to learn' she responds:

> **Gruach** Your English is a woodworker's tool.
> Siward.
> Hello, goodbye, that tree is green,
> Simple matters.
> A soldier's language sent out to capture the world in words.
> Always trying to describe. (76)

Gaelic, by contrast, is freed from such mundane illustrative function: 'We long since gave up believing in descriptions. Our language is the forest' (76). As Clare Wallace observes, throughout, 'irony is among the Scot's favoured tools for resisting or challenging English preconception' (2013: 94). When Gruach is asked by a young soldier if she eats babies, for instance, she responds by suggesting he try baby meat himself because it is 'delicious' and 'tender' (59). These jokes, and Greig's broader focus on language, are obviously understood differently by different audiences. In England, performed under the auspices of the RSC, *Dunsinane* might be read as a play about the impenetrability of tribal politics in the face of English rationalism, for example. While in Scotland, it is more straightforwardly about the arrogance of the invader's excessive cultural literalism, and the importance of linguistic fluency as a means of accessing culture. 'No doubt' as Jordan Riefe remarked reviewing the show in Los Angeles in 2015, 'future audiences will recognize conflicts of their own' (2015).

As Loren Kruger has argued, national theatres 'share with the critical and legislative texts the task of representing not merely the question of national identity but also the anxiety and aspirations invested in the articulation and resolution of that question' (1992: 28). While the NTS had largely avoided addressing this question directly, in Edinburgh in the summer of 2014, a month before the Independence Referendum of 18 September, the company staged a new trilogy of major Scottish history plays, which came close to illustrating Kruger's point. Detailing the succession of the late-medieval Stewart kings James I, II and III, Rona Munro's *The James Plays* was produced in a co-production with the EIF, and unusually, the National Theatre of Great Britain. Directed by Laurie Sansom, who had succeeded Featherstone as the NTS's artistic director in 2013, the trilogy played in repertory at Edinburgh's Festival Theatre before transferring to the National Theatre's Olivier, where it ran from late September into October. Each play functioned as a discrete entity, and Munro's subtitles gestured towards her shifting thematic focus: *James I: The Key Will Keep the Lock*; *James II: Day of the Innocents*; and *James III: The True Mirror*. Nonetheless, it was the scale and confidence of the work *as a trilogy* that was remarked upon repeatedly by reviewers and read as a marker of the authority of the NTS and the Scottish creative industries as a whole. Everything about the *James Plays* was confident and ambitious: large historical sweep; large cast; large budget; large theatres.

The trilogy spans the period from 1406, when the eleven-year-old James I is taken prisoner by the English and becomes Scotland's king in exile, to 1488 and the death of his grandson James III. The first play opens with James I's return to Scotland with his young English wife Joan, after eighteen years as a political prisoner of Henry V and here Munro consciously inverts English mythology. Henry is coarse, jaded, ruthless and dying of dysentery while James is the fresh-faced hero. Joan's unhappiness in Scotland is mirrored in his struggle to establish the rule of law, his own right to govern and his dynasty. *James II* lives in terror having witnessed the murder of his father as a child, and of having lived at the mercy of factional divides and political intrigues as various noble families fight for the regency. The now 18-year-old king revisits the horrific events of his childhood in nightmares, but eventually exercises his birthright first by overthrowing the tyrannical Lord Livingston and ultimately by murdering his boyhood friend William Douglas. The general intrigue and power play continues in *James III* with the eponymous character depicted as a sexually incontinent narcissist, whose laziness and recalcitrance contribute to his own downfall. Munro uses contemporary Scots throughout, and the productions are given additional contemporary resonance by the playful use of popular song. For *The Independent*'s Paul Taylor the 'sexy kilts-with-attitude company version of "Don't You Want Me, Baby?"' in *James III*, was 'the most elating thing' he had seen all year (2014).

Near the end of *James III: The True Mirror* (2014), the fifteenth-century Scottish queen, Margaret of Denmark, addresses a disgruntled Scottish nobility:

> You know the problem with you lot? You've got fuck-all except attitude. You scream and shout about how you want things done and when the chance comes look at you! What are you frightened of? Making things worse? (Munro 2014: 285)

This outburst, coming as it does in the month before the Independence Referendum, seems startlingly topical and explicitly political. It also appeared, to the disappointment of some Scottish critics, to be recycling a number of disabling myths about Scotland and its people, not least, as Joyce McMillan noted, the notion that the Scots are fundamentally oppositional, and that Scotland is consequently 'uniquely rough, violent and ungovernable' (2014). In August, when the outcome of the upcoming Independence Referendum was as yet unknown, the house lights were raised during the speech, so that Queen Margaret's challenge was extended into the auditorium. The audience at the Festival Theatre responded with what McMillan wryly described as 'obliging laughter', laughter that in her view evidenced Scotland's continuing willingness 'to see itself mainly through the eyes of contemptuous others' (2014). Alternatively, we can read this laughter as evidence of Scotland's self-awareness, of course, as a healthy ability to laugh at its own foibles, or as approval for the wilfully anti-authoritarian stance adopted by its imaginary ancestors. After all, as Susannah Clapp suggested in her reading of that moment: 'What could be more quintessentially Scottish than a compliment disguised as aggression?' (2014). Six weeks later, at the Olivier Theatre on London's South Bank, when the results of the referendum were known, the house lights were not raised.

In Munro's play, Margaret's accusations quickly transform into an outpouring of affection as she recalls arriving in Scotland as a 12-year-old bride: 'You showed me that the more frightened you are the better the joke you can tell about it, you taught me you can find friends wherever you share food and drink if you just wait and see how to join in the conversation' (Munro 2014: 285). This shift in tone is typical of the trilogy. By turns raucous, bawdy, sentimental, serious, comic and tragic, Munro's *James Plays* were a critical success in Edinburgh in August 2014 and on London's South Bank in the autumn of the same year, going on to win the Evening Standard and Writers' Guild of Great Britain awards for best new play. In Scotland, much was made of the energy and chutzpah of Sansom's production, which for McMillan 'firmly established [him] as a world-class large scale director, and a powerful hand on the tiller of Scotland's national company' (2014). A number of English reviewers had rather a different focus. For, Charlotte Runcie, Munro's trilogy captured 'something elusive about Scottishness: that potent mix of individual spirit, darkness, alcohol and loyalty that can seem so foreign to the rest of Britain' (2014) (Fig. 4.1).

Taken as a whole, English reviewers tended to emphasise perceived cultural differences between Scotland and England and in so doing often revealed as much about the function of Scotland as 'other' in the UK imagination, as they did about Munro's trilogy. In 2016 the trilogy was restaged and toured to Australia, Canada and New Zealand. These locations, like most of those visited by *Black Watch*, are not only former colonies which share a common language, but were also key destinations for Scottish emigrants. In a very real sense, as Ariel Watson notes, 'the nation that is performed and interpellated by these tours is not

Fig. 4.1 Matthew Pidgeon as James III in Rona Munro's *James III: The True Mirror* (directed by Laurie Sansom, National Theatre of Scotland, 2016) reproduced with kind permission from Tommy Ga-Ken Wan

simply geographical or political but also diasporic' (2014: 241). As a case in point, the Australian festival circuit has accommodated an increasing number of Scottish productions since the establishment of the NTS. *Black Watch* (Sydney and Perth Festivals 2008); David Greig's *The Strange Undoing of Prudencia Hart* (Adelaide and Perth Festivals 2013) and Shona Reppe's *The Curious Scrapbook of Josephine Bean* (Adelaide and Perth Festivals 2014). *The James Plays* (Adelaide Festival 2016) and Lee Hall's *Our Ladies of Perpetual Succour* (Melbourne Festival 2016), as Sarah Thomasson observes 'were presented as Australian exclusives' but they also 'contribute to Scottish cultural diplomacy' (2020: 137). On tour, NTS productions like *Black Watch* and *The James Plays*, operate partly as adverts for a devolved Scotland, as high-status products, packaged as gifts, that are intended to facilitate better understanding of the country's cultural distinctiveness and conviviality. In this sense, the version of Scotland that the NTS's performs abroad, cannot be easily disentangled from the wider heritage industry. David Greig's ballad play *The Strange*

Undoing of Prudencia Hart (2011), which he created for the NTS with Wils Wilson to be played in function suites and pubs, was another notable critical success for the company. It toured nationally and internationally, as far afield as Rio de Janeiro, Santa Monica and Melbourne, and was sponsored by a range of Single Malt Whisky producers. Free samples were handed out as the audience took its seats at every venue, including the McKittrick Hotel in New York where the show had a successful six-month run in 2017.

Conclusion

'National cultural institutions', as Christine Hamilton and Adrienne Scullion note, 'are a bit like national airlines: carrying national prestige abroad and providing opportunities, or fostering talent, at home' (2003: 99). Among contemporary commentators 'there were fears that any National Theatre was bound to evolve into a huge building-based institution that would sap funding and energy from an already under-funded sector' and for some the project conjured 'a nightmare vision of the National Theatre as a tweedy, inward-looking affair, projecting an old-fashioned vision of Scottish life and drama' (McMillan 2005). In the wider context, the campaign surrounding the setting up of the company was animated by complex debates around notions of Scottish cultural identity and Scottish nationalism in the years leading up to and immediately after devolution. As Tom Nairn notes, 'Donald Dewar's Devolution project... added greatly to the momentum of change in Scotland', provoking a 'general sense of an incoming tide, carrying us forward into a new period of history' (2000: 155). The enormous range, variety and vitality of the NTS's work in its early seasons were important for two reasons. Firstly, any fear of the company becoming a moribund site for the elevation of partial truths quickly receded and has not resurfaced. Secondly, it was important for the NTS to make a success of its buildingless model because some commentators had seen a future building project as inevitable. In 2002, for instance, Brian McMaster, director of the Edinburgh International Festival, raised his voice against the project insisting, 'every national theatre he had ever encountered had been hamstrung by administrative costs and overpaid backstage crews', that the virtual model, was simply 'the thin end of the wedge' and Scotland would inevitably be saddled with 'an expensive building-based company' (quoted in Garside 2002).

It now seems highly unlikely Scotland will swap its flexible and inclusive national theatre company for the kind of white elephant McMaster envisaged.

From its inception, the NTS engaged directly with communities in order to renegotiate and reaffirm local identities within the larger context of Scottish 'national' identity. Vicky Featherstone's leadership was particularly exemplary in this regard and should be applauded. As a statement of artistic intent its inaugural project, *Home*, demonstrated the existence of a confident, exciting, ambitious and forward-looking Scottish performance culture that was ready to seize its opportunity. The preponderance of new, and often experimental, work in its programme should, in this context, be considered a welcome manifestation of locally grounded and resistant performance practices working in the interests of a small nation and its diverse communities in opposition to expectations of both the cultural elite and larger centralising forces. The buildingless model on which the NTS was constituted has enabled it to repeatedly, if not exclusively, privilege the geographical periphery. This privileging, which is evidenced in the many community-based projects the NTS has facilitated, will be discussed in more detail in the next chapter.

In January 2013 the NTS announced, following a £2 m cash injection from the Scottish Government, its intention to consolidate its headquarters in a new £5.5 million home to include rehearsal, administration, technical and storage space, in the north of Glasgow. In early 2017 the building, christened Rockvilla, was officially opened by the Scottish Culture Secretary Fiona Hyslop. The NTS remains a co-producing theatre, and no performances have thus far been staged in the new building which hosts education and training events. The absence of a fixed performance venue has enabled the NTS to foreground space in its work in new and innovative ways. This has also been the aspect of the NTS model that has attracted most interest and praise. National Theatre Wales (NTW) drew heavily on the NTS model when it was set up as a buildingless company in 2009, and it remains committed to making theatre 'in unanticipated spaces: on the shore; up a mountain; on a train; in the woods. And sometimes, when you least expect it, in a theatre' (National Theatre Wales 2023). The announcement in July 2015, of the appointment of Graham McLaren, former associate director at the NTS, and Neil Murray, the NTS's inaugural chief executive, as joint artistic directors of the Abbey Theatre in Dublin, also seemed like an acknowledgement of the Scottish company's effectiveness. At home, the NTS continues to offer opportunities for the circulation of narratives about national histories, behaviours, iconography, events and preoccupations in a very wide range of settings and forms, thus opening up a space in the Scottish public sphere for consensus but also for contestation and discussion.

REFERENCES

Advisory Council for the Arts in Scotland (AdCAS) '1981–90 Correspondence'. National Library of Scotland Manuscripts Collection, Acc.10800.

Agnew, Denis (2000) 'Contexts and Concepts of a Scottish National Theatre', unpublished PhD thesis, Queen Margaret University College Edinburgh.

Alker, Sharon and Holly Faith Nelson (2007) 'Macbeth, the Jacobean Scot, and the Politics of the Union'. *Studies in English Literature*, 47:2, pp. 379–401.

Archibald, David (2007) '"We're Just Big Bullies": Gregory Burke's Black Watch'. *Drouth*, 26, pp. 8–13.

Billington, Michael (2010) 'Dunsinane Review', *Guardian*, 17 February.

Brantley, Ben (2007) 'To Tell These War Stories, Words are Not Enough'. *New York Times*, 24 October.

Brown, Ian (2013) *Scottish Theatre: Diversity, Language, Continuity*. Amsterdam, Rodopi.

Bull, John (2011) 'Anthony Neilson', in Middeke, Martin, Peter Paul Schnierer and Aleks Sierz (eds.) *The Methuen Drama Guide to Contemporary British Playwrights*. London, Bloomsbury, pp. 343–362.

Burke, Gregory (2007) *The National Theatre of Scotland's Black Watch*. London, Faber and Faber.

Burnett, Andrew (2006) 'A Ferry Tale Start for Roving Company'. *Observer*, 26 February.

Clapp, Susanna. (2014) 'The James Plays review: Rona Munro's Timely Game of Thrones', *Observer*, 17 August.

Fisher, Mark (2011) '*Dunsinane*—Review'. *Guardian*, 19 May.

Gardner, Lyn (2006a) 'Black Watch'. *Guardian*, 8 August.

Gardner, Lyn (2006b) 'Realism Review'. *Guardian*, 17 August.

Garside, Juliette (2002) 'Is it Curtains for a National Theatre?'. *Sunday Herald*, 1 December.

Greig, David (2010) *Dunsinane*. London, Faber and Faber.

Hamilton, Christine and Adrienne Scullion (2003) 'Flagships or Flagging?: The Post Devolution Role of Scotland's National Companies', *Scottish Affairs*, 42, pp. 98–114.

Harpin, Anna (2017) 'Dirty Realism', in Trish Reid, *The Theatre of Anthony Neilson*. London, Bloomsbury, pp. 171–185.

Harvie, Jen (2005) *Staging the UK*. Manchester, Manchester University Press.

Haswell, John (2006) 'Home Shetland'. *British Theatre Guide*. Available at: https://www.britishtheatreguide.info/reviews/homeshetland-rev.htm

Hauthal, Janine (2013) 'Realisms in British Drama since the 1990s: Anthony Neilson's *Realism* and Gregory Burke's *Black Watch*', in Dorothee Birke and Stella Butter (eds.) Realisms in Contemporary Culture: Theories, Politics and Medial Configurations. Berlin, Boston, De Gruyter, pp. 146–177.

Haydon, Andrew (2013) 'Theatre in the 2000s', in Dan Rebellato (ed.) *Modern British Playwriting, 2000–2009*. London, Bloomsbury, pp. 40–98.

Holdsworth, Nadine (2010) *Theatre & Nation*. Basingstoke, Palgrave MacMillan.

Isherwood, Charles (2008) 'A Greek God and his Groupies are Dressed to Kill'. *New York Times*, 5 July.

Kruger, Loren (1992) *The National Stage: Theatre and Cultural Legitimation in England, France, and America*. Chicago, University of Chicago Press.

Leach, Robert (2007) 'The Short, Astonishing History of the National Theatre of Scotland'. *New Theatre Quarterly*, pp. 171–183.

Letts, Quentin (2008) 'Black Watch: Explosive (and That's Just the Language)'. *Daily Mail*, 26 June.

McMillan, Joyce (2005) 'The Joy of Worrying Over this Crucible of Creativity'. *Scotsman*, 27 January.

McMillan, Joyce (2006) 'Home: National Theatre of Scotland'. *Scotsman*, 27 February.

McMillan, Joyce (2009) 'Review of the Decade: 2000–2009'. *Scotsman*, 17 December.

McMillan, Joyce (2011) 'Thorn in Their Side: Nursing the Thistle of Scottish Political Theatre'. *Scotsman*, 17 December.

McMillan, Joyce (2014) 'The James Plays'. *Scotsman*, 11 August.

Morris, Michael (2015) *Scotland and the Caribbean, c.1740–1833*. London, Routledge.

Munro, Rona (2014) *The James Plays*. London, Nick Hern Books.

Nairn, Tom (2000) *After Britain: New Labour and the Return of Scotland*. London, Granta.

National Theatre Wales (2023) 'About'. Available at: https://www.nationaltheatrewales.org/about

Neilson, Anthony (2008) *Realism*, in *Anthony Neilson: Plays 2*. London, Bloomsbury, pp, 287–355.

Pattie, David (2011), 'Gregory Burke', in Middeke, Martin, Peter Paul Schnierer and Aleks Sierz (eds.) *The Methuen Drama Guide to Contemporary British Playwrights*. London, Bloomsbury, pp. 22–41.

Price, Victoria (2012) '"Two Kingdoms...Compassed with One Sea': Reconstructing Kingdoms and Reclaiming Histories in David Greig's *Dunsinane*'. *International Journal of Scottish Theatre and Screen*, 5:1, pp. 19–32.

Reid, Trish (2007) '"From Scenes Like These Old Scotia's Grandeur Springs": The New National Theatre of Scotland'. *Contemporary Theatre Review*, 17:2, pp. 192–201.

Reid, Trish (2016) '"Sexy Kilts with Attitude": Scottish Theatre in the Twenty First Century', in Adiseshiah, Sian, and Louise Lepage (eds.) *Twenty-First Century Drama: What Happens Now*. Basingstoke, Palgrave Macmillan, pp. 191–211.

Riach, Alan (2021) 'What Should Our National Theatre of Scotland Be For?'. *National*, 20 December.

Riefe, Jordan (2015) 'Dunsinane: Theater Review'. *Hollywood Reporter*, 15 March.

Robinson, Rebecca (2012a) 'Funding the "Nation" in the National Theatre of Scotland'. *International Journal of Cultural Policy*, 18:1, pp. 46–58.

Robinson, Rebecca (2012b) 'The National Theatre of Scotland's *Black Watch*'. *Contemporary Theatre Review*, 22:3, pp. 392–399.

Runcie, Charlotte (2014) 'Edinburgh Festival 2014: The James Plays, Edinburgh Festival Theatre, Review: 'Astonishing''. *Telegraph*, 11 August.

Scottish Arts Council (2001) *Scottish National Theatre: Final Report of the Independent Working Group*, Glasgow.

Sierz, Aleks (2011) *Rewriting the Nation: British Theatre Today*. London, Methuen.

Taylor, Paul (2014) 'The James Plays: National Theatre Review: The Most Elating Things You'll See All Year', *Independent*, 26 September.

Thomasson, Sarah (2020) 'The Australian Festival Network', in Ric Knowles (ed.) *The Cambridge Companion to International Theatre Festivals*. Cambridge, Cambridge University Press, pp. 132–146.

Tomlin, Liz (2015) *British Theatre Companies 1995–2014*. London, Bloomsbury.

Tompkins, Joanne (2014) *Theatre's Heterotopias: Performance and the Cultural Politics of Space*. Basingstoke, Palgrave Macmillan.

Wallace, Clare (2011) 'Unfinished Business: Allegories of Otherness in Dunsinane', in Wallace, C. and Anja Muller (eds.) *Cosmopotia: Transnational Identities in David Greig's Theatre*. Prague, Univerzita Karlova v Praze, pp. 196–213.

Wallace, Clare (2013) The Theatre of David Greig Bloomsbury Publishing Plc

Watson, Ariel (2014) 'Birnam Wood: Scotland, Nationalism, and Theatres of War'. *Theatre History Studies*, 33, pp. 226–249.

Wilkie, Fiona. (2008) 'The Production of Site: Site-Specific Theatre', in Nadine Holdsworth, and Mary Luckhurst, (eds.) *A Concise Companion to British and Irish Drama*. Oxford: Blackwell, pp. 87–106.

Zerdy, Joanne (2013) 'Fashioning a Scottish Operative: *Black Watch* and Banal Theatrical Nationalism on Tour in the US'. *Theatre Research International*, 38:3, pp. 181–95.

CHAPTER 5

Engaging Audiences

Precisely five years after the launch of its inaugural *Home* project, on 25 February 2011, the NTS issued an open invitation to members of the public to submit ideas for pieces of five minute theatre. Successful applicants were to be given support to develop their work for inclusion in a 24-hour online broadcast commencing at 5 pm on Tuesday 21 June 2011. On the day, 235 performances were streamed in a 24-hour period. Around 80 of these were broadcast live, although all 235, as stipulated in the NTS brief, were performed, and recorded in front of live audiences. A total of 1000 performers—professional, amateur and novice—aged between 5 and 75 took part. 202 pieces were performed in Scotland, thirteen across the rest of the UK, four elsewhere in Europe and sixteen across the rest of the world. On the day of its initial broadcast the event attracted 6300 viewers from 51 countries who visited the site 22,000 times and in the following year the site was accessed a further 28,000 times, creating a total *Five Minute Theatre* audience of approximately 50,000. In June 2012 *Five Minute Theatre* won the CATS award for Best Technical Presentation, but by that time the format had already been deemed successful enough to be repeated in amended form. In 2012 five shorter events were scheduled. The first on the theme Protest was broadcast on 1 May, and the second on Youth on 14 July. Both dates had obvious proletarian associations and, as I have written elsewhere, these

© The Author(s), under exclusive license to Springer Nature Switzerland AG 2024
T. Reid, *Theatre and Performance in Contemporary Scotland*, https://doi.org/10.1007/978-3-031-61191-9_5

particular iterations purposefully 'provided a platform for school, community and youth theatre groups, as well as for work created in collaboration with prisoners and other marginalised constituencies' (Reid 2014: 113).

By utilising online participation as a mechanism for the extension of cultural engagement, *Five Minute Theatre* raised interesting and pertinent questions about how public space might be constituted in the digital age, and how participation in national or international theatre and performance events might be enabled via online platforms. In fact, because of its focus on widening participation, *Five Minute Theatre* was notable for its relative simplicity in this context. The internet was essentially employed as a neutral tool for the dissemination of work and participants were able to engage only within a relatively tight predetermined framework—most obviously the work could be no longer than five minutes in duration. Interactivity—a key feature of virtual theatres in other contexts—was limited to live chat facilities and Twitter and audience members, whether physically present or online, had no power to affect the course of individual performance events. In this sense, audiences for *Five Minute Theatre* had no more power to shape events than they might have in more conventional settings. A number of other signatures associated with performance and new media were also absent. The project was not immersive, for instance, nor did it involve live performers interacting with projections that had been digitally generated or manipulated. Nonetheless, *Five Minute Theatre* was clearly a digital performance project, in so far as computer technologies played a primary rather than a secondary role in its delivery.

Five Minute Theatre also privileged the idea of cyberspace as public even though, as Steve Dixon observes, 'this notion is largely metaphoric ... and indeed romantic' (2007: 462). While the individual online viewer was in a real sense simply sitting alone in front of a screen, they were aware, at least conceptually, of the presence of multiple viewers in other locations. This awareness concretised a sense that *Five Minute Theatre* was a meeting point, and thus a distinct location. Consequently, the idea of space privileged by the project gestures towards a discursive understanding of the public sphere as both a jurisdiction, where discussion of public interests can take place, and a realm of social life generated through such discussion. Public life relies on discourse and, most specifically, on the existence of a public capable of forming common understanding through conversations of one kind or another. *Five Minute Theatre* attempted to open up a space for people of shared interests to congregate and converse. This conversation took place via live chat facilities and the Twitter feed and also at the various performance hubs operating on the day where people could assemble both to view streamed performances and to participate as audience members during performances that went out live as part of the prearranged schedule. Tickets for the performance hubs were free and distributed on a first-come-first-served basis.

A significant number of *Five Minute Theatre* performances took place in streets, while others were filmed in toilets, car parks, parks, cemeteries, shopping malls, launderettes and other spaces associated with the idea of public or civic space. In providing a platform for the sharing of work that collapsed physical distance across Scotland, its focus was not on aesthetic standards or quality as such, but rather on inclusivity and access. It utilised online platforms primarily as an aid to participation but in the process also allowed individuals greater autonomy in interrogating and reinterpreting the cultural creations of others, thus facilitating a greater sense of ownership of the shared culture they occupy. This democratic impulse is worth taking seriously. NTS projects such as *Five Minute Theatre* are explicitly intended to make participants better readers of their own culture and thus potentially more critical of the culture they occupy and more self-reflective in conversations within that culture. This emphasis is even more apparent in the NTS's next iteration of the format which concerned itself explicitly with the 2014 Independence Referendum.

At 5 pm on 23 June 2014, the heavily pregnant performance artist Victoria Bianchi opened proceedings from the stage of Glasgow's Òran Mór with *ANTHEM: To a New One*, a letter to her unborn child. The NTS in collaboration with The Space, thus launched *The Great Yes No Don't Know 5 Minute Theatre Show*. Over the next twenty-four hours around 840 participants, ranging in age from three months to 80, performed over 180 bite-size works inspired by the forthcoming referendum on Scottish independence. The show was multi-authored and explicitly intended to offer multiple perspectives on the referendum debate. As with its predecessor, performances were streamed online and broadcast from various locations across Scotland and from outside its borders: East Timor, Los Angeles, Lancaster, Texas, Leeds, Istanbul, New Jersey, South Australia, Barcelona, New York, Mumbai, and Paris. Contributions were again staged and streamed live from a number of designated Hubs in Aberdeen, Inverness, Dumfries, Glasgow and Edinburgh. This time, there were also roving camera crews who captured performances in St Andrews, Angus, Prestwick, Stranraer and Falkirk.

Participants included primary school pupils, community groups, students, teenagers, visual artists and professional theatre-makers.

Although as we have seen, *Dunsinane* and *The James Plays* deal explicitly with issues of governance and cultural distinctiveness, *The Great Yes, No, Don't Know Five Minute Theatre Show* was the only work commissioned by the national company that dealt explicitly with the referendum. It was curated by two of Scotland's most celebrated theatre-makers, David Greig, who was a vocal supporter of the YES campaign, and David McLennan, a veteran of 7:84 Scotland and Wildcat, founder of the successful lunchtime theatre club A Play, a Pie and a Pint, and a confirmed NO voter. The project took shape in response to two related but distinct imperatives: on one hand, the pressure on the national company to make a direct and balanced contribution in the run up to the referendum and, on the other, its desire to consolidate and extend its reach via purposefully inclusive practice.

There are obviously benefits to the *Five Minute Theatre* model. Not least because it begins with an open call for participation it appears, to borrow Jen Harvie's phrase, to extend its 'invitation to engage socially very widely ... perhaps even democratically' (Harvie 2013: 2). In addition, its deliberate lack of sophistication models social cohesion, as does the studiedly diverse range of work it platforms. Inclusion in *The Great Yes, No, Don't Know Five Minute Theatre Show* did not depend on a demonstration of expertise, but instead on the ability to be 'representative' of the general population in terms of age, location, and differing attitudes to the question posed by September's ballot: 'Should Scotland be an Independent country?' Performances selected from outside Scotland were chosen for their resonance in relation to the referendum.

In the vast majority of cases performances occurred with no set design, on empty stages, in classrooms, gym halls and living rooms, in offices or in public spaces including the harbour at St Andrews. The absence of design magnified the significance of the people involved who became indexical of the country as a whole, or at least the project sought to gesture in that direction. *The Great Yes, No, Don't Know Five Minute Theatre Show* attempted to open up a space for people with a shared interest in, although often very different views on, the upcoming referendum to gather in a spirit of democratic engagement and tolerance. This approach resonated effectively. For instance, the Scottish critics showed little interest in evaluating, or describing, individual performances from

The Great Yes, No, Don't Know Five Minute Theatre Show. Neil Cooper's response was typical:

> What was most thrilling about watching this, be it live or virtually, was witnessing several generations of Scotland's finest theatre makers coming together with schools and community groups for a demonstration of artistic solidarity possessing an energy, generosity and spirit of inclusivity that proved truly inspiring. (Cooper 2018: 16)

This willingness to applaud the more inclusive aspects of the NTS's practice has been evident in the Scottish press since the company began making work in early 2006.

Perhaps unsurprisingly, the most widely employed dramaturgical mode across the 24-hour period of *The Great Yes, No, Don't Know Five Minute Theatre Show* was comedy: the shortened form lends itself quite easily to both the comic sketch and the satirical song. In contrast to the gloomy predictions of the Better Together campaign *The Great Yes, No, Don't Know Five Minute Theatre Show* was productively optimistic about the potentials of collective endeavour. It tended to make fun of 'Project Fear' while allowing plenty of space to those opposed to independence and to the undecided. In George Milne's *Feart*, for instance, a young couple, Alan and Linda, are preparing to make their first parachute jump from a decidedly rickety airplane. They suspect the organisers are dodgy. Their confidence fades as the moment of truth approaches. Their instructor insists that they should not be 'feart' (afraid) to make the leap. Alan retorts that he is 'feart' and asks for more substantial assurances. The instructor then has second thoughts of his own but the plane hits turbulence, and he is thrown out. Alan and Linda are left to watch him fall. Will he land safely or not?

NTS has continued to commission large-scale community projects, which are instrumental in actioning its commitment to 'make an impact for more people ... through relevant and representative theatre making' and to 'create a greater sense of connectedness throughout Scotland (National Theatre of Scotland 2023). These projects also tell us something about how the NTS conceptualises the relationship between performance and community, and by extension between a national flagship company and the nation it represents. In contrast to *Five Minute Theatre*, such NTS projects have tended to define community geographically, in relation to *where* the work takes place. The pronounced regionalism of its inaugural *Home* project established something of a pattern in this regard. For example, in 2012–13 Wils Wilson returned to Shetland to direct *Ignition*, a six-month community project produced in association with Shetland Arts and Creative Scotland, which explored the islanders' relationship with the car. Created for and with the residents of an archipelago whose economy is reliant on North Sea oil, the project culminated in one indoor and two large-scale outdoor performance events. It presented the car not in opposition to stable island culture but as essential to it and much of its final performances were experienced from inside vehicles. While being driven between sites, for instance, we picked up a hitchhiker who sang a ukulele lament. We also encountered a travelling garden gnome and its gregarious owner and, from someone's parked car, heard poetic reminiscences from older islanders of fishing disasters and car accidents recorded with great care by the choreographer Janet Parker. From the back seat of the same car, we watched teenagers perform a beautiful twenty-minute parkour routine around a wrecked Volvo, while elderly ballroom dancers waltzed serenely by. Finally, we returned to the Brae Village Hall where we were served a welcome cup of tea and treated to original songs about Shetland life, sung by and intergenerational choir of volunteers. The creation of such beautifully rich and multi-vocal work obviously requires patience and commitment and the narratives that were sutured together to create *Ignition* drew on stories collected by the performance artist Lowri Evans who for several months prior to the main events, hitchhiked across the archipelago dressed as the White Wife, a figure from Shetland folklore who is said to appear when islanders need help. These stories helped shape the final outcomes of the project. The ferry from Aberdeen to Lerwick takes around twelve and a half hours, and because of its relative inaccessibility *Ignition* was consequently a performance event made by the people of Shetland primarily for the people of Shetland. As François Matarasso notes in *A Wider Horizon* (2015), his study of Creative Arts East and rural touring, by 'gathering together in the hall, for an event that they or their neighbours have organised, people affirm not just their cultural tastes and values, but their willingness to be a community in the first place' (2015: 94).

From September 2015 to April 2016 the NTS reprised this approach in a more urban context with *Granite*, a series of performances, installations and events created in partnership with the people of Aberdeen. The collection of local stories was again figured as a core activity and the project culminated in a series of major site-specific performances in the quadrangle of Marischal College, one of the city's most prestigious buildings, and the largest grey granite building in the world. The 'privileging of localism and community engagement which these projects evidence', as I have argued in the past, 'acts in part as an antidote to the potentially centralizing effect of a national company' (2016a: 195).

Performances in and of the Rural

A major advantage of the NTS model, as Ben Walmsley has noted, is that ensures 'the existing physical infrastructure of Scottish theatre is used to the full without the wastefulness of designing, constructing and maintaining yet another expensive public building' (2020: 113). Beyond making work in partnership with existing building-based theatre companies, such as Eden Court, Dundee Rep, Perth Theatre and Pitlochry Festival Theatre, Scotland's geography also meant that rural touring was, from the outset, central to NTS strategy. Walmsley explains:

> There are several reasons why rural touring is so important to NTS: firstly, as the national theatre company in Scotland, it accepts it has an explicit duty to produce and tour work all over the country; secondly, it acknowledges that people living in rural communities are just as entitled to high quality theatre as their compatriots in Edinburgh or Glasgow; and thirdly, it values the artistic, social and audience development opportunities unique to rural touring. (114)

This commitment is evident in the early work of the company which in its first four years, in addition to the *Home* projects, toured 15 shows to local community and gathering halls across the country.

In her short and useful book *theatre & the rural* (2016), Jo Robinson argues that 'our repeated failures to fully engage with the rural in all its guises are problematic' and prevent us from engaging with 'the actual place and lived experience of the rural' (2016: 4). This problem is especially acute in Scotland where 91% of the population lives in settlements and localities which account for only 2.3% of the country's land area (National Records of Scotland 2022). An additional issue is the long-standing and persistent tendency to see the Highlands as a romanticised space 'constituting the most profoundly mythologized component of "Scottish" identity' (Śledzińska 2015: 120) 'If' as Christine Hamilton and Adrienne Scullion observe 'we continually cast the rural in this way

— without countering it with a more pragmatic reading — then we also romanticise rural policies and strategic solutions that emerge from rural areas' (Hamilton and Scullion 2004: 20). In this context the particular relationship between what is represented, and the place of performance becomes vital. In what follows I expand on my account of the benefits of the NTS's in situ performance projects, such as *Ignition* and *Granite*, with an exploration of the potentials of touring to villages and smaller towns in the more remote parts of the country. These tours represent an effort to engage audiences through, localism 'not only of material' to borrow John McGrath's phrase, but also by privileging '*a sense of identity* with the performer' (1981: 58). I follow Jo Robinson in thinking about this work taking place not only 'in the romanticised rural of our conventional imagination' but also in smaller communities that 'are just as much part of the non-urban' (2016: 39). My case studies are two NTS shows that were made around the same time, David Harrower's *Calum's Road* (2011), which was co-produced with Communicado, and Kieran Hurley's *Rantin* (2019), which was co-produced with the Arches. I also reference other work made specifically for and about the Gaelic-speaking communities of the Highlands and Islands, or to use the Gaelic term, the Gàidhealtachd.

Harrower's play is an adaptation, of Robin Hutchinson's elegiac 2008 novel of the same name which tells the true story of Calum McLeod, born in 1911 on the inner Hebridean island of Raasay. McLeod was part-time keeper at the Rona lighthouse, on the north of the island, and also a crofter, knitter, postman and writer. His celebrity status, however, derives from the fact that, driven by the desire to halt the island's depopulation, and frustrated by several decades of failed campaigning and unsuccessful grant applications, he single-handedly and over a period of around ten years from 1964, built a two-mile long road between Brochel Castle and Arnish, using little more than a pickaxe, a shovel and a wheelbarrow. To add to the drama, while McLeod's achievement was heroic, it was ultimately futile. By the time the council finally agreed to surface the road, he and his wife Lexie were the only remaining inhabitants of Arnish. In a final irony, the road is now a tourist destination.

Calum's Road is directed by Communicado's Gerry Mulgrew in a manner that resonates with the performance vocabulary of *The Cheviot, the Stag and the Black, Black Oil* (1973). Harrower and Mulgrew tell McLeod's story using an energetic ensemble, a chorus and a rich musical score performed live by Alasdair Macrae, which combines folk tunes,

Gaelic psalms and the 'hard, electronic rhythms of the world in which we all now live' (McMillan 2011). Meanwhile, John McGeoch's video design projects images of Raasay and of the road Calum laboured over for so long disappearing over a hill, thus bringing quite particular spatial and cultural imaginaries into the performance space. A pragmatic reading of the realities of island life predominates, and sentimentality is largely, if not entirely, avoided. Early in the show, Calum's daughter Julia describes her father's struggle in terms that emphasise both his extraordinary tenacity and also the harsh conditions of island life:

> And more mud and hundred year old trees and deep buried roots. It was a fight my father had. A battle. A campaign. Buried roots and rocks and rocks. Thousands of years of Lewiston and Torridonian rocks. Nothing to him. Nothing stood in his way. No-one. He would not let them'. (Harrower 2013: 3)

While Calum's heroism—and belligerence—is certainly foregrounded, we are not subjected to the conventional idealisation of island life on the lore-infused Celtic periphery.

Throughout the show, the tension in Macrae's score illuminates the play's central theme: the complexity of the relationship between traditional island culture and the attractions of contemporary urban life as represented by the major cities of the Lowlands. The return of Iain Nicolson, the son of an old neighbour who is briefly visiting to oversee repairs on his family property, invokes childhood recollections of leaving the island under cover of darkness, and of Calum pointedly turning his back on the Nicolson family as they sailed away. Iain is further unsettled by the memory of an earlier visit during which Calum spoke to Iain's young son Alex in Gaelic, only to find the boy did not understand him. This recollection produces anger and shame, a combination of emotions that like the issues of depopulation and language loss to which they refer are not easily resolved. Having left the Gàidhealtachd, Iain, like generations of parents before him, has chosen not to pass on a language he considered useless. This decision continues to manifest in feelings of estrangement both on the island and in his new home in the city. As Paula Śledzińska notes, the play is 'not so much a one-dimensional tribute to Calum, the hero in the Gaelic world' as 'an exploration of the often contradictory ... emotions held by those around him' (2015: 133). Harrower's adaptation is not without humour. In one scene Calum visits his daughter Julia who is boarding at the high school in Portree, on the Isle of Skye, only to make an early exit because he is so disquieted by the ungodly character of the town.

Episodic in structure, *Calum's Road* includes scenes set in the present and the past, and key events are revised and revisited from differing perspectives. This dramaturgical technique stresses the unresolved and perhaps unresolvable differences that animate Harrower's subject matter. Indeterminacy is apparent from the outset, as the chorus sets the scene:

> BEN. Our story begins one blustery morning
> LEWIS. Our story begins one blue sky cloudless morning
> CEIT. One rain-drenched wind-blasted morning
> ANGELA. On the island of Raasay (Harrower 2013: 2–3).

The once-upon-a-timeness of this set up permeates what follows with a whiff of folk or fairy tale, and the harsh reality of Calum's herculean self-appointed task, consisting in years of unremitting labour in the face of sublime indifference from local authorities and the wider forces of history, cannot fail to function as a powerful metaphor around which vexed questions of government complicity in depopulation of the Gàidhealtachd, absentee landlordism, respect for and resistance to the Gaelic language, and the fate of native Gaelic-speakers who move to the mainland, circulate.

Calum's Road premiered in 2011 and was revived in 2013. In total it reached thirty-three urban and rural venues across Scotland and its first run culminated in a performance in the Raasay Community Hall. In this mode of touring, as Nicole Carner observes, 'problems on the local level' are restaged as 'problems of the nation' and the connections between the two are asserted via 'a certain level of shared cultural heritage' as the show moves from small theatre to village hall to community centre (Carner 2016: 42). More expansive in content, Kieran Hurley's *Rantin* which opened at Glasgow's Cottiers Theatre in April 2013, followed a similar touring model when, early in the following year, it played at small venues across the country, including in Lossiemouth, Wick, Kirkwall, Thurso, Tongue, Durness, and Ullapool. The size of these towns and villages is important in so far as their place on the NTS touring circuit illustrates the company's approach to inclusivity. The Scottish Government offers an eight-fold urban/rural classification system under which the towns above, and many of those visited by *Calum's Road*, would be classified variously as accessible small town, remote small town, very remote small town, remote and very remote rural areas (Scottish Government 2020). The West Highland village of Tongue has a population of less than 600.

Rantin, as my earlier account of it demonstrates, can usefully 'be thought of as a state-of-the-nation ceilidh play' (2016a: 2013). Rather than focusing on one narrative, it offers a multi-vocal, convivial and celebratory exploration of contemporary Scottish identity in its various guises. It is self-consciously and purposefully inclusive and arguably an excellent example of the enactment of the Scott Hames 'trans-class people-nation' discussed in the introduction of this book (2020: 303). In a series of monologues, sketches and songs, Hurley depicts a post-devolutionary Scotland in the throes of confronting some of its more cherished myths. His vision, and that of his collaborators, Liam Hurley, Gav Prentice, Julia Taudevin and Drew Wright, is remarkably good-natured, as kind as it is satirical and unflinching, as full of optimism as it is empty of fantasy. *Rantin* seeks, to borrow Gerry Hassan's phrase, 'to understand the myths that we have created to tell ourselves how different and progressive we are, compared to the rest of the UK' but also to enact a robustly convivial version of community (2014: 15).

Both the setting and set up for *Rantin* are convivial in that they invite the audience to take its time to settle, and to co-create the space and situation for togetherness to happen:

> As the audience enters we are playing some tunes from the hi-fi. Chatting, get- ting a drink. We're setting up the space. Towards the end of this we'll encourage the audience to fill up their drinks and go for a pee and stuff. When it's time to start we open with a song (Hurley 2014: 311).

Drawing on both Scottish folk traditions in music and storytelling and current events, *Rantin* is performed in a relaxed and welcoming ceilidh atmosphere. In this regard, it echoes the radical traditions of Scottish theatre in the 1970s, particularly 7:84 Scotland and its seminal production, *The Cheviot, the Stag, and the Black, Black Oil* (1973). Hurley's play consists of a series of monologues in which characters, some narrated and some embodied, offer contrasting interpretations of what it means to be Scottish in the second decade of the twenty-first century. 'It is no coincidence' as David Overend observes that the show 'was commissioned and produced in 2013, the year preceding the referendum on Scottish independence' (2019: 175).

Howard, a 67-year-old American, arrives at Prestwick Airport on a pilgrimage, hoping to reconnect with his ancestral Scottishness: 'he was fifty years old when he watched *Braveheart* and it changed his life. Even if some of it was made up, sure, I mean Howard's nobody's fool' (Hurley 2014: 314). Meanwhile, a young man leaves his native Stornoway on the Isle of Lewis for university in Glasgow, his departure accompanied by a rendition of 'Gregor's Lament'—'Griogal Cridhe'—a very old Gaelic song: 'Gregor crosses the Minch, towards the mainland, away from Stornoway for the last time, never to return. Well, until the summer at least. I mean he'd maybe have to come back for a summer job and that. But still' (2014: 325). Elsewhere, Miriam, a Palestinian refugee long exiled from her native Ramallah, journeys to her cleaning job on a number 61 bus in Glasgow. These monologues, and others like them, form the core of *Rantin* and are punctuated by music and chat. Sometimes this involves the reworking of popular Scottish songs. A cheeky rewrite of the comic variety song 'Donald, Where's Yer Troosers (Donald, You're A Loser)', addressed to Donald Trump, brings light relief, for instance, while a new setting of Hamish Henderson's anti-imperialist 'The Freedom Come All Ye' (1960) brings added weight to the show's close.

Rantin is very much focused on the present moment and consequently on the opportunities and risks, aspirations and frustrations that were at the forefront of people's minds in the run up to the referendum. It is worth noticing the assumption of 'fellow feeling' that underwrites this piece, I think, firstly because it exists quite comfortably in an age when it is generally assumed that people are selfish and that fellow feeling is a weakness or a luxury, and secondly, because a significant tranche of contemporary Scottish theatre—including *Black Watch*, *Dunsinane* and *The James Plays*—focuses on conflict, on ruptures and discontinuities in social, ethnic, political, sexual and economic relations. By contrast, work that either articulates a vision of people living together successfully, and/or utilises a modus co-vivendi in the way it presents itself is currently employed in Scottish theatre as a tool to experiment with modes of togetherness. I use the term convivial in my account to deliberately signal the affectively at-ease relations of coexistence and accommodation that characterise this strand of contemporary Scottish theatre. My brief discussion here is focused on *Rantin* but other examples include David Greig's *Midsummer* (Traverse 2008) and *The Strange Undoing of Prudencia Hart* (NTS 2011), Graham McLaren's adaptation of Joe Corrie's *In Time O' Strife* (NTS 2013), and in David MacLennan's wildly successful A Play, a Pie and a Pint lunchtime theatre club, which since 2004 has produced around 30 new short plays a year at Glasgow's Òran Mór, all the while providing its audience with a pie—or a vegan sausage roll—and a pint by way of accompaniment. Although much of this work draws on existing popular traditions in Scottish theatre of the kind exemplified in *The Cheviot,* its resurgence demonstrates that devolution has encouraged a more immediate sense of civic responsibility and engagement, I would argue. Only through honest self-reflection, a commitment to understanding others, a healthy dose of self-deprecation, and a good old singsong, *Rantin* suggests, can Scotland understand itself. In its final scene Howard reaches for his phrasebook as his plane descends: 'Rant: verb; to frolic, romp, revel. Noun; a merrymaking rough frolic, a lively song of joy ... Ranter: verb; to sew a seam across roughly, to darn coarsely, to join, to attempt to reconcile statements which do not tally' (Hurley 2014: 351). In viewing tolerance, or the accommodation of difference, as a set of everyday practices, rather than a moral virtue, *Rantin* also draws our attention to the fact that the production of community involves actual labour, 'not just because it is hard' as Greg Noble observes 'but because it is productive, transactional and cumulative' (2009: 53).

In *Theatre's Heterotopias* (2014), Joanne Tompkins conceives of theatrical space as including:

> ... the imaginative setting created with and through a narrative, the scenic space of a production's design, the contribution to meaning that the architectural, cultural or historical surrounds of a venue might offer, and/or the efficacy of an unconventional venue (2014: 1).

The imperative to maintain, and be seen to maintain, a balance between the supposed centres of Glasgow and Edinburgh and the periphery, particularly the Highlands and Islands, and between the conventional theatre building and the alternative performance space, has shaped the NTS's work and its approach to touring form the outset. In 2011 as part of the company's Reveal season, Vicky Featherstone directed Iain Finlay McLeod's *Somersaults*, which tells the story of James, a Gaelic speaker from Lewis who leaves the island for educational opportunity and an ostensibly successful life and career in London. This narrative, which is common enough in Gaelic literature and song, inevitably 'tends to mean at least temporary abandonment of the Gael's first language' (Śledzińska 2015: 129). Initially, this does not seem to be a particular problem for

James, who is happy to be married to a non-Gaelic speaker and to teach his university friend Mark the odd phrase or two. The situation changes dramatically, however, and an existential crisis is precipitated when James realises, he cannot remember the Gaelic word for somersault, and consequently cannot conjure a joyful childhood memory accurately. The theme of language loss and its negative effects then predominates, and in this sense, *Somersaults* shares some of its preoccupations with Gaelic drama more broadly. *Somersaults* is delivered in both Gaelic and English, and in its closing scene James leaves the stage and the other actors reflect on their own experiences of Gaelic.

As Michelle Macleod notes in her introduction to the collection *Dràma na Gàidhlig: Ceud Bliadhna air an Àrd-Ùrlar* (A Century of Gaelic Drama) (2021), while it 'has always enjoyed the spoken word and performance culture ... the concept of a staged play was not one that gained much traction in Gaelic Society until the early twentieth century' when large numbers of Gaels moved into Scottish cities, especially to Glasgow and Inverness, and turned to drama as one means by which they could preserve their language and culture (ix). Many of these early plays were designed for amateur performance, and even competition, and were consequently relatively short. The post-devolutionary period has seen the production of longer plays and Macleod singles out Dòmhnall S. Moireach's WWI history play *Sequamur* (2015), which was translated into Gaelic by Catrìona Dunn, as among the finest examples. Its central character is William J. Gibson, Rector of the Nicholson Institute—the secondary school—in Stornoway on the Isle of Lewis, and it is essentially a tale of survivor guilt, not a survivor who had been traumatised in combat, but one who has actively encouraged a generation to march off to war. *Sequamur* opens after the war with Gibson, now retired, viewing the commemorative plaque that has been erected at the school and becoming distressed on learning that someone's name is missing. Thereafter it moves back in time between scenes in the school room and the battlefield. The *'sounds of explosions'* and *'pictures of war'* are projected onto a screen at the back of the stage and as stories of the horrors of the battlefields of Belgium and France, the Dardanelles and Gallipoli, reach Gibson, the headmaster gradually falls into despair (Moireach 2021: 201). The ghosts of dead teenagers, return to haunt him, in a play that explores the futility of war in a register now relatively familiar, especially in fictionalised accounts of the Great War. Coming full circle, *Sequamur* ends with Gibson unveiling the plaque, and a piper playing a lament as the '*screen shows the names of the 148 men who died*', all former pupils at the school (210). The show was performed in Gaelic—with some Latin and English in the classroom scenes—in venues across Scotland and Ireland, and at Ypres in Belgium, with a simultaneous English translation available via headphones, although the translation featured only one voice. The Glasgow-based professional company Theatre Gu Leòr has also been an 'innovator in creating drama which reaches across linguistic boundaries' (Macleod 2021: xxviii).

Like *Sequamur*, Muireann Kelly's *Scotties* (2018), which she developed with Frances Poet, is a history play that deals with trauma, and shifts between time periods. Michael, the young twenty-first-century Glaswegian son of a Gaelic-speaking mother, is doing a school project on a little known tragedy that occurred in 1937, when ten young male potato-pickers from Achill in County Mayo were burned to death in a locked farm bothy near Kirkintilloch. In Kelly and Poet's telling 'Michael dreams his way into a timeslip where he walks among the migrant workers, but is only seen by Molly', a young woman who only speaks Irish and turns out to be his great grandmother (Cooper 2018). Scotties is performed in Gaelic, Irish, English and Scots, with no surtitles or translation, and instead uses carefully choreographed stage craft and dialogue to make itself legible to monolingual audience members. Michael's journey of discovery, which is accompanied by traditional music, is one that unearths his own heritage, but also sheds light on the anti-Irish prejudice that characterised Scottish culture in the nineteenth and twentieth centuries, and indeed persists in contemporary manifestations of sectarianism. While *Scotties* is rooted in a particular incident in history, it also has obvious resonances in relation to the treatment of migrants in the contemporary moment. It was created in a co-production between Theatre Gi Leòr and the Abbey in Dublin, with supported from the NTS. It is thus, another example of how by 'embracing the value in community language' to borrow Paula Śledzińska's formulation, 'the NTS makes a clear move towards addressing the damaging consequences of the mythologization and othering performed on the landscape of the Gàidhealtachd and its people over the past centuries' (2015: 131).

As well as demonstrating a commitment to geographical and cultural inclusivity, the NTS has retained a strong focus on developing audiences via its engagement with education and young people. Between 2007 and 2009, under the heading *Transform* and in partnership with schools, for example, it created a series of performances that were again characterised by geographical inclusivity, and by the practice of bringing established theatre professionals into conversation with local communities. Projects included *Transform East Ayrshire*, *Transform Fife*, *Transform Moray* and *Transform Orkney*. *Transform Caithness* (2009) was led by John Tiffany and Steven Hoggett of *Black Watch* fame and took the form of a promenade through the streets of Thurso on a midsummer evening. Created by a company of around 170, which included 100 students from the town's High School, who were supported in developing original texts, performances, movement and music for the event. The involvement of local community groups—the Thurso Players, the Melvich Gaelic Choir, the Ormlie Youth Drama Group, the Ormlie Young Mothers' Group, the Caithness Handbell Ringers and the Kaithness Kickers—strengthened the event's sense of place as embedded in the everyday experience of local people. *Transform* is an early example of the NTS's education and outreach activity, and its commitment to young audiences, which have remained key strands in its activity, as evidenced by Featherstone's invitation to Gill Robertson, of the acclaimed Musselburgh-based children's theatre company Catherine Wheels, to direct *Home East Lothian* (2006). The introduction in 2004 of a separate CATS award category for Best Production for Children and Young People speaks to the significance of this work in the wider field of Scottish theatre.

Theatre for Children and Young People

As Liz Tomlin reminds us, prior 'to the 1990s the "Theatre in Education" (TIE) movement had driven the development of theatre for children and young people' with local education authorities across the UK directly funding companies to create work and workshop activities 'that responded to a broad educational remit' (2015: 76). The decline of this movement, in Scotland where it had never been fully embraced and elsewhere, was in part due to the introduction of Thatcherite funding models which devolved budgets to individual schools. This change eventually precipitated a move away from a focus on theatre's educative potentials—which were often viewed with suspicion by conservatives because they were felt to be too left-wing—towards a 'theatre of empowerment … characterised by collective and co-operative working, small scale touring, and a focus on children's feelings and needs' (Harman 2005: 55). Paradoxically, given its history of politically engaged theatre, Scotland has proved well placed to benefit from this shift. Catherine Wheels provides a useful representative example. Founded in 1999 by Gill Robertson, it is Scotland's most acclaimed and far-travelled children's theatre company and has won a string of awards, including Best Production at the Shanghai International Children's Festival (2008), and numerous CATS. In 2011, the Catherine Wheels show *White*, won the CATS for Best Production for Children and Young People, Best Design and Best Technical presentation, having been a critical success at the Traverse during the previous summer's Fringe, where it won a Herald Angel, a Scotsman Fringe First, a UK Theatre award, a Total Theatre award and an Edinburgh Arts Club award. Since then, *White* has gone on to tour nationally and internationally, including to Australia, China, Denmark, Japan, Mexico, New Zealand, Norway, Sweden and the US, reaching an estimated audience of 100,000.

Heather Fitzsimmons Frey has rightly noted that a major concern in theatre for children and young audiences is 'how to stage *difference*—differences like ability, non-traditional family structures, sexual orientation, religion, age, language, and culture' (2016: 81). *White* was made for very young audiences—2–4 year olds—but it nonetheless engages with these themes with subtlety and gentle sophistication. Perhaps 'nonetheless' is the wrong word here. There are a number of Scottish companies—Visible Fictions, Starcatchers, The Polar Bears, Wee Stories, TAG—working, like Catherine Wheels, with great skill and ingenuity to engage children and young people of all ages in thinking about how notions of difference, and by extension inclusion and exclusion, are produced and sustained (Fig. 5.1).

White is a 40-minute show staged in a curtained space 'in a world which is pigment free' (Manley 2017: 295). The narrative is simple. Two men, Wrinkle and Cotton, who are dressed entirely in white, inhabit a space populated with white birdboxes on stands of various heights and a small tepee, in which they sleep, and which is draped with items of white clothing and props used as they go about their daily routine. A mirror ball moon provides sparkle. On waking from their white tepee, Wrinkle and Cotton breakfast on milk and white crackers. They then tidy and clean and polish and tend to their environment and in particular to batches of white eggs which are cosseted and placed in their own bird houses. Birdsong fills the air and an atmosphere of contentment reigns. If any item is discovered that is not white, it is frowned upon and immediately placed in a white bin reserved specifically for this purpose. The dramatic stakes rise with the unexpected arrival of a red egg. Both men listen to the

Fig. 5.1 Ian Cameron as Wrinkle and Andy Manley as Cotton in *White*, 2011. Photograph by Douglas McBride reproduced with kind permission from Catherine Wheels Theatre Company

egg and hear life inside, but because it is red, they consign it to the bin. However, Cotton, his conscience clearly bothering him, sneaks back in the night and retrieves the red egg placing it in its own bird house. The introduction of this red egg has a knock on effect and little by little as colour is introduced, Wrinkle and Cotton come to embrace rather than resist it. The show ends with an explosion of multicoloured streamers which fill the set and the auditorium.

White is a show about the anxiety that can accompany the encounter with difference and about the kinds of reward that await those who are able to overcome this anxiety. It is also notable for the way it subverts gender norms by staging two men who live and work together and whose focus is entirely and contentedly on caring for others—the eggs—and each other. Indeed, the show's content and the comedy produced by its misunderstandings are almost entirely devoted to practices of care. A similar gentle subversion can be found in Ivor McAskill and Fiona Manson's *The Polar Bears Go Wild!* (2013), *The Polar Bears Go Up!* (2016) and *The*

Polar Bears Go Go Go! (2022), each of which concerns the adventures and adventurousness of two girl polar bears in fluffy white suits as they overcome various challenges ranging from pouring juice and removing their shoes to climbing a mountain and planning a tropical holiday. Also, designed for pre-school audiences, the Polar Bears shows are dialogue free, and rely on cleverly designed sets, gentle music, expert clowning and a focus on the playfully tender relationship between the bears who cuddle up to go to sleep, and spend quite a bit of time eating sandwiches.

White was widely praised by the CATS judging panel for its technical execution, the artistry of which 'was not only a marvel to watch but was integral to the overall success of the production', and in this sense it certainly evidences a shift in the esteem in which children's theatre is held in Scotland, as does the introduction in 2004 of a special CATS award category for Best Production for Children and Young People (CATS 2011). The success of *White* is emblematic of Scotland's strength in producing high quality and innovative, even radical, theatre for young audiences, but unsurprisingly its success was not achieved in a vacuum. Its creator, Andy Manley had, with fellow drama school graduate Dougie Irvine, founded the children's company Visible Fictions in 1991 and one of its early shows had signalled the change in direction that was to come. *Bill's New Frock* (1992) is an adaptation of Anne Fine's novel of the same name first published in 1989. In it, Bill wakes up one morning to find everyone is convinced he is a girl. He is subsequently required to attend school dressed in a fancy pink frock, and to experience the range of indignities and infringements associated with being a girl, including being catcalled and forced to write neatly. Unsurprisingly, his frock ends up as tattered and torn as the gender stereotypes the play quite deliberately upends. *Bill's New Frock* premiered at the Scottish International Children's Festival in 1992. The significance of the festival in enabling Scotland to emerge as a centre of excellence in this field cannot easily be overstated. Founded in January 1989 by Duncan Low, it was inspired by the Vancouver International Children's Festival, which at that time represented the largest celebration of children's dance and theatre in the world. Low borrowed Vancouver's internationalist model for the inaugural festival in May 1990, bringing together six home grown companies with visitors from Zimbabwe, the US and the Netherlands. Performances were staged inside a series of white tents in Edinburgh's Inverleith Park. Donald Smith acknowledges the impact of Low's recourse to the Canadian model in providing 'a benchmark of quality' in children's theatre, by exposing Scottish companies and audiences to international work of the highest standards (1998: 3). Joyce McMillan picks up this theme, adding that 'a decade later, during Tony Reekie's inspired 20-year directorship' the Scottish International Children's Festival, 'became Imaginate, the flourishing international festival recognised as a world leader in the field' (2017). Reekie, who took over from Low in 1996, has been the key figure in facilitating the blossoming of children's theatre in Scotland not least by developing international networks for professionalisation. In 2000, Imaginate was re-constituted as a year-round organisation promoting theatre for children and young people, with the festival at its heart. In 2004 Imaginate was, through sponsorship by the Bank of Scotland, 'the highest funded performing arts organisation in Scotland' (Reekie 2005: 38).

For Reekie the more general internationalisation of Scottish theatre in the 1980s and 90s, and in particular the influence of the City of Culture in Glasgow, which I discuss in Chapter 3, shaped the emerging artists who were to become leaders in the field:

> … when Visible Fictions first came on the scene and made *Bill's New Frock*, it was a change in terms of the way that people approached that kind of work, from Contemporary Arts Practice … they had no relationship either with the past in Scotland or with England, because none of them had any connection with Theatre in Education at all. (quoted in Fletcher-Watson 2016: 80)

Manley has also noted the influence of experimental, visual and physical theatre on his work as well as his lack of interest in using theatre as a primarily educative tool (2017: 294). *Bill's New Frock* was the first of 12 shows Visible Fictions brought to the International Festival/Imaginate, and under Irvine's continuing directorship the company remains sector leading. Children's theatre continues to be a vibrant and innovative part of Scotland's theatre ecology and to be of genuine international significance. In 2012 the French Compagnie Arcosm named their contribution to the Imaginate Festival *Traverse*, in acknowledgement of the significance of the Edinburgh theatre to their work, and of the festival to children's theatre internationally. The 2019 festival featured work from Australia, Belgium, Denmark, England, France, Germany, the Netherlands as well as Scotland itself.

In 2016 the NTS in collaboration with Imaginate, Catherine Wheels, Visible Fictions and Starcatchers established the initiative, Theatre in

Schools Scotland (TiSS), with the aim of bringing 'bold, inspiring, live theatre and dance productions into Scotland's primary schools and nurseries' (Theatre in Schools Scotland 2023). The project's primary purpose is to provide a reliable source of high quality productions which are tailored for performance in school halls and classrooms. In this way it works to develop mechanisms 'to ensure that every child in Scotland, wherever they go to school, is given an opportunity to access high quality theatre and dance' (TiSS 2019: 13). In its pilot phase, from 2016 to 2019, TiSS toured 14 shows, giving 652 performances to 52,754 children in 397 schools ranging in location from Shetland to Stranraer. The project is ongoing and among its key objectives is to continually assess and develop 'strategic priorities to strengthen relationships with theatres/venues and touring networks to ensure Theatre in Schools Scotland becomes a respected and sustainable initiative for enhancing the profile, importance and value of work for children in schools' (TiSS 2019: 4). TiSS is consequently at least partly intended to provide ongoing financial stability for Scottish artists working in this field.

Much of the discussion above has concerned theatre for very young audiences and for children of primary school age but the development of this work has been accompanied by a growth in work aimed at teenagers, which has been just as experimental and ground-breaking. Oliver Emmanuel's *I am Tiger* (2021), for instance, is an hour-long solo piece commissioned by Imaginate and produced by Perth Theatre, in which 'Chloe-Ann Tylor delivers an unforgettable performance as Laura, a teenager trying to grieve the death of an older brother' who has taken his own life (McMillan 2022). Initially too traumatised to feel much beyond intolerable pain, Laura begins to change when her parents buy her a baby tiger illegally, of course, and on impulse. Through her interactions with the tiger, Laura comes to terms both with the scale of her rage at her brother's passing and her own inner strength. A powerful soundscape by Danny Krass and beautiful movement direction by Jack Webb combined in *I am Tiger*—which was directed by Perth Theatre's artistic director Lu Kemp—with Jamie Vartan's cleverly designed set and Simon Wilkinson's lighting to produce a piece of total theatre which dealt with difficult subject matter head on and with sensitivity and skill. Covering different, but similarly challenging, terrain in 2018, Untitled Projects teamed up with London's Unicorn Theatre to produce *The End of Eddy*, an adaptation by Pamela Carter of Edouard Louis's autobiographical coming-of-age novel *En Finir Avec Eddy Bellegueule* (2014), about growing up gay in a working-class town in Picardy. Eddy's environment is characterised by violence, judgement and small-mindedness and his attempts to fit in are fraught with danger. Themes of sexual awakening, masculinity, bullying and the conflict between desire and the desire to fit in are explored by two performers, both playing Eddy and all supporting roles. Stewart Laing, who directs and designs, makes use of four television screens to variously provide a backdrop to the action, props and other characters and these have the added benefit of gesturing towards a culture of surveillance which is a recognisable affective structure in teenage experience. Laing and Carter are not alone among theatre-makers who work predominantly for adult audiences in producing work for teenagers. One key example is David Greig, whose association with TAG has resulted in several plays for teenagers, notably *Dr Korczak's Example* (2001), *Yellow Moon: The Ballad of Leila and Lee* (2006) and *The Monster in the Hall* (2010). These last two were later successfully revived at the Traverse, the Citizens, and by the NTS, and are worth further discussion because of what they tell us about the sophistication of theatre for young audiences in contemporary Scotland.

Yellow Moon draws its tragic subject matter and its linear narrative energy from the ballad tradition which its title references. Its protagonist, 17-year-old Lee McAlinden lives in Inverkeithing in Fife with his mother, Jenni, and her boyfriend Billy. His estranged father Dan, we learn, is living in the Highlands where Lee mistakenly believes him to be a wealthy landowner. One evening, after stealing an engagement ring from Billy, Lee meets a girl from school—'silent' Leila Suleiman—at the all-night superstore. They decamp for a drink in the local cemetery where an enraged Billy tracks them down. In the ensuing scuffle Lee fatally stabs Billy. Panic ensues. Lee decides to go in search of his estranged father. He asks Leila to go with him and they catch a train north. 'This is the part of the story' the narrator of Scene Eight tells us 'where Leila and Lee go on the run to the highlands and nearly die' from hypothermia (Greig 2006: 20). Luckily, they are rescued by Drunk Frank, the estate keeper. Frank gives them the unwelcome news that Lee's father has died but offers to put them up in return for their helping him with his work. Leila and Lee work the estate for three months. They learn a lot about the estate and each other and almost forget why they ran away in the first place. Eventually, Lee realises Frank is his father and confesses the murder of Billy Logan to him. However, Frank proves incapable of dealing with this kind of intimacy, and he lashes out at Lee who steals a car in order to escape.

Unable to bear the loss of his son a second time, Frank shoots himself. Finally, Leila tracks Lee down to a mountain cave where he sits hunched over his father's body. As police helicopters draw closer, Lee cuts out his father's heart and buries it in the cave. Leila and Lee give themselves up.

Yellow Moon utilises a number of motifs found elsewhere in Greig's work. The figure of Leila Suleiman, whose family we are told 'came to Scotland in the 1990s' as 'refugees from some sort of war', reflects Greig's interest in the effects of displacement in the aftermath of conflict, which is a focus in *Europe* and *The American Pilot* (2005) (206: 6). Metaphors of travel also reoccur in his work and his characters regularly get lost, as in *One Way Street* (1995), *San Diego* (2003), *Pyrenees* (2005) and *The Strange Undoing of Prudentia Hart* (2014). On one level *Yellow Moon* is about the kinds of crises that can ensue when intergenerational authority breaks down. Lee's family has disintegrated. His father has abandoned him, and his mother is a depressive alcoholic who is unable to provide even cursory support. When he finally tracks his father down, he finds an older man unable to respond to his son's needs. Similarly, when we first meet Leila, she is an elective mute, locked into the obsessive consumption of celebrity magazines, and a cycle of self-harming. For much of the play her story is narrated. 'When Leila Suleman cuts herself', we are told in scene four, 'she feels like she is real' (2006: 8). The developing romance between Leila and Lee pours light into this darkness. It forms the emotional core of Greig's play and enables its young protagonists to make genuine connections. Leila's silence and her self-harming signal an acute estrangement from her own body and it is this alienation that is dissolved as the young couple fall in love.

Especially in the first half of the play, Greig uses narration to produce a sense of his young characters being acted upon: as powerless in the face of the breakdown of adult authority. The story begins in crisis and quickly moves to the murder of Billy Logan. These techniques call to mind the ballad tradition with its tendency to begin in *media res* and its focus on action rather than exposition or character motivation. We never fully understand why Leila cuts herself, why Frank abandons his family in the first place, why he takes his own life, and, perhaps most significantly, why Lee cuts out his father's heart at the end of the play. Such opacity is typical in traditional ballads where ironic juxtapositions leave gaps that must be filled by the listener. Greig uses it in *Yellow Moon* to encourage young spectators into awareness of the power of their own imaginations to interpret and enhance the performance. Towards the middle of the play

Leila speaks her first line, when she demands Lee take off his clothes. In what follows Greig moves the ground of representation explicitly into the realm of the imagination:

> Lee takes off his clothes.
> He is a prize.
> You take off your clothes.
> Lee sees your body
> Old cuts like tribal markings.
> And he touches you.
> You are a prize.
> Imagine what that would be like.
> That's what it was like (42).

This strategy, which is partly designed to develop the young audience's critical capacities as theatregoers, is explored at greater length and in more detail in my article 'Teenage Dreams: Power and Imagination in David Greig's *Yellow Moon* and *The Monster in the Hall*' (Reid 2016b). For Clare Wallace, both plays are marked by a 'lightness of touch and a stripped back attitude to dramatic situation' as well as a focus on 'potential states of alienation and points of human contact' (2013: 57).

The Monster in the Hall is more explicitly concerned with social themes than *Yellow Moon*, and it emerged directly from Greig's engagement with the charity Fife Young Carers. Set in Kirkcaldy, its heroine is 16-year-old Duck Macatarsney, who has a rich fantasy life and wants to be a novelist, but is responsible for looking after her father Duke, who suffers from multiple sclerosis. One morning, Duke wakes up blind and Duck learns that Social Services are planning to pay a visit. An already stressful situation is then complicated by the arrival of Lawrence Lofthouse, the 'most beautiful boy in the school' and Duck's partner in a drama project (Greig 2011: 30). Lawrence's reputation as a heterosexual lothario, it transpires, has been seriously compromised by rumours of his interest in fashion and textiles. He has come to ask Duck if she will simulate giving him a blowjob—'tonight at half past six, behind the wall near the chippie'—in order to demonstrate to their peers that he is not gay (38). Lawrence's arrival is closely followed by that of Agnetha Bergholm, a Scandinavian dominatrix, who has become romantically attached to Duke after meeting him in an online fantasy universe. Finally, the social worker, Linda Underhill, appears and chaos ensues. Fearing that she will be taken into care, despite repeated assurances to the contrary, Duck steals the social worker's moped, and an unlikely motorbike chase ensues, which sees Duck survive a crash unharmed. Much of the show's impact is in the frequent and imaginatively handled transitions in which the four-strong cast performs in the manner of a sixties-inspired girl group, the Duckettes, and also acts as a chorus providing exposition and commentary when necessary and Greig brings the play to a satisfying close 'with a happy ending of pure girl-group dreaminess' (Fisher 2010).

In *Monster in the Hall*, Greig again explores the power of the imagination to provide relief from the harsh realities of life, both in Duck's novel, which she writes every morning before school, and in Duke's alternative existence in the online fantasy world. The 'monster' of the play's title is the Ducati Monster 796 series once owned by Duck's mother and kept in the hallway as a kind of memorial. Duck, short for Ducati, is named after the bike. Although never represented visually, the bike is at once an obstruction—Duke in particular keeps bumping into it—and an object of admiration. Lawrence describes it as 'the most beautiful object I have seen in my entire life' (Greig 2011: 43). The monster in the hall also functions as a metaphor for the things in life the characters struggle to face, including Duke's chronic degenerative condition and Duck's need to access support. Greig is careful not to characterise Duck as an unwilling carer and to show that for the most part she experiences 'a sense of specialness and usefulness that counterbalances the negative effects' of her situation (Kerig 2014: 18). The social worker, Underhill is described in the play as someone who every day 'is invited into the lives of people who are teetering on the edge of catastrophe ... and every day does her best to bring them back' (80). That she often does this by handing out 'leaflets that describe courses' speaks to the light-hearted tone of the piece as a whole, but also to Greig's genuine belief in the power of education to transform people's lives (81). The leaflet handed to Duck at the end of the play is for a two-day residential creative writing course in Dunfermline and Underhill also promises to 'organize some care at home' for Duke, so that Duck can attend (95).

Yellow Moon and *The Monster in the Hall* are designed to be performed in the round, in school halls, in broad daylight with no lighting and very little in the way of props and costume. In these environments young audience members were invited to become especially aware of themselves—their peers, and their teachers—as spectators. Greig exploits this context by drawing attention to the relative merits of showing and telling. For example, Duke is given his happy ending with Agnetha. 'And just at that moment they kissed', we are informed, 'which is something it's not necessary for us to see' (2011: 101). In using elements of chorus, direct address, farce and music theatre to explore serious social issues, *The Monster in the Hall* in particular, locates itself in a long tradition of politicised popular theatre, which has retained its place and power in Scotland, in spite of the expansion in vocabulary described in the earlier chapters of this book. The imperative to entertain audiences using performance modes they recognise and cherish has persisted and resulted in some of the most successful productions in twenty-first-century Scotland.

Reclaiming a Politics of Sincerity

Written in working-class Scots and telling the story of her father Garry, his friends and their amateur football team in a small, depressed Renfrewshire town the late 1980s, Eilidh Loan's debut play *Moorcroft* (2022) began life at the Tron in February 2022 and, after universally positive reviews and a CATS nomination for Best New Play, was revived the following year for a national tour in co-production with the NTS. Moving from comedy to tragedy as it explores the lives of seven working-class men, *Moorcroft* is remarkably direct and unflinching, but also tender and empathic. Each of Loan's characters is a victim, in his own way, of poverty, low expectations or simply the vagaries of fate. The play begins as Garry, who is celebrating his fiftieth birthday, looks back to when he was 'a good lookin nineteen-year auld' and persuaded, and in some cases bribed, six of his closest friends to set up an amateur football team, known as Moorcroft, or more affectionately, The Croft (Loan 2023: 5). 'The thing is', Garry tells the audience in the opening scene, 'we lived a life where everything was so boring and shite, ye couldny be arsed brushin your teeth some mornins' (4). From then on, Garry narrates their story, stepping in and out of the action and, so, back in time. This is a particularly striking effect, where the older actor, in this case Martin Docherty, gets to play his younger self and (re)embody experiences now out of reach because he has lost three of his friends to illness and suicide. The toxic aspects of west of Scotland working-class masculinity, including sexism, racism and homophobia, are explored by Loan through a highlighting of their negative effects on a group of young men who are prohibited by the rules of culture from expressing emotions openly. The high energy ensemble playing, careful choreography and knock-about banter nevertheless establish the group as held together by love. Loan also directs. Her juxtaposing of sincerity with satire, and her use of an eighties soundtrack, allows the young men, among other things, to dance to Joy Division and Madness. These elements combine to make *Moorcroft* a male-centred working-class comedy in the tradition of John Byrne's *Slab Boys* trilogy. As Mark Fisher observes, the fact that 'every off-colour remark is countered by an enlightened liberal argument' stretches credibility somewhat, but the show nonetheless delivers a richly satisfying emotional experience for its audiences and in so doing places the social, economic, political and cultural crises suffered by working-class men centre stage (Fisher 2022).

Cora Bisset and David Greig's musical *Glasgow Girls* (2012) is an equally significant example of the re-emergence of a more direct and populist form of political engagement in Scottish theatre. Based on real events, the show tells the story of seven Glaswegian schoolgirls and their teacher who in 2005 conducted an award-winning campaign against dawn raids on asylum seekers in their local community. Set in Drumchapel, a peripheral housing estate in the northwest of the city, *Glasgow Girls* is an uncomplicatedly joyful celebration of working-class solidarity. Merle Hensel's bleak rendering of the housing estate, built in the 1960s as an exercise in slum clearance and perennially associated with the lower working class, recalls Marc Augé's notion of substantive place, which he defines as 'relational, historical and concerned with identity' (1995: 77).

A relatively high number of asylum-seeking families were dispersed to Glasgow in the late 1990s and in the period in which the events that form the backbone of the show took place, around one in ten pupils at Drumchapel High School was an asylum seeker. Half of the students at the school were in receipt of free school meals, a key indicator of poverty and a figure almost double the average in Glasgow. The school was performing well below the national average across a range of metrics including progression to higher education. 'Nevertheless', as Susan Haedicke notes 'Drumchapel became the site of effective youth activism as seven schoolgirls led a strong campaign against dawn raids on families with children and influenced UK immigration policies' (2017: 217). Their story challenges the abjection that has typically marked representations of the working class in recent years, and it captured the public imagination and has been retold in a number of formats. As well as Bisset and Greig's stage musical there have been two BBC Scotland documentaries in the series, 'Tales from the Edge'—The Glasgow Girls' (2005) and 'The Children Who Disappear' (2006)—a BBC 3 television drama in 2014 and in 2015, the documentary, 'The Glasgow Girls' Stories' (BBC

2), which caught up with the girls a decade on as they reflected on these various versions. Bisset and Greig's musical is my main concern here.

In this supposedly grim environment, Euan Girvan is given the task of teaching English as a foreign language to a group of pupils at Drumchapel High School and, carried along by their enthusiasm and righteous anger, becomes instrumental in supporting Amal Azzudin, Jennifer McCann, Emma Clifford, Toni-Lee Henderson Roza Salih and Ewelina Siwak in their campaign for the release of their friend 15-year-old Agnesa Murelaj, a Roma refugee from Kosovo who has been in Scotland for five years, when she is arrested along with her family early on a Sunday morning in March 2005. The initial campaign led to the release of the Murelaj family, although some other Kosovan families were deported, but the girls did not stop there. By successfully refiguring dawn raids as a children's rights issue, they put pressure on the Home Office and the Scottish Government, and shifted public opinion, effectively making the practice of dawn raids unacceptable. In doing so, they also highlighted tensions in the constitutional settlement:

> The expulsion of the Kosovan asylum seekers provoked one of the most serious confrontations between the Scottish Office and Whitehall since 1999. For many, it summed up the inadequacy of a devolution settlement which allows the Scottish parliament to voice its unanimous condemnation of dawn raids, but also allows the UK government to disregard it. (Macwhirter 2005)

Immigration policy is reserved, and the Home Office continued to insist there would be no separate protocol for Scotland. The girls extracted a promise from the Labour First Minister Jack McConnell that child deportations would end in Scotland, but McConnell was unable to deliver on that promise. Nonetheless, the Glasgow girls succeeded in exponentially raising public awareness about the inhumane treatment of asylum-seeking children.

As Susan Haedicke suggests, Greig and Bisset's musical seeks to 'have an impact on the spectator's understanding of asylum issues primarily through encouraging *affective* responses: emotive reactions and aesthetic pleasure' (2017: 224). The show's music, inflected with multicultural influences, and performed with gusto, certainly plays a significant part in the generation of affect but a particular motif that runs through the show, and this is perhaps unsurprising as it deals with teenage outrage at injustice, is the moment of pure sincerity. In general, Greig's dialogue utilises the sophisticated language of Glaswegian urban life, often for comic effect, but at moments of extreme emotion the characters express themselves in unabashed and guileless tones. For instance, on discovering that Agnesa has been arrested, Emma responds: 'It's just not right. It's cruel. I can't believe this is happening in Scotland!' (Greig 2012: 14). Later in an attempt to explain her involvement in the campaign to her sceptical father Jennifer says:

> So one night I'm walking home – the sun's catching the top of the Scotstoun flats making them glow red. I can hear the traffic on Great Western Road, I can hear kids out playing in street and I'm just thinking it seems - mad – that all this could be just taken away from you – as if a great big hand could reach down out of the sky and snatch you. (Greig 2012: 43)

There is a deliberate artlessness to the organisation of the sentences, here, that gestures beyond them in a manner that compels emotionally and theatrically. The girls' ambitions for their campaign sometimes appear decidedly unworldly—they are devastated when they fail to prevent the deportation of a mother and her young son, for instance, but their actions exemplify the child's appetite for justice, and this might seem sentimental were it not for the cruelty and brutality that surrounds them. The show as a whole exposes itself to sincerity and attempts to challenge cynicism in its moments, mostly musical, of breath-stopping exuberance. Such tactics demand a corresponding openness from the audience, similar to that achieved by *Moorcroft*. I saw *Glasgow Girls* twice, once at the Citizens in Glasgow and once at the Theatre Royal Stratford East in London. On each occasion the evening culminated in an extended standing ovation. At such moments, as Richard Dyer has argued 'the utopianism is contained in the feelings it embodies … in what utopia would feel like rather than how it would be organized. It thus works at the level of sensibility' (Dyer 1992: 18).

The dramaturgies of *Moorcroft* and *Glasgow Girls* are not fiercely dialectical nor are they intended to pull productively against the limitations of realism, although in his review of the latter Mark Brown suggested that not 'perhaps, since 1973 – when John McGrath and his 7:84 theatre company staged their legendary play *The Cheviot, The Stag And The Black Black Oil*—has Scottish musical theatre packed a political punch as hard as *Glasgow Girls*' (2012). I would argue instead that these shows privilege emotional space. In *Glasgow Girls* many significant events take place in between scenes—the arrest of Agnesa and her family, the deportation of the mother and son—so that rather than concretise these highly charged moments in a particular representation Bisset and Greig open up spaces in the dramaturgy for the intense emotional responses of the young protagonists to inhabit, allowing such emotions to situate themselves beyond the precise world of the play, in the auditorium.

Such a reading is of course unashamedly optimistic and aligns itself neatly with Jill Dolan's arguments in *Utopia in Performance* in which she insists on:

> ... the potential of different kinds of performance to inspire moments in which audiences feel themselves allied with each other, and with a broader more capacious idea of a public, in which social discourse articulates the possible, rather than the insurmountable obstacles to human potential. (Dolan 2005: 2)

In some ways, the success of *Glasgow Girls*, like that of *Black Watch* before it, signalled the return in a new incarnation of the kind of politicised populism that had characterised Scottish theatre in the 1970s. It also demonstrated a continuing appetite for 'celebrations of Scottish working class culture and identity' which has been embraced by the national company and is further evidenced by the success of NTS shows like Lee Hall's *Our Ladies of Perpetual Succour* (2015), Douglas Maxwell's *Orphans* (2022) and Gary McNair's *Dear Billy* (2023) (Maloney 2011: 72). This last show, subtitled *A Love Letter from the People of Scotland to the Big Yin*, is essentially a one-man show, performed by McNair accompanied live by musician-composers Simon Liddell and Jill O'Sullivan, about the legendary Glaswegian shipyard worker turned comedian Billy Connolly.

Dear Billy is an intimate 90-minute piece performed on a carpeted stage, in which, McNair who bears a strong physical resemblance to Connolly, performs a selection of stories, and half-remembered Connolly routines, donated by a range of ordinary Scots via a series of interviews conducted up and down the country. Much hilarity ensues, but again, the work is punctuated with moments of sincerity. Many contributors, as Joyce McMillan's review stresses:

...try to put into words how Connolly has helped them find a new way of being Scottish, and particularly of being male and Scottish; how to be raised amid violence and punitive forms of religion, and yet to be neither violent nor punitive themselves, but instead to become funny, self-aware, creative, and generous. (2023)

The aesthetics of the performance thus lead to moments of affective and effective feelings and expressions of love, not just for Connolly, although that love is certainly tangible, but for a more abstracted sense of community, for Scotland itself and its people. What emerges, is what Mark Fisher describes as 'a democratic tapestry with Connolly as its guiding spirit' (2023). *Dear Billy* finished its run—after visiting venues in Kilmarnock, Edinburgh, Ayr, Dundee, Banchory, East Kilbride, Hawick, Dumfries, Lyth, Strathpeffer, Nairn, St Andrews, Cumbernauld, Largs, Dunoon and Perth—at the King's Theatre in Glasgow, the large council-owned receiving house where Connolly played a two-week sold-out run in the 1970s. Primarily the venue for touring musicals, comedy and popular dance, since the early 1960s the King's has been famous for its annual pantomime featuring stars including Stanley Baxter, Rikki Fulton, Gerard Kelly and Elaine C Smith. The theatre is thus synonymous with the popular audience and in closing *Dear Billy* there, the NTS not only acknowledged the importance of the comedian to his home city, but of the popular audience to its mandate. A revival of *Glasgow Girls* played there in early 2019, and *Orphans* toured to the King's Theatre in Edinburgh, a venue similarly associated with popular entertainment. The King's Theatre in Glasgow also played host to the final performances of Isobel McArthur's spectacularly successful *Pride and Prejudice (sort of): After Jane Austen* (2018), which began life at the Tron, was revived for a UK tour in 2019, when it visited Birmingham, Bristol, Edinburgh, Leeds, Oxford and Southampton, and again for a West End run in 2021, where it won the Olivier for Best Entertainment or Comedy Play. In McArthur's retelling, six female actors play servants from Austen's novel, who retell its well-known narrative playing multiple characters while utilising well-chosen karaoke versions of contemporary popular songs. The result is a deliciously delightful romp. A second UK tour ran from autumn 2022 to summer 2023 taking in, among other places, Bath, Cardiff, Coventry, Newcastle, Norwich and Nottingham, and more dates are planned for 2024.

This chapter has concerned itself with developments in contemporary Scottish theatre that relate specifically to the expansion and consolidation of audiences beyond those typically engaged by theatre made in subsidised urban venues for adult audiences. Audiences who have attended these performance events have sometimes been asked to log in and provide feedback via Twitter, to wear waterproof outdoor clothing, to gather in the village or school hall, to take off their shoes and recline on beanbags and to sing along. Scotland's theatre-makers have devised new methods for attracting audiences and found that the creative landscape of the devolved nation presents new opportunities. Audiences who prefer to sit quietly in conventional theatres are, of course, also participants in the theatrical event, their presence felt by performers and fellow audience members alike. While sitting comfortably in the dark in upholstered seats, audiences 'might be swept along by the emotion and atmosphere of the performance or find themselves resistant or immune to its contagious effects' (Harpin and Nicholson 2017: 1–2). In the next chapter, I examine an eclectic range of plays that have been produced in the post-devolutionary period for more conventional theatre spaces, but which have nevertheless explored the fertile breeding ground generated by the blurring of boundaries between 'new writing' and 'new work' that has marked theatre practice in Scotland and elsewhere in the UK in the twenty-first century. Many of these plays look inward to examine Scotland, its current realities, ambitions and disappointments, and others are more ostensibly outward-looking in focus, marked by a progressive spirit of exploration, embracing indeterminacy and suspicious of nationalist discourse in all its forms. Taken as a whole, this work endeavours to bring new perspectives to the ethical challenges that persist in everyday Scottish life and to contribute to the public good by offering alternative realities and insights.

References

Augé, Marc (1995) *Non-Places: Introduction to an Anthropology of Supermodernity*. Translated by John Howe. London, Verso.
Brown, Mark (2012) 'Glasgow Girls Review'. *Sunday Herald*, 4 November.
Carner, Nicole (2016) 'Re-constructing Heritage: The National Theatre of Scotland's *Calum's Road*'. *Scottish Journal of Performance*, 3:1, pp. 29–44.
Cooper, Neil (2018) 'Theatre Review: Scotties, Tron, Glasgow, Four stars'. *Herald*, 17 September.

Critics' Awards for Theatre in Scotland (2011) Available at: https://criticsawards.theatrescotland.com/2011-winners/
Dixon, Steve. 2007. *Digital Performance: A History of New Media in Theater, Dance, Performance Art and Installation*. Massachusetts, MIT Press.
Dolan, Jill (2005) *Utopia in Performance: Finding Hope at the Theater*. Ann Arbour, University of Michigan Press.
Dyer, Richard (1992) *Only Entertainment*. New York, Routledge.
Fisher, Mark (2010) 'The Monster in the Hall review'. *Guardian*, 5 November.
Fisher, Mark (2022) 'Moorcroft Review: Bittersweet Football Comedy Is Right on Target'. *Guardian*, 21 February.
Fitzsimmons Frey, Heather (2016) 'Producing Meanings About Cultural Differences and Identities in Canadian TYA: Three Case Studies'. *Youth Theatre Journal*, 30:1, pp. 81–87.
Fletcher-Watson, Ben (2016) 'Interview: Tony Reekie'. *The Scottish Journal of Performance*, 3:1, pp. 79–95.
Greig, David (2006) *Yellow Moon: The Ballad of Leila and Lee*. London, Faber and Faber.
Greig, David (2011) *The Monster in the Hall*. London, Faber and Faber.
Greig, David (2012) *Glasgow Girls*. Unpublished Rehearsal Script.
Haedicke, Susan (2017) 'The Glasgow Girls: Many Faces of Child Asylum Seekers' in Bishnupriya Dutt, Janelle Reinelt and Shrinkhla Sahai (eds.) *Gendered Citizenship: Manifestations and Performance*. Basingstoke, Palgrave Macmillan, pp. 215–232.
Hamilton, Christine, and Adrienne Scullion (2004) *The Same But Different: Rural Arts Touring in Scotland. The Case of Theatre*. University of Glasgow, Centre for Cultural Policy Research.
Hames, Scott (2020) *The Literary Politics of Scottish Devolution: Voce, Class, Nation*. Edinburgh, Edinburgh University Press.
Harman, Paul (2005) 'Window on the World' in Stuart Bennett (ed.) *Theatre for Children and Young People: 50 Years of Professional Theatre in the UK*. London, Aurora Metro, pp. 53–58.
Harpin, Anna and Helen Nicholson (2017) 'Performance and Participation' in Anna Harpin and Helen Nicholson (eds.) *Performance and Participation: Practices, Audiences, Politics*. London, Bloomsbury, pp. 1–16.
Harrower, David (2013) *Calum's Road*. Unpublished rehearsal script.
Harvie, Jen (2013) *Fair Play: Art, Performance and Neoliberalism*. Basingstoke, Palgrave.
Hassan, Gerry (2014) *Caledonian Dreaming: The Quest for a Different Scotland*. Edinburgh, Luath Press.
Hurley, Kieran (2014) '*Rantin*', in Trish Reid (ed.) *Contemporary Scottish Plays*. London, Bloomsbury, pp. 305–354.

Kerig, Patricia, K. (2014) *Implications of Parent–Child Boundary Dissolution for Developmental Psychopathology: "Who Is the Parent and Who Is the Child?"*. London, Routledge.

Loan, Eilidh (2023) *Moorcroft*. London, Methuen.

Macleod, Michelle (2021) (ed.) *Dràma na Gàidhlig: Ceud Bliadhna air an Àrd-Ùrlar. A Century of Gaelic Drama*. Glasgow, Association for Scottish Literary Studies.

Macwhirter, Iain (2005) 'Power failure Events of 2005: Dawn Raids'. *Herald*, 18 December.

Maloney, Paul (2011) 'Twentieth-Century Popular Theatre', in Brown (ed.) *The Edinburgh Companion to Scottish Drama*. Edinburgh, Edinburgh University Press, pp. 60–72.

Manley, Andy and Ben Fletcher-Watson (2017) 'How Low do You Go? Andy Manley in Conversation'. *Contemporary Theatre Review*, 27:2, pp. 293–296.

Matarasso, François with Rosie Redzia (2015) *A Wider Horizon*. Wymondham: Creative Arts East.

McGrath, John (1981) *A Good Night Out, Popular Theatre: Audience, Class and Form*. London, Methuen.

McMillan, Joyce (2011) 'Theatre Reviews: Calum's Road/The Hunted/Twelfth Night'. *Scotsman*. 6 October.

McMillan, Joyce (2017) 'The Edinburgh International Children's Festival'. *Scotsman*, 4 April.

McMillan, Joyce (2023) 'Theatre Reviews: Dear Billy/Beautiful People'. *Scotsman*, 22 May.

McMillan, Joyce (2022) 'Theatre Reviews: I Am Tiger/Plock/Little Top'. *Scotsman*, 9 May.

Moireach, Dòmhnall S. (2021) '*Sequamur*', in Michelle Macleod (ed.) *Dràma na Gàidhlig: Ceud Bliadhna air an Àrd-Ùrlar. A Century of Gaelic Drama*. Glasgow, Association for Scottish Literary Studies, pp. 185–210.

National Theatre of Scotland (2023) Strategic Framework April 2023–March 2026. Available at: https://www.nationaltheatrescotland.com/about/reports-and-documents

National Records of Scotland (2022) '91% of Scotland's Population Live in 2% of Its Land Area'. Available at:https://www.nrscotland.gov.uk/statistics-and-data/statistics/statistics-by-theme/population/population-estimates/settlements-and-localities/mid-2020

Noble, Greg (2009) 'Everyday Cosmopolitanism and the Labour of Intercultural Community' in Amanda Wise and Selvaraj Velayutham (eds.) *Everyday Multiculturalism*. Basingstoke, Palgrave Macmillan, pp. 46–65.

Overend, David (2019) '*Rantin* and Raving: Kieran Hurley's Aesthetic Communities'. *Contemporary Theatre Review*, 29:2, pp. 166–179.

Reekie, Tony (2005) 'Revival of Theatre in Scotland: the Cinderella Story of Scottish Children's Theatre' in Stuart Bennett (ed.) *Theatre for Children and Young People*. London, Aurora Metro Press, pp. 38–42.

Reid, Trish (2014) 'Staging Scotland: National Theatre of Scotland and Shifting Conceptions of Scottish Identity', in Huw Jones (ed.) *The Media in Europe's Small Nations*. Newcastle, Cambridge Scholars Press, pp. 105–120.

Reid, Trish (2016a) '"Sexy Kilts with Attitude": Scottish Theatre in the Twenty First Century', in Adiseshiah, Sian, and Louise Lepage (eds.) *Twenty-First Century Drama: What Happens Now*. Basingstoke, Palgrave Macmillan, pp. 191–211.

Reid, Trish (2016b) 'Teenage Dreams: Power and Imagination in David Greig's Yellow Moon and The Monster in the Hall'. *Contemporary Theatre Review*, 26:1, pp. 60–70.

Robinson, Jo (2016) *Theatre & The Rural*. Basingstoke, Palgrave Macmillan.

Scottish Government (2020) *Scottish Government Urban Rural Classification*. Available at: https://www.gov.scot/publications/scottish-government-urban-rural-classification-2020/documents/

Śledzińska, Paula (2015) 'Revisiting the Other: National Theatre of Scotland and the Mythologization of the Highlands and Islands'. *The Canadian Journal of Irish Studies*, 39:1, pp. 118–141.

Smith, Donald (1998) '1950–1995'. Bill Findlay (ed.) *A History of Scottish Theatre*. Edinburgh, Edinburgh University Press, pp. 253–308.

Theatre in Schools Scotland (2019) 'Pilot Report'. Available at: https://www.theatreinschoolsscotland.co.uk/uploads/8/2/5/9/82595058/tiss_report_2019_41.pdf

Theatre in Schools Scotland (2023). Available at: https://www.theatreinschoolsscotland.co.uk/

Tomlin, Liz (2015) *British Theatre Companies 1995–2014*. London, Bloomsbury.

Tompkins, Joanne (2014) *Theatre's Heterotopias: Performance and the Cultural Politics of Space*. Basingstoke, Palgrave Macmillan.

Wallace, Clare (2013) *The Theatre of David Greig*. London, Bloomsbury.

Walmsley, Ben (2020) 'National Theatre of Scotland and its Sense of Place'. *Marketing Review*, 10:2, pp 109–117.

CHAPTER 6

Plays and Playwrighting

Since breaking through with her second play, *Further Than the Furthest Thing* (2000), Zinnie Harris has created a substantial body of intensely poetic original work as well as a number of radical adaptations of European classics. Her most recent retelling, *Macbeth (an undoing)*, opened at the Lyceum in Edinburgh in early February 2023 and was successful enough to warrant a revival at the same theatre, where Harris is an associate director, in May 2024. Harris' feminist reworking of Aeschylus' *Oresteia*, *This Restless House*, won the 2016 CATS award for best play, and she has also produced radical adaptations of Ibsen, Shakespeare, Strindberg and Webster, as well as a diverse range of original plays for a variety of stages including the Citizens, the Donmar Warehouse, Hampstead Theatre, Leeds Playhouse, the NTS, the Royal Court, the Lyceum, the Royal National Theatre, the RSC, the Traverse and the Tron. Her work has been translated and performed abroad, and she has a growing reputation as a director. Harris is also a woman, and her sustained success can be read as indicative of a shift in Scotland's playwrighting culture towards greater gender equality. In the twenty-first-century Scottish playwrights have, to borrow Adrienne Scullion's formulation, continued the work of 'reassessing and re-creating in the context of existing cultural codes and conventions, thereby exposing the emotional uncertainties beneath totemic structures and, finally, taking knowing responsibility for the nature and effects of our own culture' (Scullion 1995: 203).

© The Author(s), under exclusive license to Springer Nature Switzerland AG 2024
T. Reid, *Theatre and Performance in Contemporary Scotland*,
https://doi.org/10.1007/978-3-031-61191-9_6

The establishment of a devolved Scottish Parliament in 1999 has only intensified this scrutiny.

Among other things, devolution had provoked a focus on the past and its relationship to the present and the future. In her essay 'Devolution and Drama: Imagining the Possible', Scullion picks up this theme by reading David Greig's history play *The Speculator* (1999) as primarily concerned with 'the possibilities afforded by an aspirational future bold enough to confront and progress away from the assumptions and prejudices of the past', for example (2007: 71). The road to devolution was long and bumpy but, as Tom Nairn observes, the opening of a new Scottish Parliament created cultural momentum and provoked 'a general sense of an incoming tide' which compelled re-imaginings of Scotland and Scottishness (2000: 155). For theatre-makers the creation of what David Pattie describes as 'new maps to help us negotiate the difficult terrain ahead' became one among a number of imperatives (Pattie, 2008: 143).

In 2022 the Scottish Society of Playwrights, the organisation established in 1973 'to develop support for playwriting and to act as a new channel for playwrights to speak collectively', had 166 members (Brown, 2013: 90). The SSP has continued to represent the collective interests of playwrights through advocacy, specific negotiations, and public debate. For example, it reached an agreement with the NTS on playwright's renumeration in the mid-noughties. In the same period, under Nicola McCartney's leadership, the SSP developed best practice guidelines for dramaturgs and contributed to debates around the establishment of Creative Scotland. In the meantime, discussions involving the SAC, playwrights, theatre companies, the SSP and educational institutions resulted in the establishment of Playwrights' Studio Scotland (PSS) in 2004. This organisation took over much of the developing and mentoring work that had been done by the SSP in its early years. Based at the CCA in Glasgow, PSS is funded by Creative Scotland and remains 'the only arts organisation in the UK exclusively dedicated to the artistic development of writers for live performance' (Playwrights' Studio 2023). Its aim is to support playwrights based in Scotland at all stages of their careers and to this end it 'has established a lively programme of activities that serves Scottish theatre and its playwrights outstandingly' (Brown 2013: 97). Currently operating under the chairpersonship of Rona Munro, the PSS database lists 307 playwrights.

If the numbers above suggest a relatively active playwriting culture, they also mean many playwrights will be excluded from my discussion in this chapter, although some of them make appearances elsewhere in this book. Omissions are no reflection of the quality of the work. In making my selection I have privileged work that has attracted sustained national and international attention. Scotland is a small stateless nation operating in an increasing connected world and its playwrights have, perhaps unsurprisingly, asked questions about the discursive regimes that underpin contemporary global power relations. They have also sometimes dealt explicitly with how these questions pertain to Scotland. I am also keen to acknowledge, following Nadine Holdsworth, that 'many of the plays and productions considered here have evoked a strong sense of emotion and/or recognition of my own classed, gendered and political positioning' as well as my awareness of the shifting meanings of my own Scottishness (2020: 8). Their inclusion consequently speaks to my interest in theatre's affective power. Finally, I have attempted to capture some sense of the diversity of form currently being employed by Scottish playwrights across a range of scales and career stages. As Elin Diamond et al. remind us 'resistance has many registers', and the plays discussed here are far from uniform in approach (2017: 4). This brings me neatly back to Zinnie Harris.

While varied in scale, Harris' work has been characterised by a focus on female experience and feminist concerns, and on questions of identity particularly as they relate to place. Setting is consequently a preoccupation in her work. From the *'terrible rumbling ... under the water'* that permeates *Further than the Furthest Thing* (2000), to the barren landscape of the post-conflict *Midwinter* (2004), and the war-torn wasteland of *The Wheel* (2011), her emphasis on environment places eco-feminist concerns centre stage (Harris 2019: 9). *Further than the Furthest Thing* is set in the early 1960s on a remote mid-Atlantic volcanic island based—loosely Tristan da Cunha—from which its inhabitants are forced to flee. Its subject matter of migration and exile, and the fragility of the frameworks of civilisation under pressure, remains relevant for twenty-first-century audiences, and it was revived in 2023 in a production for the Young Vic directed by Jennifer Tang. Harris' islanders are a peculiar hybrid of cultures and periods, part Napoleonic, part Victorian and part modern, and the play performs the valuable work of making strange ideas of community and island identity as its characters move from volcanic eruption to mass evacuation, to exile, to potential return.

In *The Wheel*, which was commissioned by the NTS, Harris' heroine 'Beatriz travels across the war-torn world and the bloody centuries, gathering a creche of children along the way and carrying them into the future' (Gardner 2011). *Midwinter*, which is the first in a trilogy for the RSC and the Traverse, that continues with *Solstice* (2005) and *Fall* (2008), is set in the bleakest of seasons at the end of a ten-year conflict that has left all of its soldiers blinded by a mysterious parasite. In a motif reminiscent of Brecht's *Mother Courage*, a woman guards and sells off pieces of a dead horse to survive. Characters are continually displaced. Harris returns repeatedly to the subject matter of migration and exile, which is central to *Solstice* and again to *How to Hold Your Breath* (2015). This last play, which was commissioned by the Royal Court and directed by Vicky Featherstone, sees its heroine Dana, a stylish customs relations expert played by the activist and actor Maxine Peake, suffer a loss of privilege after a seemingly straightforward sexual encounter with a man named Jarron, who mistakes her for a prostitute and offers her money. Dana's rejection of his offer leaves him notionally beholden to her and leads to dire consequences. In a Faustian twist, Jarron, who claims to be a demon who works for the United Nations, casts Dana into an economic doomsday scenario in which migrant routes and patterns of economic collapse are inverted.

Sometimes Harris' plays are more personal and intimate. *Meet Me at Dawn* (2017), which opened at the Traverse in the summer of 2017 as part of the EIF, was partly inspired by the legend of Orpheus and Eurydice, but also intended to chime, as Harris has said, with the 'collective grief and loss' people were experiencing in the aftermath of the Brexit referendum (quoted in Hart 2023: 23). A couple in their forties, Helen and Robyn, are marooned on an island in the Firth of Forth, after a boating accident. They are soaking wet. Robyn is feeling shocked and nauseous, Helen exhilarated and by her own admission 'kind of buzzing' (Harris, 2017: 13). At first, we assume these are simply contrasting responses to their near-death experience. They talk, bicker and banter about the accident, about suing the company from whom they hired the boat, about getting off the island, about the cold, about being lost and having no phone. They try to find the funny side of their situation. They expect they will be home soon, possibly with the help of a mysterious third woman who is also on the island. We come to understand that they love each other very much. Robyn is haunted, however, by images of another, parallel and more terrible, version of reality, in which Helen has died in the accident while she has survived, condemned to live alone in the house, and life, they once shared. This later version gradually takes precedence, and the audience begins to realise that Helen is dead, and that the action of the play is taking place in some kind of alternative supernatural temporal reality in which the flow of time has been suspended, at least for the duration of one day.

This kind of supernatural ghosting, which obviously operates at some distance from naturalism, also occurs in *This Restless House* in which the figure of Iphigenia haunts the stage, and in Harris' adaptation of Webster's *The Duchess of Malfi*, which opened at the Royal Lyceum in Edinburgh in May 2019 and later transferred to the Glasgow Citizens at the Tramway, where I saw it in September 2019. In this instance, Harris holds focus on the Duchess—and the play's other female characters—by extending the echo in the tomb motif of Webster's play, to a full-scale ghostly afterlife which keeps the female characters on stage and the Duchess to some extent in control of the action. Webster's play is unremittingly grim, of course, but Harris introduces gentle rituals—involving music and tender washing—that liberate her female characters, after their on stage deaths, from the constant threat of male violence. One by one, having fallen victim to this violence, the women are tended, washed and revived. They spend the rest of the play, watching, repeating their ritual, remaining and persisting. They refuse to leave the stage and in so doing, they repudiate causation. This seems important because causation has been central to the way power—and indeed conventional tragic plotting—has been understood to operate (Fig. 6.1).

Harris is a playwright of considerable skill and formal ingenuity and, by defying easy categorisation and resisting the urge to conform to any pre-existing notion of what it means to be a Scottish playwright, she has actively 'contributed to the creation of a public sphere where women are better able to define those categories for themselves' (Maguire, 2011: 164).

In the next section I want to return to developments in the earlier part of the new century, and thus in the more immediate aftermath of devolution. In his book *Modernism and Scottish Theatre Since 1969* (2019), Mark Brown singles out Harris, along with David Greig, David Harrower and Anthony Neilson, as 'arguably, the four most important writers' of what he calls 'the golden generation of Scottish playwrighting' (2019: 113). This is a large claim, of course, and is consequently open to challenge. Nonetheless, having opened this chapter with a discussion of

Fig. 6.1 Fletcher Mathers, Leah Walker, Georgette McMillan and Kirsty Stuart in Zinnie Harris' *The Duchess (of Malfi) after John Webster* (directed by Zinnie Harris, Royal Lyceum Edinburgh and Glasgow Citizens', 2019) reproduced with kind permission from Mihaela Bodlovic

Harris' work, an assessment of the contribution made by Greig, Harrower and Neilson in the post-devolutionary period seems as good a place to start as any. All three originally came to attention in the 1990s.

Established Voices

As the various discussions of his work elsewhere in this study demonstrate, David Greig remains the most critically reviewed of contemporary Scottish playwrights, his work having generated numerous chapters and articles, a number of edited collections and several scholarly monographs including Anja Muller and Clare Wallace (eds.) *Cosmotopia: Transnational Identities in David Greig's Theatre* (2011), Clare Wallace, *The Theatre of David Greig* (2013) and Verónica Rodríguez *David Greig's Holed Theatre* (2019). In 2016 a special issue of the journal *Contemporary Theatre Review* was dedicated to Greig's work, and its contents give some sense of the breadth of interest he has provoked, as scholars focused variously on his treatment of national identity, globalisation, multiculturalism, dissensus, participation, historical truth, utopian performatives and the power of the imagination. The special issue is an acknowledgement of Greig's status as a major playwright. Along with Burke, Harrower and Neilson, he is one of four Scottish playwrights to have a dedicated chapter in *The Methuen Drama Guide to Contemporary British Playwrights* (2011) and a chapter on his work by Nadine Holdsworth appears in *Modern British Playwriting 2000–2009* (2013). His inclusion in this 2000–2009 volume, as Verónica Rodríguez points out 'indicates that he has been canonised as a post-millennial playwright rather that a 1990s' one' (2019: 10). Given the critical success of plays like *Europe*, *The Architect* (1996) and *The Cosmonaut's Last Message to the Woman he Once Loved in the Former Soviet Union* (1999), this categorisation reflects the by now widespread assumption that the 1990s was the decade of the Royal Court and the in-yer-face aesthetic. Greig has been associated with neither.

At least until he took over the artistic directorship of the Royal Lyceum in June 2016, Greig was extraordinarily prolific as a playwright, producing around fifty play texts in the first couple of decades of his career, and generating a large body of work in a variety of forms, for a wide range of audiences. In the year 2000, for instance, *Outside Now* was produced at the Prada Showroom in Milan, *Swansong* for BBC Radio 4, *Candide 2000* for Suspect Culture, *Oedipus (after Sophocles)* for Tramway and Theatre Babel and *Victoria* for the RSC at the Pit, London. This last play is worthy of closer attention not least because of its ambitious scope and structure.

'It is difficult to imagine', as Clare Wallace notes, 'a work greater in contrast to the comic, ironic, urban qualities of *Caledonia Dreaming*'— which I discuss in the introduction to this book—than *Victoria* (2013: 74). The latter is a large cast, three-act, monumental history play, that spans 60 years and traces the impact of modernisation and in particular the vicissitudes of global capital on one small West Highland community. Like a number of other post-devolutionary plays discussed in this book, *Victoria* draws on the mythology of the Highlands and Islands, a landscape which remains central to cultural evocations of Scotland. 'The "Scotland" of our imaginations', as David McCrone stresses, is 'not only rural but largely Highland, replete with tartanry and clans' (2001: 6). In the event, the idea of the Highlands functions in a number of complementary and contradictory ways. For instance, since 1707 it has, according to the historian Tom Devine, effectively 'answered the emotional need for the maintenance of a distinctive Scottish identity without in any way compromising the union', at least until recently (2006: 244). As the historical elements of Gregory Burke's *Black Watch* show, Scotland's rise to prosperity depended on the continuation of its relationship with England, and 'the indissoluble link between tartanry, the Highland soldier, patriotism and imperial service' (Devine, 2006: 244). Greig draws on these complex and contradictory discourses in his play.

The three acts of *Victoria*, which are organised in 72 scenes, span three generations. In 1936 fascism is taking hold in Europe. In 1974, the North Sea oil boom is beginning to impact the lives of Highland communities and in 1996, the promise of devolution and the inexorable force of globalisation are starting to impact village life. In performance, the play is sutured by the appearance of three Victorias, all from different generations, but played by the same actress. The result is an epic that explores the limitations of human agency by excavating intergenerational conflicts between landowner/developers, and the community their actions impact, against a backdrop of inexorable twentieth-century modernisation. The landscape of the Highlands plays its part. In the first act the ancient pull of the land is represented by the mountain, which seems to hold onto the characters preventing their escape. By the end of the nineties, the same mountain is being ground down for granite aggregate, which is being shipped across the globe to build motorways.

Across *Victoria*'s three acts Greig distinguishes his characters in relation to socio-economic status and political affiliation—in 1936 the landowner's son is a Nazi sympathiser while some of the estate workers are preparing to travel to Spain to fight Franco, for instance. Throughout, the 'theatrical use of doubling', as Nadine Holdsworth notes, along with recurring motifs of inherited trauma, 'highlights connections between characters and across historical periods', providing thematic continuity (2008: 135). Janelle Reinelt admires the dialectical structure of a play in which the 'Highlands are confining and provincial, but they are also beautiful and bounteous' and where 'characters are drawn to the terrain but also long to escape it' (2011: 209). *Victoria* is a study of how individuals are shaped by place, and how place is in turn shaped by individuals and their competing desires, both personal and political. These themes are developed further in another of Greig's history plays, *Outlying Islands* (2002).

It is 1939 and Europe is poised on the precipice of war. Two young Cambridge ornithologists are despatched by the government to a remote Hebridean island, forty miles from the mainland, ostensibly to make a record of the wildlife, although it is later revealed, much to their dismay, that the government is interested in using the island as an anthrax testing site. The narrative premise is simple enough. The young men are marooned in this 'almost pristine habitat' for a month with only the island leaseholder Kirk and his niece Ellen for company (Greig 2002: 155). Although much simpler in structure than *Victoria*, the play again works through a series of oppositions. The leaseholder, as his name suggests, is a testy old Calvinist who seeks to control his more free-spirited niece, and sees the land as something entirely at his disposal. The young ornithologists are very different in temperament. 'Nature divides us into the gambler and the saver', Robert tells his assistant John: 'I'm a gambler. You're a saver' (149). Utilising the activity of bird watching as a metaphor, *Outlying Islands* explores processes of looking and being looked at as, in the aftermath of Kirk's sudden death from a heart attack, erotic tensions rise between the three young people. Ostensibly trapped in the male gaze—she is photographed by Robert while bathing, for instance—Ellen converts this objectification into something empowering as she comes to terms with her own desires. Although Robert is the more confident and strident, and hence more vocal in expressing his desire for her, it is John she makes love to in the penultimate scene, while Robert watches in silence. The play ends as the boat arrives to take them back to the mainland, and we discover that Robert has jumped to his death from a cliff edge. 'He walked out into the storm', Ellen recalls, 'Up the Hill he walked to the cliff top ... And he made a short run ... He ran at the cliff edge and spread his arms out and flew' (230). For John, by contrast, Robert simply fell. In this way, the metaphorical and the literal remain in play until the end, although we are perhaps encouraged towards the former. *Outlying Islands* won the CATS Award for best new play in 2003.

Among Greig's major plays of the noughties set outside Scotland, *San Diego* (2003) and *Pyrenees* (2005) have attracted particular critical attention. For Marilena Zaroulia, *San Diego*, which moves between 27 different locations, is nothing less than 'a play-critique of mobility and its impact on individual and collective identities' (2011: 37). The play, which was a co-production between the Tron and the EIF, opens with a young Scottish playwright named David Greig, boarding a flight to California to see a production of one of his plays. This is his first trip to the US. He wears a t-shirt bearing his own name. We might expect that what follows will be a self-reflexive account of the perils and pleasures of authorship, but we are quickly disabused of this notion when this particular version of David Greig is fatally stabbed by an illegal immigrant shortly after arriving in the US. Thereafter other Davids populate the scenes, and are given the opportunity to reflect on a range of themes from colonial violence, hospitality, transnationalism, migration, homelessness, alienation and the comfort of strangers. Determinedly eschewing closure, *San Diego* ends back on the plane with the pilot's announcement: 'Ladies and gentlemen, welcome to San Diego. We hope you've enjoyed flying with us today' (Greig, 2003: 116). In the interim, the play is 'filled with images of international travel and migration, identities echoing and shifting in transit' (Rebellato, 2016: 9).

With *Pyrenees* Greig returns to a more condensed two act structure, and a fixed setting—the action unfolds on the terrace of a hotel in the south of France in off season—but continues his exploration of identity and its attendant geographies. A man is found unconscious in the snow on the Camino de Santiago. The Man, as he is designated in the text, has suffered total amnesia and the plot revolves around the search for his true identity. Anna, who works for the British consulate in Marseilles, arrives to interview him and establish whether he is British. She records his voice in the hope of identifying linguistic signifiers related to place, telling him 'people carry a landscape in their voice' but manages to miss these when they do occur (Greig, 2010: 244). His use of the Scots word clanjamfrie to signify confusion and chaos is the most obvious example (274). Over the course of the first act sexual chemistry develops between the two, but the relationship is interrupted by the arrival at the beginning of Act Two of Vivienne, who claims to be the Man's wife. Tensions between the two women culminate in Anna suffering an epileptic fit, and the play closes with the Man's rueful acceptance of Vivienne's account of his identity: that he is an errant civil servant with the Fisheries Department in Edinburgh by the name of Keith Sutherland. This conclusion is juxtaposed with the Man's earlier account of moment he wakes up in the snow, as a kind of rebirth: 'I really remember the moment. Very intense …That moment's where I start from. Now. New' (Greig, 2010: 271). This is a play about identity, then, and Greig uses the comic figure of the hotel Proprietor 'for thematic amplification' (Wallace 2013: 131). He identifies himself as variously African, American, Basque, English, French, Galician,

German, Spanish and Portuguese, as well as both male and female, thus illustrating Greig's conviction, articulated in this play and others, that identity is always contingent and often fluid. This is not to suggest that Greig is unaware of how identity markers reflect actual power relations in the real world. *The American Pilot* (2005) and *Damascus* (2007) raise quite different questions to the work discussed above, and their treatment of power relations between East and West are discussed in some detail by Nadine Holdsworth (2013)** and Janelle Reinelt (2011).

It is possible, of course, to read *Pyrenees* and *San Diego* as plays about the possibility of personal transformation, and Greig returns to this theme, more explicitly and light-heartedly in the hit shows *Midsummer* (2008) and *The Strange Undoing of Prudencia Hart* (2011). *Midsummer*, 'a play with songs' written by Gordon McIntyre of the indie group Ballboy, is a lo-fi musical rom com, which functions partly as a hymn to its setting, the gorgeous city of Edinburgh, and also nods cheekily in the direction of Shakespeare's *A Midsummer Night's Dream*. When the show visited Sydney in 2012, the programme included a map of the Scottish capital that traced the Bacchanalian progress of its characters the unlikely couple, Helena and Bob, who hook up in a bar on the longest day of the year. What follows is a feelgood tale of mid-life crisis, casual sex, weekend binge, ukuleles, stolen goods and ultimately true romance. *The Strange Undoing of Prudencia Hart* (2011)—which I reference above in reference to the NTS approach to international touring—reaches back beyond musical theatre and variety to utilise older popular forms. Drawing on the conventions of the medieval border ballad, it is designed to be performed by a small group of actor musicians in pubs, howfs, function rooms and community halls, and consequently sits comfortably within the traditions of the ceilidh play.

Greig's heroine, Prudencia, is a folklorist and academic who has devoted her life to the study of folk ballads. One winter's night she travels to Kelso in the borders to collect song material for her thesis, *Paradigms of Emotional Contact in The Performance and Text of Traditional Folk Song in Scotland 1572–1798*. Partly due to deteriorating weather conditions, she is caught up in a lock-in with a bunch of locals on the night of the 'Devil's Ceilidh', and they hear of the existence of a song beyond song, an original and uncollected song, a song of undoing (Greig 2011: 35). While hiding in the toilet planning her escape—she is not good at parties—Prudencia spots a card advertising a local B&B at Goodman's field and steps out into the snowy night. Her subsequent journey takes her into supernatural realms. At the final stroke of midnight Nick from the B&B appears to lead her to shelter, and the seductive allure of his large library. 'Every book that's ever been is here and every book that's never been as well', he explains, and 'also a pretty extensive collection of rare vinyl'(55) Subsequently, Prudencia spends two thousand years with the devil—for Nick's identity is now clear—researching his archive and being drawn in by his strange methods of courtship. They fall in love. Eventually, she is rescued by a colleague, but in the play's final scene, she comes to the realisation that 'to find your song' you must 'first find who to sing it to' (82). She belongs with the devil and ideally, according to Greig's text, *'the song she sings is Kylie Minogue's I can't Get You of My Head'* (83).

In combining folk tradition with contemporary pop culture, *Prudencia Hart* demonstrates the continuing efficacy of popular forms in Scottish theatre. More seriously perhaps, in their utopian affirmation of the possibility of change, both *Midsummer* and *Prudencia Hart* link Greig's persistent interest in experimenting with theatrical form to the political dimension of his work, which is perhaps more obvious in *Europe* or *San Diego*. 'What I would call political theatre', Greig writes, 'makes interventions into ideology … It poses questions about society to which it does not already know the answer. And perhaps most importantly, political theatre has at its very heart the possibility of change' (in Edgar, 1999: 66). In contrast much of David Harrower's work is marked by ambivalence about the possibility of change, and instead tends towards indeterminacy and opacity.

Caridad Svitch observes that Harrower pays 'particular attention to the fragmentary nature of thought (and how thought and its expression are revelatory of fragmented souls)' (2008: 88). His characters speak in a kind of broken poetry, and articulate self-expression and effective communication remain largely out of reach. Indeed, while it allows for the extended exploration of difficult subject matter, Harrower's pessimism is not without risk. In *Knives and Hens*, for instance, his linking of knowledge, specifically female knowledge, with violence and deceit, as Clare Wallace argues, 'inevitably suggests the fall of man' and can thus be read as rather regressive (2011: 248). Harrower's work, nonetheless, defies easy categorisation. In *In-Yer-Face Theatre*, Aleks Sierz suggests that in *Knives and Hens*, violence is 'shrouded in words' concluding that the 'intense and sensuous language, and the production's restrained mime of the killing, distanced the audience' (2001: 2008). Not quite in-yer-face, then.

Indeterminacy can be a powerfully affective tool in the theatre, of course, and Harrower has made productive use of it. As my account of *Callum's Road* in the previous chapter demonstrates, he has also shown a consistent interest in adaptation and an attendant preoccupation with older dramaturgies and forms. His other adaptations include Pirandello's *Six Characters in Search of an Author* (2001), Büchner's *Woyzeck* (2001), Chekhov's *Ivanov* (2002), Horváth's *Tales from the Vienna Woods* (2003), Schiller's *Mary Stuart* (2006), Brecht's *The Good Soul of Szechuan* (2008) Schnitzler's *Sweet Nothings* (2009), Ibsen's *Public Enemy* (2013) and Muriel Spark's *The Prime of Miss Jean Brodie* (2018). This strand of Harrower's work has added a certain richness to the texture of Scottish theatre. More recently he has moved into writing for film and television, but although fewer in number than Greig's, his original plays have nevertheless attracted significant critical attention.

If *Knives and Hens* is unsettling in its ambivalence, Harrower's next major play, *Blackbird* (2005), is disturbingly so. Along with his debut, it is also his most widely revived and translated play. Originally staged at the EIF in the summer of 2005 in a production by the eminent German director Peter Stein, *Blackbird* transferred to the Albery in London in 2006, and was revived at the Manhattan Theatre Club in April 2007. The Edinburgh and London productions won the CATS and Olivier awards for Best New Play. In 2011, a revival by Rogue Machine in Los Angeles won the LA Drama Critics Circle Award for Best Writing. Its inaugural production on Broadway, which starred Michelle Williams and Jeff Daniels, was nominated in the Best Revival of a Play category in the 2016 Tony Awards and Harrower also adapted the play for the Ben Andrews film, *Una* (2016). *Blackbird's* premise is straightforward enough. Una, a woman in her late twenties, confronts Ray, a man in his mid-fifties, in an anonymous litter strewn staff common room. She has tracked him down after seeing his picture in a trade magazine and it soon becomes apparent the two had a sexual relationship fifteen years earlier, when she was twelve years old, for which Ray has served a prison sentence. He is now living under a new identity.

Inspired by the real-life news story of US Marine Toby Studebaker's abduction of a twelve-year-old girl from Manchester, at one level *Blackbird* is a conventionally realist play, an intense two-hander about the impact of the past on the present. Crucially, Harrower's decision 'to locate the abuse in the past', as Anna Harpin observes, 'allows for the density of the subject to be approached in a discursive mode' and he is not solely focused on moral arguments but also excavating the vivid intensity of desire, be it aberrant or culturally sanctioned (2013: 176). One of the more problematic aspects of Harrower's dramatisation, however, is that Una's exact motivation in confronting Ray remains clear. Does she want to accuse him, humiliate him, attack him, extract an apology or rekindle their sexual relationship? Boundaries between moral categories are also blurred because the adult Una is a damaged, erratic and destructive presence, and therefore not easily recognised as a victim. The implication that their earlier illegal sexual relationship was in some meaningful sense consensual is also given some credence. Most disturbingly, in the absence of an actual child onstage, the audience is left to imagine the twelve-year-old Una who is constructed retrospectively as Wallace observes, 'as endowed with adult agency and self-aware sexuality', while Ray's responsibility 'as an adult *not* to respond is obscured by the assertion of consensual love' (2011: 256–257). Moreover, Ray is staged as the more sympathetic and stable character and Harrower's sustained ambivalence, especially around the figure of Una, effectively compromises the audience's ability to interpret the narrative ethically. This is obvious in the language used by many of its reviewers. Nicholas de Jongh posed the question: 'Was Ray a genuine paedophile?', for instance (2006). For Georgina Brown, Una 'was clearly a precocious child, just as she is now a predatory woman', a reading that implies a degree of culpability and is certainly inflected by the ambiguity that surrounds the capability of preteens, especially girls, to consent to sexual activity (2006). According to Charles Spencer, 'Harrower leaves no doubt that what happened between these lost and lonely souls was indeed love' (2006). Such readings are possible, of course, precisely because the child is absent, and indeed the erasure of the child's voice is largely achieved in *Blackbird* via the sexualised characterisation of the adult Una. In this way, the passage of time and Una's adult presence combine to destabilise notions of truth and moral responsibility in Ray's favour. Harpin sums up the effect nicely. The 'mediation of their illegal sexual past through the body and voice of a mature woman affords a generosity towards Ray that would be wholly absent if the play was re-set to the original scene of the affair' (2013: 176). In Stein's original production, the final scene shifted from the office to a carpark where Ray and Una physically wrestle with each other. In Harrower's text, Ray pushes Una aside to re-join his new partner and her daughter. Either way, one feels simultaneously transfixed and horrified. 'Charged with grim visceral emotion', as Wallace concludes, 'Blackbird is a mesmerising work' which continues to draw the attention of directors and audiences (2011: 257).

Like *Knives in Hens*, *Blackbird* is not geographically specific. It focuses instead on individuals isolated within their subjective realities and locked into their unfolding drama. For Steve Cramer this absence, or relegation, of social context as a determinant of human behaviour is a defining feature of Harrower's work, which, he argues, is informed by 'the post-Thatcher era's extreme paranoia and individualist ethos' (2011: 173). Cramer has a point, of course, but Harrower's work is not easily categorised, and his next major critical success was with a play very much rooted in the specific culture of the city of Glasgow where he makes his home.

Ciara (2013) is a solo piece, a monologue delivered by the daughter of a deceased Glasgow crime lord. She is now pursuing a respectable and profitable career as a gallery owner but cannot quite shake off her family's dark past. She is elegantly attired, the kind of woman who attends 'restaurant openings, catwalk shows, charity auctions' and 'testimonial dinners', and from the outset her monologue is laden with colloquialism, poetry, and metaphor (Harrower 2013: 13). Her husband Bryan, a former protégée of her father's, likes to provoke 'blue-nosed business associates', for instance, and 'belt to out multi-versed rebel songs at the limit of his lung power' (13). The former activity is a derogatory reference to supporters of Rangers football club, and the latter a clear expression of his affiliation to Glasgow Celtic. Indeed, many of the play's jokes rely on a working knowledge of the sectarian aspects of Glaswegian culture, and most are at the expense of Rangers and its fan base. For instance, Ciara's father is buried in 'Janefield Cemetery so he can hear the roar from Paradise', a synonym for Celtic Park (29). Her monologue is peppered with references to her Catholic upbringing.

In the play's opening sequence, Ciara describes a painting of an enormous woman lying 'on her side and sleeping, peacefully sleeping' on the Glasgow skyline (12). This 'sleeping giantess held calmly in Glasgow's embrace' is her favourite artwork, and it serves as a metaphor for Ciara and for the city itself, steeped in the masculinist traditions of football, heavy industry, and gangsterism, yet hungry to embrace gentrification and the promise of a brighter future (22). Far from being out of her depth in this world, Ciara proves more than capable of handling herself as her family's brutal past bears down mercilessly on her present. Harrower's very considerable skill as a writer is showcased in *Ciara*, which won the CATS Award for Best New Play in 2014. His storytelling is masterful, and on continuous display in the rather exposed monologue form: always in command of what is happening in the space, always alive to the potentials of language to change the situation, and always in control of the shape of the action and its tempo.

Questions about the shape and tempo of the action have also preoccupied Anthony Neilson, a playwright who like Greig and Harrower came to prominence in the 1990s, although he has been categorised rather differently. Alongside a number of young London-based playwrights, Neilson was grouped by Aleks Sierz under the heading in-your-face, and moreover was identified as a progenitor of the movement. 'Long before Sarah Kane and Mark Ravenhill hit the headlines in the mid-nineties', writes Sierz, 'Neilson was exploring the darker side of the human psyche' (Sierz 2001: 68). Subsequently, Neilson's early plays, which included *Normal* (1991), *Penetrator* (1993) and *The Censor* (1997)—which are all discussed by Sierz—were rarely categorised as Scottish. In an essay on emerging Scottish dramatists published in 1996, for instance, Peter Zenzinger makes no mention of Neilson. *The Censor* and *Stitching* (2002), which respectively won The Writer's Guild Award and the Time Out Off West End Award, were primarily understood as intense and troubling relationship plays. Toby Young's description of *Stitching* as 'a mesmerising two-hander about a dysfunctional sexual relationship' is typical (2002). Neilson's strong association with London was diluted in the early years of the new century. In 2004 Simon Stokes and David Prescott at Plymouth Theatre Royal agreed to co-produce a new play, *The Wonderful World of Dissocia* (2004), with Glasgow's Tron Theatre and the EIF. The production went on to win five of the ten awards at the Critics' Awards for Theatre in Scotland, including Best Direction and Best New Play for Neilson, and Best Theatre Production for the company. In 2015 it was reissued in the Methuen Modern Classics imprint, and in 2023 in a student edition by the same publisher. 'This play', as Anna Six states boldly in her introduction to this latest edition, 'stands as Neilson's most unambiguous and enduring theatrical success' (Six, 2023: 1).

In 2005 Vicky Featherstone commissioned Neilson to direct one of the NTS's inaugural projects, *Home Edinburgh*, and to write and direct *Realism* (2006) for the company's first summer season. In 2007, the national company also revived *Dissocia* for a UK tour. This activity enabled a re-evaluation of Neilson as a more specifically Scottish artist.

Soon after, Adrienne Scullion identified him as one of a number of contemporary Scottish playwrights wrestling with identity politics by employing 'a catalogue of relevant metaphors of mutable edges and liminal terrains' (2007: 74). Elsewhere, Ian Brown located Neilson's work within an identifiably Scottish tradition in relation to its 'strategic use of register shifts' to subvert dominant or conventional modes of perception (2007: 127). My own article 'Deformities of the Frame' (2007), makes similar claims, arguing that because 'the Scottish theatre tradition has generally been thought of as more varied and populist, and less text-bound than its English counterpart … understanding Neilson's work as part of it, enables a shift in emphasis away from content towards form and texture' (2007: 491).

In *Dissocia*, as elsewhere in his work, Neilson is concerned with characters that occupy the margins and with the affective staging of their subjective realities. His heroine, Lisa Jones, is suffering from a dissociative mental disorder that—because she refuses medication—allows her access to a simultaneously seductive and terrifying world inside her own head. Supporting characters, like those in *Realism*, sing and dance, adopt foreign accents, wear animal costumes and funny hats, return from the dead and exist only in the mind of the protagonist. As the play opens, we find Lisa at home in her flat dressed for an evening out with her boyfriend Vince. She is feeling depressed. After a brief hiatus she is visited by a diminutive Swiss watch-mender, Victor Hesse, a figure who 'bears more than a passing resemblance to how we imagine Sigmund Freud' (Neilson 2015: 26). Hesse has been attempting to fix Lisa's broken watch, and after assuring her there is nothing wrong with it, he offers her an unusual explanation for her persistently low mood. At some point on a flight across the Atlantic, he explains, she has lost an hour. She needs to journey immediately to the magical country of Dissocia to retrieve it and thus restore her equilibrium. Lisa's flat then transforms into an elevator, and she descends into a colourful and sometimes threatening new world where she spends the remainder of Act One. Eventually, Dissocia's inhabitants confess that the considerable energy generated by her missing hour is fuelling their country's existence. Without it, they insist, Dissocia will be destroyed by the forces of evil in the form of the Black Dog Army. As the act builds to its climax, an ominous rumbling in the distance signals the approach of the enemy. The Dissocians declare Lisa their Queen, vow to protect her and march bravely into battle, where they are all killed. Left alone on stage, Lisa watches '*helplessly in and fear and sorrow*' (2015: 94).

Finally, a '*shadowy figure emerges from the carnage*' (94). Lisa recognises him as the Black Dog King. We recognise him as her boyfriend Vince. The act ends in '*blackness*' (94).

Act Two unfolds in a private room in a secure mental hospital and consists of sixteen short scenes that chart the slow and painful progress of Lisa's recovery from the psychotic episode we now understand to be the substance of Act One. In the opening scene a nurse enters, gently nudges Lisa awake and administers medication. This action is repeated by a different nurse in the second scene and on five other occasions. In the third scene Lisa attempts to leave the hospital, insisting she is ready to go home and promising to take her medication. A nurse persuades her back to bed. The action continues much in this way with Lisa making incremental improvements and responding to her treatment variously with resentment, frustration and docility. In Scene Eleven she is visited by her sister Dot who is angry at her failure to take her medication, and accuses her of selfishness. In the penultimate scene, Vince visits. They have a difficult conversation about the recurring pattern of Lisa promising to take her medication, failing to do so, and ending up in hospital, but he agrees to pick her up from hospital at the weekend. In the final scene it is dark. Lisa is asleep. In her arms she holds a small polar bear. Eventually, we hear music and see coloured lights dancing around her head. '*Dissocia still exists*' the stage directions tell us, and we are left in '*little doubt that she will return to her kingdom*' (2015: 110).

Dissocia is an extraordinary play. Its innovative structure and pronounced theatricality combine to trouble received attitudes about its subject matter in ways that are genuinely progressive and unusual. Most obviously, by positioning us alongside his heroine rather than at an objective distance, Neilson disturbs preconceptions about the fundamental 'otherness' of those suffering from mental disorders. The play, as Anna Harpin has noted, 'reveals the world of Dissocia to the audience in the same instant that it is revealed to Lisa and in so doing aligns an audience's perspective with hers' (Harpin 2014: 195). Neilson also utilises a clash of theatrical styles to great effect. If joyful overabundance and a chaotic arrangement of signs are the dominant stylistic feature in Act One, Act Two is its '*polar opposite*', with '*no overt colour used in set design, costume or lighting*' (Neilson 2015: 95). It is characterised by silence, slowness and repetition and it thus purposefully removes the suspense from its own disclosure. No sounds are heard apart from footsteps which only occur before and after the scenes in which Lisa is medicated. This is in stark contrast to Act One which has a continuous and often riotously noisy soundtrack. The general muffledness was enhanced in Miriam Buether's design for the original production in which 'the hospital room was enclosed in a box, the front of which was clear Perspex' (Neilson 2015: 95). The actors were obliged to use microphones, and were thus able to speak in hushed tones. The multiplication of frames—the framed hospital room viewed within the frame of the proscenium arch—also troubled the illusion of the single frame on which dramatic theatre depends, and instead drew attention to the theatre's own representational forms and to how they are perceived. In purely theatrical terms, *Dissocia*'s effects rely considerably on the perceptible concentration and then dilution of signs. Act Two contains no flights of fancy and no jokes. Indeed, the play as a whole can be said to operate around a dialectic of semiotic surplus and famine. For John Bull, this is typical of Neilson's insistence on offering 'fantasy and uncertainty, where an audience conventionally seeks seriousness and fixity' (2011: 343). *Dissocia* is a play that asks us to think differently about mental illness. Neilson's innovation is in aligning our perspective so intimately with a person who cannot, as I have written elsewhere, 'conform to normality either in behaviour of thought, much as she might like to' (Reid, 2017: 85).

In *Dissocia* and *Realism,* Neilson privileges felt experience over culturally imposed notions of normality by staging—in a cocktail of memory, fantasy, nightmare and reality—the insides of his characters' heads. An almost complete absence of reference to contemporary Scottish political debates in these plays means that his work, like Harrower's, succeeds in qualifying reductive or essentialist constructions of Scottish identity. This is in no way to imply that contemporary Scottish theatre as a whole has avoided overt engagement with issues of national identity or abandoned its existing iconography. The extraordinary success of *Black Watch* demonstrates the continuing appeal of familiar martial and masculinist tropes. Burke and Tiffany had worked together successfully on *Gagarin Way* (2001), another play which featured an all-male cast but also drew on Fife's traditions of working-class militancy. Through bold politicisation of the thriller format—two disaffected factory workers take company executive hostage—*Gagarin Way* articulates the powerlessness and rage felt by workers across Scotland, as they witnessed industries and livelihoods being passed from Japanese to American hands without their consent or knowledge.

In the small Fife town of Lumphinnans, there is a street named in honour of Yuri Gagarin, the famous Russian cosmonaut. This naming, and that of Burke's play, references the area's long history as a centre for left-wing activism. In 1935 the communist Willie Gallacher was elected MP for the West Fife parliamentary constituency, a significant number of men volunteered for the International Brigade, and the Fife coalfields provided the environment for this radicalism to be kept alive. By the time Burke wrote his debut play, the mines had closed. In this context, David Pattie rightly notes that *Gagarin Way's* two kidnappers, Gary and Eddie, are versions of established 'Scottish character types' (2011: 25). Gary is the kind of militant left-wing activist familiar from plays like Bill Bryden's *Willie Rough* (1972) while Eddie is a working-class autodidact, whose characterisation draws on Scotland's longstanding reputation for high levels of literacy, and worker's education. They are joined by the recent politics graduate and security guard Tom, and Frank, the company executive who turns out not to be Japanese or American, but a local man who has become a rather reluctant global capitalist. All four are the sons or grandsons of miners. *Gagarin Way* is a high-octane darkly bleak comedy about the loss of political identity, status and agency. Burke adds complexity by making Gary an ineffective activist resigned to his own pointlessness, and Eddie a sadistic nihilist, who in the play's violent dénouement stabs both Tom and Frank. The two men have briefly deluded themselves into believing they can interrupt the course of capitalist history. *Gagarin Way* established Burke as an emerging talent, but its success was overshadowed by *Black Watch* five years later, and he has not written for the stage since *Hoors* (2009). In the next section, I consider the work of a younger group of writers, who came to attention more recently, and who have utilised more diverse performance modes.

Newer Voices

Rob Drummond's *Bullet Catch* (2012), while ostensibly dealing with an event in the past, owes much of its theatrical power to its mobilising of recent developments in participatory performance. It re-enacts the notorious 'bullet catch' trick, an illusion in which a magician appears to catch a bullet directly fired at him/her, as performed in 1912 by William Henderson, a gifted young illusionist and protégé of Houdini. Henderson handed a gun to a labourer who had been randomly selected from the audience. The gun misfired, Henderson was killed, and Garth, for that was the unfortunate labourer's name, found himself embroiled in a murder trial. In *Bullet Catch*, Drummond both narrates Henderson's story and plays him, while at each performance a different co-star, or Garth, is selected from the audience. The piece is thus a solo show for two performers that relies on audience participation.

The new century, as Jen Harvie observes, has witnessed the 'proliferation of performance and art practices that engage audiences socially — by inviting those audiences to participate' (2013: 1). It is worth paying attention to this trend because it raises interesting questions about how theatre-makers are engaging with shifting ideas about social relations. This is certainly the case in David Greig's larger experiments in participation *The Events* (2013)—in which every performance on tour is accompanied by a different community choir—and *The Suppliant Women* (2016)—which uses an amateur chorus of local women. In *Bullet Catch*, Drummond's investigation into Henderson's death, which may or may not have been suicide, becomes the means of exploring not only the trick, but larger questions about illusion, pretence, and physical and emotional risk. Although Drummond performs a number of impressive magic tricks in the course of the show, the most striking way the audience bears witness to the power of theatrical transformation is in watching the journey undertaken by the second member of the cast. This co-star is different in every performance, but his or her relationship with Drummond remains central because the climax to Henderson's story, and also Drummond's show, depends on Drummond convincing an audience member to shoot a loaded gun into his face. Occasionally, a volunteer refuses. Each performance of *Bullet Catch* therefore carries a potential risk of failure, or rather foregrounds the risk of failure that accompanies all live performance. The show won a Herald Angel and a Total Theatre Award at the Fringe in 2012.

Drummond is a Glasgow-based theatre-maker with a reputation as an innovator and as someone who immerses himself in his projects in a manner that might seem extreme. For his 2011 show *Wrestling*, he spent five months in training as a professional wrestler, for instance, and as a result of his preparation for *Bullet Catch*, is an extremely competent magician. His other theatre credits include *Mr Write* (2010), an improvised NTS show for teenagers, *Top Table* (2011), a dark comedy set at a wedding party in which the father of the bride gives the wedding speech from hell, *The Majority* (2017), in which the audience is invited to vote, and *Eulogy* (2018), a companion piece to *Top Table* in which the father of the bride has died and is submitted to character dissection by his surviving relatives. All of these shows have participatory elements. In 2013 Drummond's *Quiz Show*, a clever and disturbing take on the light entertainment industry of the 1970s, presumably written at least partly in response to the Jimmy Saville scandal, was produced at the Traverse. It went on to win a CATS for Best New Play in the following year.

Top Table and *Eulogy* were produced at Glasgow's Òran Mór, the venue for the lunchtime theatre club, A Play, a Pie and a Pint (PPP), which has become a major player in the development of new writing in Scotland. Founded in 2004 by David MacLennan, a veteran of 7:84 Scotland and Wildcat, PPP is Scotland's largest de facto commissioner of new plays, providing a relatively accessible training ground for emerging writers and directors, and also a platform for more established dramatists. In the last decade Òran Mór has hosted an average of 34 premieres, a year and has co-produced with the NTS, the Traverse, Paines Plough, Live Theatre Newcastle, Bewley's Dublin, Bristol Tobacco factory and Dundee Rep. Many of its premieres have transferred to other venues. When its first edited collection was published in 2020, PPP had produced an astounding 500 new plays. Its formula is by now tried and tested. For around £15, audience members get a 50-minute play, a pie, and a pint— or a vegan sausage roll and a glass of wine—all in the space of a lunch hour. More recently the success of PPP has attracted additional scrutiny. Because it was established on a shoe-string budget, a PPP contract covers a 'platforming' short of a full production, and consequently pays a lower fee. Should a PPP show be picked up by another theatre—which has happened more than once—a new fee might be negotiated, but the problem remains that Scotland's leading producer of new writing does not fully recompense its playwrights. Nonetheless, like many playwrights of his generation, Drummond has been well placed to benefit from McLennan's ground-breaking initiative, but he has also received support from elsewhere. In 2011, along with Kieran Hurley and Gary McNair he was selected for the NTS's inaugural Auteurs project. Conceived in collaboration with The Arches, the project was designed specifically to support the development of emerging Scottish theatre artists and was consequently tailored to meet individual needs. Hurley's *Rantin* (2013), which is discussed more fully in Chapter 5 of this book emerged from this project.

Hurley, who was the NTS's Pearson Playwright in Residence in 2013, made a significant impact with his monologue *Beats* (2012), a coming-of-age tale about the mid-1990s rave culture and the efforts of the establishment to suppress it, which toured the UK in 2013 and was made into a film directed by Brian Welsh in 2019. His earlier Fringe show *Hitch* (2010) used live music to accompany an autobiographical monologue about Hurley travelling, with little money or sense of direction, to the G8 conference in L'Aquila in 2009, pausing along the way to attend a Patti Smith concert in Rome. Like *Beats*, *Hitch* is relatively simple in structure, but it deals, with intelligence and subtlety, with a number of issues of striking relevance, particularly to young people. Like *Rantin*, it is about, among other things, the challenges of becoming politically engaged in an increasingly confused world; the kindness of strangers; the hesitancy one inevitably feels in a world so overwhelmingly large; and how one might connect with others and consequently make a meaningful contribution.

Hurley's *Heads Up* (2016), revives the minimalist aesthetic of *Beats*: Hurley sits alone at a desk and uses a sampler to accompany four intersecting monologues in which an office worker, a school girl, a barista, and a rock star deal with personal breakdown against the backdrop of the imminent end of the world. Both *Beats* and *Heads Up* won CATS for Best New Play. Hurley also writes plays for other people to perform: *Mouthpiece* (2018) is an extraordinarily acute two-hander, which details the relationship between Libby, a middle-aged Edinburgh playwright whose star has waned and Declan, the unemployed teenager she meets on Salisbury Crags, which are part of Arthur's Seat, and whose abject working-class life she exploits for the content of a new play that revives her career. In the play's dénouement Declan arrives at the Traverse—where the play about his life is being performed—and seizes control of the resolution from the playwright, insisting on his right not to end his own life for the entertainment of the middle-class audience. In this way the play adopts and then subverts the cultural trope of the abject working-class subject, which has dominated representation across a range of media for a number of years. Hurley's version of Ibsen's *An Enemy of the People* (2021) for the NTS and Dundee Rep, confirmed his commitment to advocacy.

If a range of perspectives on Scottish identity can be illuminated by close reading of the work of a further selection of younger playwrights, then Caithness-born Henry Adam provides an interesting starting point. In the first decade after devolution, his work engaged with notions of identity in a variety of scales. His first full-length play, *Among Unbroken Hearts* (2000), as Ian Brown observes, 'problematises the clash of cultures within traditional Scotland', by bringing the language and culture of the marginalised rural North East to the stage (2007: 324) Dealing explicitly with issues surrounding the efficacy and sustainability of regional identities within Scotland, *Among Unbroken Hearts* was particularly praised for its melancholic emotional intensity and the lyrical richness of its Doric dialect. It shared the 2002 Meyer-Whitworth Award with *Gagarin Way*. It tells of Ray, a young heroin addict who makes an ill-fated return to the far northeast after a prolonged urban sojourn. Its tone is melancholic and pessimistic: Ray's identity crisis is understood as the product of various interactions between self-absorption and immaturity on one hand and the appeal of his childhood landscape, language, and friendships on the other. Ultimately, he cannot escape the narcissistic cocoon of his own drug addiction and the play closes with the inevitable drugs overdose.

Issues of identity, tolerance and acceptance are again foregrounded in Adam's next major work, *The People Next Door* (2003) which offers a satirical, and often hilarious, examination of how paranoia about terrorism in the aftermath of 9/11 not only encourages excessive and counter-productive responses from the authorities, but warps relationships with neighbours and friends. Marooned in a block of housing association flats somewhere in London, Adam's characters exist on benefits. The narrative is simple enough. Nigel, a mixed-race British Asian on disability allowance, is harassed and blackmailed by Phil, a maverick gun-wielding, drug-taking policeman, who is convinced Nigel's estranged half-brother Karim is a terrorist. Coerced by Phil into spying at a local mosque, Nigel begins to acquire emotional stability. His newfound strength is drawn both from his encounter with Islam and his developing friendships with his neighbours, Marco, a black teenager neglected and physically abused by his mother, and Mrs Mac, an elderly Scottish widow who carries a poker in her handbag. Together the trio form an unlikely alliance, a family of sorts, and in an improbable utopian finale, manage to murder Phil and convince the police it was suicide. The play ends with the trio watching television together, in a scene of domestic contentment. The definition of family, offered here, is hybrid, inclusive and essentially optimistic. *The People Next Door* won the inaugural CATS Award for Best Play.

A number of other voices from the North East have made themselves heard in the post-devolutionary period. Matthew Zajac's *The Tailor of Inverness* (2008), produced by his Dingwall-based company Dogstar, explores the ambiguities inherent in sustaining more than one identity by making use of Zajac's Polish father's personal history as a soldier, migrant and refugee during and in the aftermath of WW2 and Zajac won Best Male Performance at the 2009 CATS for his work as the title character. Around the same time, Morna Pearson's short play *Distracted* (2006) won the Meyer-Whitworth Award for new writing in 2007, and immediately established her as an acute, if idiosyncratic, observer of her native North East. Her portrayal of a boy scarred by the death of his drug addict mother, living in a caravan park with his domineering grandmother and a lascivious neighbour, is as vivid as it is tender. Pearson was born in Elgin in Morayshire, and her most successful play to date has been *The Artist Man and the Mother Woman* (2012). Like *Distracted*, this full-length play deals with intergeneration tension and evidenced Pearson's flair for a kind of dark, skewed poetry rooted in her local dialect. Mark Fisher commented on Pearson's ability to root 'doric poetry in a disturbingly credible world' (2012). An indicator of the esteem in which Pearson was already held, was evidenced by the fact the Traverse production was directed by Orla O'Loughlin in her first show as Artistic Director of the theatre.

Edie, the mother woman of the play's title, is a disturbing mixture of middle-aged sensuality and smugness, outwardly serene, but vicious when thwarted. She imposes total domestic control and is extremely hostile to the exposure of her son to anything of a sexual nature, preferring to keep him permanently infantilised. 'Mither pulled me ooto French classes at school', he recalls, she 'telt the heidmaster the language wid corrupt my innocence. I wis allowed tae dae mair art instead' (Pearson, 2012: 32). Unsurprisingly, although already in his thirties, the unfortunate Geoffrey, who now works as an artist and teacher, is a stranger to his own passions. The status quo is disrupted when, while in the local Sainsbury's, he runs into Evelyn, an attractive former pupil. Thereafter, Edie and Geoffrey's domestic situation becomes increasingly fraught as the latter attempts to break free. For Danièle Berton-Charrière this central relationship functions in Pearson's play as a metaphor for all 'unnatural unions leading to stifling and painful existences' and for 'domineering/dominated couples' locked in unhealthy power dynamics (2015: 79). In a play that mixes moments of grotesque comedy, hyper-realism and finally horror, Geoffrey's obsession with Evelyn leads to a restraining order and a violent dénouement in which Evelyn is brutally murdered by Edie. This disastrous outcome puts an end to Geoffrey's bid for freedom and the final scenes mirror the opening ones while simultaneously inverting the power dynamic between mother and son. Geoffrey, by now accused of the murder, remains trapped at home, looking after his deranged mother.

More recently Morna Young has emerged as another significant voice from the North East. Born in Elgin by the Moray coast, she was just five years old when her crewman father fell overboard from a trawler in the Norwegian sector of the North Sea. His body was never recovered. Her first full-length play, *Lost at Sea* (2019), is an elegy, not just to her father, but 'to all the other men and boats who've been lost from Burghead and all the other coastal towns over the years' (Young, quoted in Alexander, 2019). Young's fictional protagonist, Shona, is the journalist daughter of a fisherman lost at sea, who returns to her home village in search of answers about the death of her father. There she encounters the deep-rooted reticence typical of communities that have long been obliged to absorb grief and hardship. Young's thematic backdrop covers the continuing struggle to ensure the survival of fragile fishing communities, the temptation faced by fishermen in the 1980s, when there were enormous sums of money to be made working lengthy trips in dangerous conditions, and the age-old struggle with the sea itself. In Joyce McMillan's view, *Lost at Sea* is 'more like a chorale than a conventional drama' (2019). Its twenty-two scenes include interpersonal and familial exchanges, and material drawn from interviews conducted by Young, but the action is overseen by the quasi-mythical figure of the Skipper, who summons discrete characters from the nine strong Chorus which acts as '*the voice of the community, of the ocean, of the dead*' (Young, 2019: 14). As if to stress this community aspect, in the final scene the Chorus lists the names of Scottish fishermen men lost at sea, beginning with Young's father: 'Donnie Young, 43, Lost from the "Ardent II", 1989' (Young, 2019: 107). With its extensive use of music and folk song, its ensemble cast, its populism and its radical sincerity, *Lost at Sea* continues a long tradition in working-class drama about uncelebrated Scottish communities, which stretches back as far as *Joe Corrie's In Time O' Strife* (1926). Ian Brown's production won Best Ensemble at the 2020 CATS.

It is impossible to close this section about playwrights from the North East without mentioning Rona Munro, of course, who is by some distance the most established playwright from the region. Long before garnering international acclaim for *The James Plays*, Munro emerged as an important figure, coming to prominence, and winning the Evening Standard Most Promising Playwright Award with *Bold Girls* (1991), which tells the story of three Belfast women against the backdrop of the Troubles. Munro's work has since focused substantially if not exclusively on female experience. In *The Last Witch* (2009), she gives a fictional account of the life of Janet Horne, who in 1727 became the last woman to be burned as a witch in Scotland. Set in the village of Dornoch in Sutherland, the play imagines Janet as a strong, willful and eccentric fantasist and the superstitious and claustrophobic community that turns on her as profoundly misogynistic. For Lyn Gardner, in Munro's re-imagining, the devil 'appears in many guises, but all of them male' (2009). In particular, the expression of female sexual desire—for Janet is free with her favours—provokes a disproportionally violent male response and in this regard *The Last Witch* echoes Munro's earlier play *The Maiden Stone* (1995) which draws on and inverts local myths of chastity to attack the demonisation of female sexuality. In terms of her current profile, Munro is most closely associated with the contemporary Scottish history play. She has extended her exploration of the medieval Stuart dynasty with *James IV: Queen of the Fight* (2022) and *Mary* (2022). The former, which was commissioned by the NTS, traces the impact of the arrival of two Moorish women, Lady Anne and Lady Ellen, at the fifteenth-century Scottish court, and the latter is a less expansive closet drama about the systematic dismantling of the reputation of *Mary Queen of Scots* during her own lifetime, in which Mary herself does not appear. September 2023 saw an announcement of the next play in the series, *James V: Katherine*, which will be produced in 2024, and will again shift focus away from the male monarch, this time onto the figure of Katherine Hamilton, sister of Patrick Hamilton, Scotland's first martyr of the Reformation who was burnt at the stake for heresy in St Andrews in 1528. Munro's continued reframing and destabilising of the myths of Scottish history thus continues unabated.

Munro is not the only Scottish playwright to have begun a career in the 1980s and to continue to command major Scottish stages. Among veterans of the 1985 Traverse season, Peter Arnott, Jo Clifford and to a lesser extent Chris Hannan have returned to prominence after a hiatus in the 1990s, when, according to Steve Cramer 'the need to develop the new generation manifested itself' and the spotlight fell on Greig and Harrower (2011: 176).

The Old Guard

Peter Arnott's *Group Portrait in a Summer Landscape*, which arrived on the stages of Pitlochry Festival Theatre and the Lyceum in Edinburgh in the autumn of 2023, looks back almost a decade to the summer of 2014, and the feverish atmosphere of heightened political engagement that surrounded the upcoming independence referendum. It is set in the Perthshire country house of an affluent couple: George Rennie, a charismatic academic on the brink of retirement, and his disaffected wife Edie. Jessica Worrell's set is limited to a few pieces of tastefully expensive looking furniture in front of a large expanse of rolling Perthshire countryside, which dominates throughout. The setting, like the drama it forms the backdrop to, is recognisably Chekhovian. Conversations are erudite. Relationships are fraught and tangled. Everyone is a little jaded and time passes slowly. 'There wasn't a book in the house' one character recalls of his earlier visits 'that wasn't worth reading ... and a lot of them were signed by the folk that wrote them' (Arnott, 2023: 7).

A party has been arranged to celebrate George's retirement and the couple is joined by their daughter Emma, a London-based art curator, two of George's former students, Frank and Charlie, both of whom have previously been involved with Emma and are accompanied by their current partners, and finally Jimmy Moon, an ageing actor and Edie's gay best friend. As old tensions rise to the surface, characters sit around drinking wine and arguing about politics, jazz, the meaning of life, and the disappointments of the past. George is disappointed his daughter never finished her Cambridge degree; Jimmy is disappointed Edie gave up a promising acting career; Frank still carries a torch for Emma who may still carry a torch for Charlie; George and Edie are more or less estranged. Hovering over proceedings, visible to the audience, and the reason for the couple's estrangement, is their son Will, who some fifteen years ago died of a massive brain aneurism. As the play opens in the kitchen of the summer house '*Will, a ghost, forever 19, is haunting*' his mother (Arnott, 2023: 1). The ghost literalises the impact of the past on the present, and the weight of grief at his passing, especially for Edie, inhibits meaningful engagement with the present, and by extension the future. 'Do you want to be alright?', Will asks his mother in the play's penultimate scene (69):

> Do you want to go back downstairs in a minute ... where they're washing the dishes ... and find out what everyone's laughing at ... Or do you want

to stay up here with me. Do you want them to come and find you in half an hour or so. Because you can't take me down there with you mum. You can stay with me or you can go to them (69).

The revelation that George has arranged the gathering to announce he has pancreatic cancer which has metastasised, and that consequently he intends to take steps to end his own life, raises the stakes around the need for reconciliation with the past and heightens the sense of a family at a crossroads. In production, the Perthshire hills, ancient and beautiful, provided an additional temporal frame.

Group Portrait in a Summer Landscape was billed as a 'bold, funny and deeply thoughtful play about family and the forces that shaped the country we live in today' (Pitlochry Festival Theatre, 2023). While most reviewers agreed with the first half of this statement, and referenced Chekov by way of comparison, some were less sure about the second. For Joyce McMillan, for example, the play failed to link 'the demise of the Rennies to the questions raised by the Scottish independence referendum of that summer', or at least to make the link sufficiently explicit (2023). The imminent vote is discussed, some characters are Yes, some No, some ambivalent and some undecided. Perhaps it is the atmosphere of elegiac indeterminacy that pervades the production, that is its most striking achievement. It offers no easy answers, and in this respect, it accurately reflects the political situation in Scotland at the end of 2023, where support for independence is at times polling at 53% but no clear path to achieving another referendum appears viable.

Arnott's other major successes of recent years include an adaptation of Compton Mackenzie's 1941 satirical novel *The Monarch of the Glen* for Pitlochry Festival Theatre, which won the CATS Award for Best New Play in 2018. Like Mackenzie's novel, Arnott's adaptation features bagpipes, bens, glens, tartan and a laird, Sir Donald McDonald of Macdonald who, with the assistance of his friend and neighbour Killwhillie, hatches a scheme to extract money for the building of a golf course from a wealthy American tourist, Chester Royde. In Ken Harrison's design, the Pitlochry stage is festooned with tartan like 'a badly furnished Highland hotel' and the ensuing chaos involves a love triangle and a clash between the landowners and a group of socialist hikers (Cooper, 2017). Insurgent Scottish nationalism in the form of the Glasgow poet and architect Alan Macmillan is pitted against the laird himself, who is a staunch unionist widely known by his nickname, Ben Nevis. MacDonald's butler Prew acts as a sardonic narrator, and the whole thing is delivered with gusto and heightened levels of self-awareness.

Arnott's plays *Tay Bridge* (2019) and *The Signalman* (2019) are much more serious in tone and intent. Inspired by conversations with the actor Tom McGovern, they each revisit the Tay Bridge disaster of December 1879 when, during a violent storm, the bridge collapsed while a North British Railways passenger train was crossing, killing all on board. Rather than exploring the causes or aftermath of the disaster, Arnott's first play takes the form of a series of vignettes, featuring passengers travelling in what Mark Fisher evocatively describes as a 'ghost-train-in-waiting' (2019). Arnott's characters—the servant; the predatory womaniser; the American salesman; the pair of young lovers; the minister's wife—ostensibly share little but their fate, but their composite stories reveal much about the economic and moral inequities, of Victorian Dundee. The audience's certain knowledge of their shared fate gives the whole piece a powerfully mournful quality.

The Signalman is *Tay Bridge's* companion piece. Forty years after the disaster Thomas Barclay sits in his signal box on the south side of the bridge and looks back on that fateful night when as a young man of twenty-four, he waved the ill-fated train through. Utilising the monologue form—Barclay was played by Tom McGovern in an award-winning tour de force—and drawing on transcripts of the public inquiry into the disaster, Arnott unpacks the investigators' obsession with allocating blame, and Barclay's acute awareness that had things played out differently, he might easily have become their preferred scapegoat. This theme has obvious contemporary resonances, but *The Signalman* also works extremely powerfully as a rumination on fate and the futility of the search for meaning in the face of catastrophe. Speaking from his vantage point in 1919 in the immediate aftermath of the Great War, Barclay's bleak conclusions linger long after the play closes, they:

> … just happened to be on that train that night … just visiting their parents … or just coming back tae work after the weekend … It means nothing, naebiddy chose them … naebiddy punished them … it doesnae mean a bloody thing'. (Arnott, 2019: 60)

The Signalman also won the CATS Award for Best New Play, and McGovern Best Male Performance.

Arnott is not the only playwright produced in the Traverse 85 season to continue to make an impact. Chris Hannan's *The Three Musketeers and the Princess of Spain* (2010) was lauded as the best Christmas show for years when it arrived on the stage of the Traverse, and it picked up a CATS for Best New Play. However, Jo Clifford has arguably made a more sustained and nuanced contribution. She is by now an elder stateswoman of Scottish theatre. The author of over 100 plays, many of which have been performed internationally, she is also a translator and adaptor of considerable experience. Most recently, her 1998 translation of Pedro Calderón de la Barca's Golden Age drama, *Life is a Dream*, was revived to rave reviews in 2021 at the Lyceum in Edinburgh. Originally programmed for 2020, the production was chosen to mark the theatre's re-opening to the public and it proved a tour de force, and a reminder that translation and adaptation continue to be key elements in Scotland's theatre ecology. A summary of Calderón's great play is perhaps useful here since some readers may not be familiar with it.

Life is a Dream (1636) is a philosophical and political allegory. Basilio, the fictional King of Poland is an astrologer and mathematician who has his son, Segismundo, imprisoned in a tower from birth because he has predicted through a horoscope that the prince will eventually become a tyrant, bringing chaos to the kingdom and shame upon his father. Early in the play Basilio designs a test to prove the accuracy of his horoscope. While asleep Segismundo is brought to his father's castle and the court is ordered to treat him as the crowned prince. Exposed to luxury, power and freedom for the first time, Segismundo behaves outrageously. 'Naturally', as Mark Fisher observes, in Clifford's translation as in the original, 'the brutality of his upbringing turns him into exactly the monster his mother feared' (2021). He is duly returned to the tower, again while in a drug-induced sleep and on waking is convinced, by his jailer Clotaldo, that the interlude in the palace was merely a dream. However, this dream-as-deception plot devised by Basilio to justify his actions becomes something else for Segismundo. From the time of his second awakening, he begins to understand human existence as an experience to be lived according to the metaphor 'life is a dream'. Subsequently, when the people learn the truth about Basilio's legitimate heir, they revolt and make Segismundo their leader. Instead of humiliating his father as predicted in the original horoscope, Segismundo acknowledges Basilio's position as his father and king and Basilio is then ready to accept his son's right to the succession. Calderón's play is consciously metaphoric and therefore intrinsically poetic.

The Lyceum production brought together some of Scotland's most accomplished theatre-makers. A thrust stage was constructed that reached into the auditorium, covering the stalls, and allowing a section of the audience to be seated behind the proscenium. In this way 'boundaries between performers and spectators, between real and imaginary' were effectively blurred and a familiar space was made strange (Brennan 2021). Foregrounding the play's theme of the relationship between reality and the imagination, the costumes utilised a dressing-up-box aesthetic—'part underwear, part punk-royalty'—and characters moved in and out of character in full view of the audience. Kai Fischer's ravishing golden lighting design was accompanied by a 'haunting musical soundtrack co-ordinated by Davey Anderson' (McMillan, 2021). Rave reviews were followed by a strong showing at the CATS. For his work in the role of Segismundo, Lorn Macdonald lifted the award for Best Male Performance, Wils Wilson won Best Director, and Georgia McGuinness, Alex Berry and Kai Fischer, design awards for set, costume and lighting respectively. In the confidence of its execution and its ambitious scope, *Life is a Dream* was generally welcomed as a superb showcase for Scottish theatre as it emerged from the darkness of the pandemic. In my next, and concluding chapter, I turn to some of the new imperatives that have shaped theatre and performance in the last decade. These include a renewed awareness of the history and continuing legacies of racial injustice, gender inequality and LGBTQ+ rights.

References

Alexander, Michael (2019) 'Lost at Sea: Why the Loss of Her Trawlerman Father Inspired Playwright Morna Young to Become a Writer'. *Courier*, 8 April.

Arnott, Peter (2019) *Two Plays: Tay Bridge, The Signalman*. London, Salamander Street.

Arnott, Peter (2023) *Group Portrait in a Summer Landscape*. London, Salamander Street.

Berton-Charrière, Danièle (2015) 'Irony and the Construction of Scottish Memory and Identity in Contemporary Plays'. *International Journal of Scottish Theatre and Screen* 8:2, pp. 73–90.

Brennan, Clare (2021) 'Life is A Dream review'. *Observer*, 7 November.

Brown, Georgina (2006) 'Blackbird Review'. *Mail on Sunday*, 19 February.

Brown, Ian (2007) 'Alternative Sensibilities: Devolutionary Comedy and Scottish Camp' in Berthold Schoene (ed.) *The Edinburgh Companion to Contemporary Scottish Literature*. Edinburgh, Edinburgh University Press, pp. 319–327.

Brown, Ian (2013) 'More to Come: Forty Years of the Scottish Society of Playwrights'. *Edinburgh Review*, 137, pp. 90–99.

Brown, Mark (2019) *Modernism and Scottish Theatre Since 1969*. London, Palgrave Macmillan.

Bull, John (2011) 'Anthony Neilson', in Middeke, Martin, Peter Paul Schnierer and Aleks Sierz (eds.) *The Methuen Drama Guide to Contemporary British Playwrights*. London, Bloomsbury, pp. 343–362.

Cooper, Neil (2017) 'Monarch of the Glen review'. *Herald*, 30 October.

Cramer, Steve (2011) 'The Traverse, 1985-97', in Ian Brown (ed.) *The Edinburgh Companion to Scottish Drama*. Edinburgh, Edinburgh University Press, pp. 165–176.

De Jongh, Nicholas (2006) 'Blackbird Review'. *Evening Standard*, 14 February.

Devine, Tom (2006) *The Scottish Nation: 1700-2007*. London, Penguin.

Diamond, Elin, Denise Varney and Candace Amich (eds.) (2017) *Performance, Feminism and Affect in Neoliberal Times*. Basingstoke, Palgrave.

Edgar, David (1999) (ed.) *State of Play: Playwrights on Playwriting*. London, Faber and Faber.

Fisher, Mark (2012) 'The Artist Man and the Mother Woman review'. *Guardian*, 8 November.

Fisher, Mark (2019) 'Tay Bridge Review: Adventurous Story of Ghost-Train-in-Waiting' *Guardian*, 2 September.

Fisher, Mark (2021) 'Life is a Dream Review'. *Guardian*, 3 November.

Gardner, Lyn (2009) 'The Last Witch'. *Guardian*, 25 August.

Gardner, Lyn (2011) 'The Wheel Review'. *Guardian*, 11 August.

Greig, David (2002) *Outlying Islands*. London, Faber and Faber.

Greig, David (2003) *San Diego*. London, Faber and Faber.

Greig, David (2010) 'Pyrenees' in *David Greig: Plays 1*. London Faber and Faber, pp. 233–339.

Greig, David (2011) *The Strange Undoing of Prudencia Hart*. London, Faber and Faber.

Harpin, Anna (2013) 'Unremarkable Violence: Staging Child Sexual Abuse in Recent British Theatre'. *Contemporary Theatre Review*, 23:2, pp. 166-181.

Harpin, Anna (2014) 'Dislocated: Metaphors of Madness in British Theatre', in Anna Harpin and Juliet Foster (eds) *Performance, Madness and Psychiatry: Isolated Acts*. Basingstoke: Palgrave Macmillan, pp. 187–215.

Harris, Zinnie (2017) Meet Me at Dawn. London, Faber and Faber.

Harris, Zinnie (2019) 'Further Than The Furthest Thing', in Zinnie Harris: Plays 1. London, Faber and Faber, pp. 3–160.

Harrower, David (2013) *Ciara*. London, Faber and Faber.

Hart, Katie (2023) *Re-imagining Scotland: Scottish Women's Cultural Leadership in the Theatre Sector 2011–2021*. Unpublished PhD thesis. Available at: https://theses.gla.ac.uk/83520/

Harvie, Jen (2013) *Fair Play: Art, Performance and Neoliberalism*. Basingstoke, Palgrave.

Holdsworth, Nadine (2020) *English Theatre and Social Abjection: A Divided Nation*. London, Palgrave Macmillan.

Maguire, Tom (2011) 'Women Playwrights', in Ian Brown (ed.) *The Edinburgh Companion to Scottish Drama*. Edinburgh, Edinburgh University Press, pp. 154–164.

McCrone, David (2001) *Understanding Scotland: The Sociology of a Nation*. Second edition. Edinburgh, Edinburgh University Press.

McMillan, Joyce (2019) 'Lost at Sea, Perth Theatre'. *Scotsman*, 29 April.

McMillan, Joyce (2021) 'Life is a Dream review'. *Scotsman*, 5 November.

McMillan, Joyce (2023) 'Theatre Reviews: Group Portrait in a Summer Landscape' *Scotsman*, I September.

Nadine Holdsworth (2008) 'The Landscape of Contemporary Scottish Drama: Place, Politics and Identity', in Holdsworth, Nadine and Mary Luckhurst (eds.) *A Concise Companion to British and Irish Drama*. Oxford: Blackwell, pp. 125–141.

Nairn, Tom (2000) *After Britain: New Labour and the Return of Scotland*. London, Granta.

Neilson, Anthony (2015) *The Wonderful World of Dissocia*. London, Bloomsbury.

Pattie, David (2008) 'Mapping the Territory: Modern Scottish Drama', in D'Monté, R. and Saunders, G. (eds.) *Cool Britannia? British Political Drama in the 1990s*. Basingstoke, Palgrave Macmillan, pp. 143–157.

Pattie, David (2011), 'Gregory Burke', in Middeke, Martin, Peter Paul Schnierer and Aleks Sierz (eds.) *The Methuen Drama Guide to Contemporary British Playwrights*. London, Bloomsbury, pp. 22–41.

Pearson, Morna (2012) *The Artist Man and the Mother Woman*. London, Methuen.

Pitlochry Festival Theatre (2023) 'Group Portrait in a Summer Landscape'. Available at: https://pitlochryfestivaltheatre.com/whats-on/group-portrait-in-a-summer-landscape/

Playwright's Studio Scotland (2023) 'About Us'. Available at: https://playwrightsstudio.co.uk/about-us-2

Rebellato, Dan (2016) 'Local Hero: The Places of David Greig'. *Contemporary Theatre Review*, 26:1, pp. 9–18.

Reid, Trish (2007) '"Deformities of the Frame": The Theatre of Anthony Neilson' *Contemporary Theatre Review*, 17:4, pp. 487–498.

Reid, Trish (2017) *The Theatre of Anthony Neilson*. London, Bloomsbury.

Reinelt, Janelle (2011) 'David Greig', in Martin Middeke, Peter Paul Schnierer and Aleks Sierz (eds.) *The Methuen Drama Guide to Contemporary British Playwrights*. London, Bloomsbury, pp. 203–222.

Rodríguez, Verónica (2019) *David Greig's Holed Theatre: Globalization, Ethics and the Spectator*. Cham, Palgrave Macmillan.

Scullion, Adrienne (1995), 'Feminine Pleasures and Masculine Indignities' in Christopher Whyte (ed.) *Gendering the Nation: Studies in Modern Scottish Literature*. Edinburgh, Edinburgh University Press, pp. 169–204.

Scullion, Adrienne (2007) 'Devolution and Drama' in Schoene, B (ed.) *The Edinburgh Companion to Contemporary Scottish Literature*. Edinburgh, Edinburgh University Press, pp. 68–77.

Sierz, Aleks (2001) *In-Yer-Face Theatre: British Drama Today*. London, Faber and Faber.

Six, Anna (2023) 'Introduction: Will the Real Anthony Neilson Please Stand Up?', in Anna Six, Anthony Neilson (ed.) *The Wonderful World of Dissocia*. London, Bloomsbury, pp. 1–26.

Spencer, Charles (2006) 'Blackbird Review'. *Daily Telegraph*, 14 February.

Svitch, Caridad (2008) 'Ordinary Sites of Transgression (review)' in *PAJ A Journal of Performance and Art*, 30:2, pp. 88–92.

Wallace, Clare (2011) 'David Harrower', in Middeke, Martin, Peter Paul Schnierer and Aleks Sierz (eds.) *The Methuen Drama Guide to Contemporary British Playwrights*. London, Bloomsbury, pp. 243–262.

Wallace, Clare (2013) *The Theatre of David Greig*. London, Bloomsbury.

Young, Morna (2019) *Lost at Sea*. London, Oberon Books.

Young, Toby (2002) 'Stitching Review'. *Spectator*, 24 August.

Zaroulia, Marilena (2011) '"What's Missing Is My Place in the World": The Utopian Dramaturgy of David Greig', in Muller, Anja and Clare Wallace (eds.) *Cosmotopia: Transnational Identities in David Greig's Theatre*. Prague, Univerzita Karlova v Praze, pp. 32–49.

CHAPTER 7

New Imperatives

In 2009 Zinnie Harris produced a historically displaced version of Ibsen's *A Doll's House* for the Donmar Warehouse which was revived at the Lyceum in Edinburgh in a co-production with the NTS in 2013. Her interest in the play is shared by Stef Smith, a younger female playwright whose 2019 version *Nora: A Doll's House*, features three Noras situated within three different time periods: 1918, 1968 and 2018. Each of Smith's Noras is walking a tight rope between the dominant gender politics of her time and the promise of freedom. In 1918 she is preparing to vote for the first time, for instance, while in 1968 she is just about able to apply for her own credit card. Meanwhile, 2018 Nora is attempting to reconcile her own experience of entrapment by her husband with the revelations of #metoo. Smith's Noras are also, as in Ibsen's famous play, trapped by economic circumstances and the playwright uses this recurring theme of financial dependency and precarity to demonstrate how women's agency continues to be limited. Feminist and anti-capitalist critiques thus come together powerfully in Smith's reworking. Tom Piper's set for the original production at Tramway featured three door frames, 'three pairs of chairs and, above, three frames marking different eras in iron, concrete and LED' (Fisher 2019a). In this space three Noras dressed in claret play their part in the centuries-long struggle for women's liberation, and in so doing expose some of the ways gender politics have changed over the last hundred years or so, and more importantly how they have not. As their respective doors slam, they remain resolute. 'Because we are angry', Nora 1 explains in the play's closing sequence, because 'we are fucking furious' adds Nora 2, 'we are coming for your daughters, your sisters, your mothers [and] your lovers', concludes Nora 3, and 'we won't stop' (2019: 95).

Smith came to prominence with the Edinburgh Fringe production *Roadkill* (2010), a site-specific piece about human trafficking which begins on a bus and drives its audience to an ordinary house, which is being used as a brothel. We follow the story of Mary, a 13-year-old Nigerian girl, forced to work as a prostitute after being lured to the city by her 'auntie' Martha. Conceived and directed by Cora Bissett, *Roadkill* is an extraordinarily affecting and effective piece of theatre, and it won an array of awards including a Fringe First, Best Production at CATS 2011, and the Olivier for Best Production at an Affiliate Theatre when it transferred to London in 2012. Elsewhere, Smith's work reflects the preoccupations of its time, especially in its focus on gender politics and female empowerment. *Nora* was shortlisted for the Susan Smith Blackburn Prize, the world's oldest prize for female playwrights, and in 2022 Smith won Best Writer at the Royal Television Awards for her BBC Scotland mini-series *Float*, a coming-of-age lesbian love story, and a 'rare depiction of LGBT+ relationships in small town Scotland' (Ferguson 2021). Read alongside Harris', Smith's work provides a snapshot of the richness and diversity of Scottish women's writing for the stage which has been in good health in the new century. Women playwrights and performance makers of particular significance, some of whom have already been mentioned, include Cora Bisset, Jo Clifford, Isla Cowan, Sue Glover, Maryam Hamidi, Jackie Kay, Hannah Lavery, Eilidh Loan, Isobel McArthur, Nicola McCartney, Linda McLean, Rona Munro, Morna Pearson, Frances Poet, Julia Taudevin, Jenna Watt and Morna Young.

When considered alongside other events such as Jackie Wylie's appointment at the NTS, the success of these women, is indicative of a larger shift in Scotland's theatre sector towards greater gender equality. Two recent reports commissioned by the Edinburgh-based intersectional feminist theatre company Stellar Quines provide hard evidence to support this claim. The second of these, *Where are the women? Part 2*, was published by Christine Hamilton Consulting in July 2020 following 'a similar exercise that examined women in creative roles in Scottish theatre in 2014/15' (Hamilton 2020: 5). The first research project drew on data collected from twenty-four companies and the second from twenty-six. The resulting reports consequently offer some useful comparisons against which progress can be measured. In some areas, it was minimal. In the year to July 2020, 41% of commissioned playwrights were women, for example, as opposed to 39% in 2014/15, and women directed 48% rather than 47% of shows (Hamilton 2020: 5). Elsewhere the picture was more encouraging. In 2020, half of Scotland's twenty-six publicly funded theatre companies were artistically led solely by women, an increase of 33% in 2015 when only four out of twenty-four had female Artistic Directors. Moreover, in 2020 48% of creative roles across all categories went to women, which represents an improvement of 9% on 2014/15. This data, as Hamilton concludes 'suggests that in term of opportunities for women Scottish theatre is, by some way, in a better position in terms of this measure of equality than similar organisations in England and in some other European countries' (Hamilton 2020: 5).

While some of the statistics above are undoubtedly encouraging, like Hamilton, I want to resist the idea that struggles for gender equality in Scottish theatre are over. The statistics only tell part of the story. At the time of writing, of the country's six most generously subsidised producing theatres beyond the NTS, only Pitlochry Festival Theatre is currently run by a woman, Elizabeth Newman, although Jemima Levick—formerly of Stellar Quines and currently of A Play, a Pie and a Pint—will become Artistic Director of the Tron Theatre in Glasgow in April 2024. Dundee Rep, Edinburgh's Lyceum and Traverse, and the Citizens in Glasgow are all run by men. Moreover, Harris' CATS win for Best New Play, with this *Restless House*, was also something of an outlier. Since the award was inaugurated in 2003, only one other woman has won: Ursula Rani Sarma for *The Dark Things* (2009). Women thus account for 5% of winners in the category, a percentage equalled by four male playwrights, Peter Arnott, David Greig, David Harrower and Kieran Hurley, all of whom have won twice. Harris remains the only female playwright based in Scotland to have won the award.

In the summer of 2017 Harris took centre stage at the EIF with three shows. *This Restless House* was revived and the EIF also programmed a new Harris play, *Meet Me at Dawn* (2017) at the Traverse, and a version of Ionesco's *Rhinoceros*, adapted by Harris for a co-production with DOT Theatre, Istanbul. That year the EIF programme also included Glasgow-based Vox Motus' *Flight*, an adaptation by Oliver Emmanuel of Caroline Brothers' novel *Hinterland* (2012) about two orphaned Afghan boys and their journey across Europe towards a 'better' life in London. The production, which has since toured extensively, utilises Vox Motus' signature immersive storytelling approach, which relies on beautifully rendered visuals: co-artistic director Jamie Harrison created the magic and illusion for *Harry Potter and the Cursed Child* which has been running at London's Palace Theatre since June 2016. *Flight* is very different in scale.

Seated in individual booths and through a succession of little windows, audience members watch Aryan and Kabir, recreated as tiny model figures, undertake their arduous, desperate and hazardous journey by way of a series of tableau in an exquisitely crafted diorama. Mark Melville's sound design, which is experienced via headphones, includes pre-recorded dialogue and original music. *Flight* is 'rendered on a Lilliputian scale' and requires 'you to do nothing but watch and listen' and perhaps lean in, as the boys are treated as slave-labour in an orange grove, marvel at the hustle and bustle of Athens, or are stashed away in a refrigerated meat truck (Collins-Hughes 2018). For Michael Billington, Emanuel's adoption of 'a studiously non-political tone' and his refusal to situate 'the story in the wider context of the global refugee crisis' is a source of frustration, but I think this is to miss the point (2017). It is precisely the forced passivity, the isolation, which intensifies our experience of a show which not only, as Nathan Jones observes, 'conveys more about those who make the journey than has been managed by years of often unsympathetic press coverage' but also heightens our awareness of our own lack of political agency and the ways in which the suffering of others has become a kind of ambient background noise to privileged Western lives (2021). *Flight* is an intimate Scottish show about a global crisis.

In the run up to and aftermath of devolution, Scottish theatre-makers continued to be animated, like theatre-makers elsewhere, by emerging global crises including the effects of the financial crash of 2007—especially austerity—mass-migration, the climate emergency, the global pandemic and a renewed awareness of the continuing legacies of racial injustice and gender inequality, as well as by constitutional questions and issues of Scottish identity. These crises have developed against the backdrop of rapid technological advance which has also impacted the sector. Scottish theatre-makers have responded to these pressures in inventive and creative ways, often focusing on misfits, outsiders and the marginalised, while moving between local and global concerns. My argument in this book has been that, taken as whole, their practice has provided a useful antidote to some of the underlying discourses of Scottish nationalism which might, if left unchallenged, tend towards the ethnocentric or exclusive. By engaging with other discourses of identity like class, gender, race and disability, theatre-makers have insisted that, if we are to be honest about the idea of post-devolutionary Scotland developing a new non-threatening brand of nationalism, one that accommodates both the country's internal plurality and its ambition towards international engagement, we must carefully consider how these positive ambitions are culturally animated and not simply take them for granted. In this context, it is crucial not to ignore the gap between progressive rhetoric and the reality on the ground. In this concluding chapter, I want to think about the question of contemporary Scotland as a community, how it is constituted and how Scotland's theatre-makers have variously celebrated and problematised it. My first example is *Scenes for Survival* (2020), a series of short digital artworks co-created by the NTS and BBC Scotland during lockdown which deals variously with themes of isolation and precarity, and as we might expect given the context, with notions of community under pressure.

SCENES FOR SURVIVAL

Until 2020 digital performance had been a small if significant area within the wider field of theatre and performance in Scotland, however, when the COVID-19 crisis obliged theatres to close, digital practices moved swiftly into the mainstream where they have remained. For many theatres this was straightforwardly a matter of increasing the amount of streaming they engaged in, or of engaging in streaming for the first time, but the activity quickly moved beyond streaming previously recorded productions online, or indeed live productions from empty theatres. The pandemic was a state of exception which reproduced, materialised and intensified—from the individual to the population as a whole—the dominant forms of biopolitical management already operating over sexual, racial or class minorities. In Scotland the management of the COVID-19 crisis staged an idea of community but, as elsewhere, it also revealed society's immunitary fantasies.

As its title suggests, *Scenes for Survival* was in part a creative response to theatres being closed and theatre workers experiencing varying degrees of often extreme economic hardship. In this context, the NTS commissioned around 200 writers, actors, directors and designers and worked with an unprecedented number of partner organisations including

Aberdeen Performing Arts, Birds of Paradise, the Citizens, Dumfries & Galloway Arts Festival, Dundee Rep, Imaginate, Eden Court in Inverness, Lyth Arts Centre in Caithness, Playwrights Studio, Queen Jesus Productions, the Royal Lyceum, Shetland Arts, Summerhall, Stellar Quines, Theatre Gu Leor, the Tron Theatre and the Traverse. The resulting digital artworks were broadcast over a period of weeks in the summer of 2020, and eventually grouped under twelve headings which included Scenes with Lockdown Loneliness, Scenes About Surviving, Scenes from the Frontline and Scenes about the Future. The project developed as it did partly because the NTS had a history of curating large online performance events. Its Five Minute Theatre projects, which are discussed more fully in Chapter 5, established the format.

Unlike its Five Minute predecessors, however, the 55 individual digital artworks that make up *Scenes for Survival* were broadcast in batches of five or six over several weeks, beginning in May 2020. They therefore lacked something of the 'eventness' of their predecessors, and obviously the opportunity for an audience to congregate was missing. They also, as Davis Pollock emphasises in his review for *The Stage*, offered 'a proliferation of those walls the NTS has previously disregarded' because in most cases writers and directors came together to reveal what life was like under lockdown from within the confines of the performer's own home, often their bedroom (2020). This was certainly the case in the first batch of six, all of which were also monologues. Responding to its moment, *Scenes for Survival* privileged narratives of social isolation and vulnerability, evidencing how the pandemic created widespread crises that were nevertheless unevenly distributed, predicated as they were on the structural positioning of individuals in line with existing socio-economic groups and identity categories. Taken as a whole, the series charted the complex, and intersecting, dimensions of precarity, and can be read as a barometer of the shifting but shared anxieties of the first lockdown. The project also offered respite to its audience and, as its title suggests, gestured towards the notion that the survival of the individual is predicated on the survival of the collective. Scenes remained available on YouTube months after their original broadcast, emphasising the NTS's longer-term commitment to public engagement.

In Jenni Fagan's *Isolation*, directed by Debbie Hannan and performed by Kate Dickie, the lock down poses a direct threat to its protagonist's already poor mental health. An unnamed woman speaks to us from her bedroom. She is coughing and has some difficulty breathing. Her son, who she occasionally addresses directly, has been sent to stay with his father to avoid catching the virus. Beyond the disease's physical aftershocks, she struggles with forced isolation, repeatedly insisting that the experience has changed her. She is paralysed by indecision, afraid to ask friends and neighbours to provide her with groceries, and she is missing her son dreadfully. We get close-ups of the woman disinfecting his plastic toy animals and resorting to strange acrobatics so as not to touch the tap when washing her hands. Her only link to the outside world is the sudden eruption of clapping for healthcare workers, which is obviously in tension with the protagonist's mental state and also faintly recalls the applause of an audience in the theatre.

In *John Rebus: The Lockdown Blues* Ian Rankin's legendary Edinburgh detective, who in spite of his solitary lifestyle is usually a man engaged in the world, be it the city mortuary or the Oxford bar, is also struggling. Left with nothing but memories, beer bottles and his record collection he is simultaneously funny and sad. He also looks old. The contrast with our previous experience of Rebus as a character who is active and ultimately in control, foregrounds the vulnerability of ageing generally, but more specifically in relation to the COVID-19 virus which was especially lethal to the elderly. The scene calls to mind Elinor Fuchs' reflections on the staging of ageing as 'a late life developmental moment in which the familiar becomes strange' (2014: 70). For Fuchs, in this kind of age-conscious alienation effect, 'the aging figure may be seen as if for the first time, or the scene may depict a late life experience in which the old are estranged from their former selves' (70). Played by a haunted-looking Brian Cox, lockdown Rebus hovers on the edge of existential despair. He is not alone. In other examples, Kevin Gilday's *Courier Culture*, follows a fast-food delivery driver, played by Jatinder Singh Randhawa, cycling through the deserted streets of lockdown-Glasgow because like a significant number of people he is denied the opportunity to 'work from home', while Janey Godley's *Alone* explores the increased risk of domestic violence suffered by many women during lockdown. Among other things, then, *Scenes for Survival* raises interesting questions about the extent to which public performances of vulnerability can be mobilised in forms of resistance beyond the theatre itself, as tools for community building. Taken as a whole, it constitutes, or at least attempts to constitute, a coalition of vulnerability and this coalition pertains especially acutely to the theatre sector itself.

Financial Pressures

If *Scenes for Survival* was created during a particularly difficult period for theatre and live performance in Scotland, it was also made against the backdrop of longer-term standstill funding which had already left the sector beleaguered and hanging on by a thread. This is a situation that pertains across the UK, of course, where arts funding has fallen victim to austerity politics at least since 2010. In October 2023, Creative Scotland revealed it was facing 'a gap of more than £50 million from organisations, venues, festivals and events seeking long-term funding' and that it would consequently be offering long-term funding to far fewer organisations unless there was a major government rethink (Ferguson 2023b). In December of the same year Creative Scotland ramped up pressure on the Scottish Government to deliver on its pledge to more than double arts funding in the next five year period. The *Scotsman's* Arts Correspondent Brian Ferguson puts it plainly: 'the government has been under growing pressure over the past 18 months to … to reverse a trend that has seen Scotland slump to 28th out of 34 European countries for spending on arts and culture per head' (2023a).

New Labour's commitment to the arts had been significant in the immediate aftermath of devolution. Writing in 2005, for example, Jen Harvie emphasises how far 'New Labour political discourse about the importance of the creative industries … helped secure much needed funding for the arts, and particularly for theatre in Scotland' (Harvie 2005: 32). More recently, as the discussion above shows, austerity measures have complicated the landscape of arts funding and the relationship between artists and funding bodies has become acrimonious and fraught. In June 2012, for instance, controversial changes to funding were announced by Creative Scotland which involved forty-nine of its flexibly funded organisations moving over to a system based on project funding. Such an arrangement was inevitably seen as threatening the continued health of companies, by limiting their ability to maintain a core team or engage in effective forward planning. The Scottish arts sector—the proposed changes are not confined to theatre—staged a fight back, however, which led to the resignation of Creative Scotland's Chief Executive, Andrew Dixon in December 2012. It is by now clear, however, that artists and commentators have been winning battles rather than the war. In early 2018 Maria Oller was in the middle of rehearsals for a new production of Chekhov's *Three Sisters* when the news came through that

Lung Ha, the theatre company working with learning disabled adults she had led since 2009, had lost its main funding from Creative Scotland. Up until then, Lung Ha, like Scotland's other major disability theatre company Birds of Paradise, had been a Regularly Funded Organisation (RFO), and consequently guaranteed at least three-year's security to plan ahead. For companies such as Lung Ha and Birds of Paradise, such guarantees are especially vital, because of their practice of working with and through people with disabilities. Following a public outcry, Creative Scotland reversed their decision and announced £2.6 m additional funding to re-admit five organisations into the network RFOs, and also to undo a planned 22% funding cut for Stellar Quines. Along with Lung Ha and Birds of Paradise, the two other companies that had been excluded were Catherine Wheels and Visible Fictions, the acclaimed children's theatre companies discussed in more detail Chapter 5 of this book. 'We have listened to the extensive and constructive feedback we received from many individuals and organisations working across the arts and culture in Scotland', explained Ben Thomson, Interim Chair of Creative Scotland, by way of explanation for the climbdown (Creative Scotland 2018).

Clearly, Creative Scotland's initial decision—although the organisation is obliged to make difficult decisions—demonstrated an alarming lack of awareness of the importance of improving diversity, inclusion, and access, not only to the theatre sector, but to Scottish culture more generally. The contributions made by Birds of Paradise and Lung Ha, for example, as Paul Darke has argued about disability arts more broadly, are 'based upon legitimizing the experience of disabled people as equal within art and all other cultural practices' and the work consequently constitutes 'a challenge to, an undermining of (as a minimum) traditional aesthetic and social values' (2003: 132). The significance of such work should be self-evident. Lung Ha's production of Linda McLean's singular and surprising musical *Castle Lennox* (2023), which tells the story of 16-year-old Annis who in 1969 is abandoned at the gates of Scotland's foremost institution for people with learning disabilities and other perceived mental disorders, reaffirmed the company's status as a leader in European disability arts, while bringing the deplorable treatment of learning disabled people by the state in earlier decades into the spotlight. It won the CATS for best ensemble. The Birds of Paradise and NTS musical *My Left Right Foot* (2018), was nominated in the same category, and the company has dealt variously with issues of brain injury in *In An Alien Landscape* (2013), mental illness in Nicola McCartney's drama-come-cabaret *Crazy Jane*

(2015) and growing up with cerebral palsy in Jack Hunter's *One of Two* (2022).

Nicola McCartney has been a stalwart of the Scottish theatre scene in the post-devolutionary period, working as a playwright, director, dramaturge, teacher and applied theatre practitioner. Her breakthrough play, *Heritage* (1998) 'is an examination of the politics of memory and identity in the context of sectarianism carried by the Irish emigrant community to Canada' (McKean 2011). Originally from Belfast, McCartney's career has been marked by eclecticism and versatility. She directed the national tour of Harry Gibson's adaptation of Irvine Welsh's *Trainspotting* (1996), for instance while her play for Catherine Wheels, *Lifeboat* (2002), won the TMA/ Equity Best New Show for Children & Young People and was revived for a school's tour as recently as 2020. In 2019 she collaborated with the Kosovan refugee Dritan Kastrati to write *How Not to Drown*, which won a Fringe First before touring the UK in 2023 and told the harrowing story of Kastrati's journey to the UK as a child migrant. *How Not to Drown*, is an extension of McCartney's work with marginalised communities which has included projects with refugees and asylum seekers, people impacted by the criminal justice system, and young people in the care of the state. She led the NTS listening project Care in Contemporary Scotland, which resulted in the film, *Holding/ Holding On* (2021), scripted by McCartney and inspired by conversations with care-experienced people, sector professionals and volunteers. *Holding/Holding On* was subsequently staged at the Scottish Parliament as part of the 2022 Festival of Politics in 2022. In March 2024 the NTS announced *Caring Scotland*, a new three-year project, led by McCartney, created in partnership with Who Cares? Scotland—the country's only national independent membership organisation for Care Experienced people—which 'will culminate in a new oral history audio archive at the National Library of Scotland and a touring immersive installation in 2027' (NTS 2024). In 2019 the NTS staged Jenni Fagan's stage adaptation of her debut novel *The Panoptican* (2013), which draws on her own experiences growing up in the Scottish care system. Fagan's heroine, fifteen-year-old Anais Hendricks is clever, witty, fierce and determined, and Anna Russell Martin won the 2020 CATS for Best Female Performance in the role. 'Never off the stage' as Mark Fisher remarked, Russell Martin played Anais 'without sentiment, offering no special pleading, the better to show the brutalising impact of a loveless childhood' (Fisher

2019b). Among other things, McCartney's work in this space has sought to evidence the positive impact of the arts on marginalised communities.

Unfortunately, there is a discernible gap between the rhetoric of the SNP administration around the value of culture and the reality on the ground. In its 2021 Manifesto, the Party insists 'culture is central to who we are as a nation' and further that:

> In government the SNP has always valued culture and creativity, but the pandemic has demonstrated more than ever how vital it is to our well-being, mental health and sense of belonging as well as to our economy and society. (2021)

These claims are not supported by the facts. More recently, during a period of appalling cost crises, a range of organisations representing the sector—including the Federation of Scottish Theatre, The Musician's Musicians' Union, Campaign for the Arts, the Museums Association, and the Broadcasting, Entertainment, Cinematograph and Theatre Union—expressed dismay at the decision outlined in the 2023/24 Scottish Government budget, to reduce funding to Creative Scotland by over 10%. On 21 February 2023, in the face of widespread criticism, the Scottish Government announced the reversal of the proposed 10% cut, but again provoked fury in September 2023 by reinstating it, citing the impact of public sector pay deals by way of explanation. Creative Scotland was obliged to draw on its financial reserves to fill the £6.6 m hole in its budget, and avoid passing the cut on to the 121 organisations on long-term funding. It is quite possible to argue, of course, that this is a reasonable and judicious use of Creative Scotland's reserves, since it in not clear what function they serve beyond providing a safety net for just such an eventuality.

Nonetheless, despite Government promises of an increase of £100 million in arts funding to 2028, the outlook remains relatively bleak, especially since government rhetoric does not match its actions which are marked by U-turns and inconsistency. To add to the misery, cash-strapped local councils have also reduced or withdrawn support. At Glasgow's Tron, the loss of its £130,000 council grant—which accounts for 10% of its annual budget—in early 2023, makes invidious choices unavoidable. More broadly, a combination of cuts, standstill funding and inconsistency inhibits any serious or strategic long-term planning either by Creative Scotland or the arts organisations it supports. By the close of 2023 the funding body was warning it had received applications from 361 cultural organisations to the value of £96 m per year. It currently has £40 m in its budget. In a move bordering on the comedic, in March 2024, it put crucial funding decisions on hold after having withdrawn funding from Leonie Rae Gasson's installation *Rein*, when it emerged, she was planning to film performers having 'non-simulated' sex as part of her project. Extra layers of scrutiny, risk evaluation and due diligence were conducted on dozens of application when the Scottish Culture Secretary Angus Robertson told the Scottish Parliament the Gasson project should never have been funded in the first place. On 25 March Holyrood's culture committee announced the launch of a probe into Creative Scotland's decision to fund Gasson and the funding body was instructed to provide details of the full criteria and process for handling applications. None of this is confidence inspiring.

New Imperatives

Clearly, there remains a need for careful interrogation of the complacency that underwrites the utopian conceptions of Scotland's cultural distinctiveness privileged not only by the Scottish Government, but by a range of mainstream commentators. In 1994, Lyndsay Paterson argued that Scotland provided 'a template from which other nations can learn how to develop a non-threatening conception of nationalism, one that is tolerant both of internal plurality and of flexible subversions of its sovereignty' (1994: 180). Almost a decade later, and after the establishment of the new parliament, Cairns Craig reiterated this conception when describing Scotland as 'a beacon for a new and non-threatening civic nationalism, which will be the basis for a new international order' (2001: 21). Ian Macwhirter, meanwhile, explained his decision to vote Yes in the 2014 referendum by praising the SNP's 'social democratic policies and their commitment to social justice, nuclear disarmament, racial integration, open borders, increased immigration, and the defence of public services' (2014: 105). Such declarations, as Gerry Hassan and Simon Barrow point out, are 'for many, the official stories of modern Scotland: a confident, competent social democracy, increasingly asserting the politics of difference from the rest of the UK' (2017: 19). In reality, however, although the SNP has done many progressive things—scrapping prescription charges and tuition fees, for example—and has expressed good intentions, it has not overseen a significant redistribution of wealth towards the poorer sections of society, nor has it campaigned purposefully for a more radical conceptualisation of social justice. Nevertheless, the frame of Scottish 'difference' is a key structuring motif for these statements and, as I have argued in this book, it effectively establishes the discursive space in which Scottish theatre-makers operate. In my next and concluding section I turn my attention to the ways performance has engaged with some of the tensions implicit in the discussion above. In particular, I want to think about how theatre-makers have asked necessary questions and contributed to debates in the public sphere by offering more nuanced and complex versions of Scottishness than those provided by some mainstream commentators.

On 3 May 2015, 31-year-old Sheku Bayoh died after being restrained by six police officers in a street in Kirkcaldy, Fife. The resulting police investigation sparked outrage and a public inquiry which is ongoing at the time of writing. As this incident demonstrates, and has come to symbolise, particularly in its excessive use of force, Scotland has a problem with racism that marks black people, and especially black men, as aggressive and as outsiders in a way that obfuscates other markers of citizenship. Bayoh, after all, had lived in Scotland since he was a child. Scottish teachers report race-based bullying as the most pervasive form of prejudice-based bullying in schools, and people of African descent wait the longest for housing referrals: 261 days against an average of 184 (Centre for Race and Equality Rights 2023). Racial motivated crime remains the most commonly reported hate crime in Scotland. All of this, in spite of repeated claims that Scotland is somehow more egalitarian and inclusive than its larger southern neighbour. A number of interventions have been made by contemporary Scottish theatre-makers to confront these issues, most of which necessarily involve a reckoning of some kind with Scotland's imperial past.

Scotland's relationship with its involvement in Empire, and its complicity in the construction and maintenance of racial hierarchies, has undergone something of a transformation since devolution. During the 1970s and 1980s, Michael Hechter's opinion that 'the [English] core is seen to dominate the periphery politically and exploit it materially' supported the view held by many in the SNP that Scotland was an English colony (Hechter 1975: 5). Thankfully, this view did not go unchallenged, even at the time. Tom Nairn, Scotland's leading nationalist intellectual of the period, detailed a markedly different perspective in *The Break-Up of Britain* (1977). For Nairn, imperialism had enabled Scotland to occupy a leading position at the heart of the world system and dissatisfaction with the Union had been enlivened by its failure to provide the same advantages after the dissolution of empire. Nairn's thesis gained ground, especially after the establishment of the new parliament, and Hechter's victimhood argument has largely been repudiated, at least among Scottish historians, who have tended to draw conclusions that much more closely resemble Nairn's. For instance, Stephen Mullen's *The Glasgow Sugar Aristocracy* (2022) demonstrates in evidence that Scotland had the status of an imperial core between the eighteenth and twentieth centuries, and moreover that it played a disproportionately large role in Britain's Atlantic slave economy. Similarly, David Alston's *Slaves and Highlanders* (2021) which won the 2022 Saltire Society Scottish Book of the Year Award, uncovers the extent to which Highlanders, often represented in simple terms as victims of the Clearances, were involved in every aspect of the slave trade as perpetrators. These contributions to Scotland's reckoning with its own past are of course most welcome, and there have been similar attempts to uncover such hidden histories in the field of theatre and performance. The manner of Sheku Bayoh's death, and public responses to it, also provoked a response from Scotland's black and global majority theatre-makers.

Near the beginning of Hannah Lavery's *Lament For Sheku Bayoh* (2020), which was live streamed during lockdown, and performed live at the EIF in 2021, four black female performers set out the requirements of being Scottish as they see it: 'We walk our preserved battlefields. Laying stone on towering cairns. Kilted and tearful in school assemblies we sing of our beautiful defeats, our fallen. Ignoring anything, anyone who may dispute the telling' (2021: 8). Having established this present reality, they ponder their own exclusion from the dominant narratives of Scottish history. 'What would it cost us' they ask, 'to lift him broken from a Kirkcaldy street, to cradle him as our own?' (2021: 8). In what follows, Lavery is at pains to show that, as she argues in the foreword to the published edition of the play, Scotland is not 'not the country we promote to others and more importantly to ourselves. People in Scotland who experience racism have to spend so much time getting people to admit racism actually exists' (2021: 5). The show begins with the musician Beldina Odenyo's haunting rendition of Burns' 'A Man's A Man For a That', a song deeply associated with Scotland's supposed egalitarianism, before offering a meditation on the country's misplaced sense of innocence on the subject of race and empire (Fig. 7.1).

Fig. 7.1 Belinda Odenyo in Hannah Lavery's *Lament for Sheku Bayoh* (Directed by Hannah Lavery, National Theatre of Scotland, 2020) reproduced with kind permission from Mihaela Bodlovic

The show's energy is partly fuelled by righteous anger at the injustice of Bayoh's death. Attention is paid to officers repeatedly describing him as 'massive' although they were considerably larger than he was, for instance, and the fact that no officer has been charged despite heroically relentless pressure from Bayoh's family, acts as a constant reminder of the structural operations of racial injustice. Lavery's play also, as its title suggest, opens a dramatic space for specifically Scottish form of lamentation and grief. It is intended, she notes, as a 'a keening for a man who has been much maligned' (2021: 5). In the Gaelic tradition, a keening is a graveside lament, typically performed by women, and here it is extended beyond Bayoh to encompass all those who know that 'the belonging is conditional — only skin deep' (2021: 37). '*Lament For Sheku Bayoh*' as Joyce McMillan observes, 'sets down a vital marker in the story of Scottish theatre, challenging the nation to seek justice for Sheku Bayoh as one of our own, or to abandon the myth of Scotland as a land of equality and humanity, once and for all' (2021).

Questions of Scotland's historical involvement in racial injustice has been explored in different registers. In 2021, Adura Onashile's app-based performance *Ghosts*, created with the NTS, explored Glasgow's historical ties to the slave trade via a 70-minute guided walk, intended as 'an evocation of those whose enslavement made the imposing architecture' of Glasgow's Merchant City possible (Fisher 2021). *Ghosts* involved an affective encounter with the city itself and its material spaces, seen anew through the lens of colonial violence and injustice. Enhanced graphics made the Museum of Modern Art, once the home of slave-owner William Cunningham, appear to fall to the ground and at one point, for instance and while gazing at the river Clyde, I saw a series of forgotten names drift tenderly skyward, drawing attention to the way enslaved peoples have been erased from the city's landscape, despite being crucial to its economy for centuries. The topic of chattel slavery was returned to in more conventionally dramatic form, in May Sumbwanyambe's, *Enough of Him* (2022), which was described concisely by Joyce McMillan as 'a lush and intense 80 minute meditation, featuring four actors, on the emotional and psychosexual structure of the slave economy that helped shape modern Scotland' (2022).

Sumbwanyambe's protagonist is the historical figure Joseph Knight, a black slave brought to Scotland from Jamaica by the eighteenth-century Perthshire laird John Wedderburn, who had made his fortune in slave sugar. In *Enough of Him, as in history*, when Knight tries to leave Wedderburn's service, the latter has him arrested, arguing that as his property Knight owes him service in perpetuity. Knight's legal challenge begins in 1774 in the Justices of the Peace court in Perth, where he argues that, although he had been purchased by Wedderburn years earlier in Jamaica, the act of landing in Scotland freed him from perpetual servitude, because slavery was not recognised in the country. The Justices of the Peace find in favour of Wedderburn, but Knight appeals to the Sheriff Depute, John Swinton, who concludes in his favour 'that the state of slavery is not recognised by the laws of this kingdom, and is inconsistent with the principles thereof' (Sumbwanyambe 2022: 54). Wedderburn then appeals to the Court of Session, Scotland's supreme civil court, which in 1778 also finds in Knights favour by a majority of eight to four, basically upholding Swinton's judgement that Scots Law would not uphold the institution of slavery. Knight's is an historic victory then, but Sumbwanyambe's play is far from celebratory in tone. 'Written economically in spare, fragile scenes' *Enough of Him*, as Mark Fisher notes, presents the case as 'fractious and troubled, a game of chess that cannot be won' (2022). Staged in a co-production between the NTS and Pitlochry, *Enough of Him* won best new play at the CATS in 2023, as well as Best Director for Orla O'Loughlin. In the play's closing scene, Joseph is legally free, but unable to experience any real sense of liberation, scarred as he is by his relationship with Wedderburn who treats him as a kind of protégé come pet. Nonetheless, the stories told in *Enough of Him*, and in Rona Munro's *James IV*, evidence a long black presence in Scotland, one that disrupts what Sivamohan Valluvan identifies as residual belief in 'a permanent chain of historical whiteness that has only been undone, rashly' in the postwar period (2019: 10). As Valluvan acknowledges, and as the ambivalent tone of Sumbwanyambe play indicates, however 'the national myth does not reel in defeat when presented with the corrected historical record' (102). David Alston gives a detailed account of the factors that until relatively recently led Scottish historians to downplay the extent of country's involvement in slavery, but also notes that 'in a single week in August 2020', the *National* 'published contributions that included the historian Michael Fry's claim that "Edinburgh's part in the Caribbean slave trade was minimal" and a reader's comment that "the vast majority of Scots were in no position to have either profited or prospered from the slave trade as they were often little better than slaves themselves"' (2021: 11).

Hate crimes are, as Sara Ahmed shows, examples of how the individual stands in for the entire group, and they consequently expose the extent to which 'violence against others involves forms of power that are visceral and bodily, as well as social and structural' (2004: 56). 'Sexual orientation aggravated crime' is the second most commonly reported type of hate crime in Scotland, and has been on an upward trend since 2014–15, with a 10% rise between 2021 and 2022 (Crown Office and Procurator Fiscal Service 2022: 6). 'In 2021–22', moreover, '84 charges were reported with an aggravation of prejudice relating to transgender identity, 87% more than the 45 charges reported in 2020–21' (7). These last numbers are not large, of course, but they are particularly alarming when considered alongside the low numbers of transgender people in the population, and the growing climate of unwarranted hostility in which they are obliged to live. The presence of gay characters on Scottish stages has been minimal before minimally consistent since the 1980s, when playwrights including Iain Heggie, and John Binnie as discussed in Chapter 2, had, explored the experience of being gay in a country where heteronormativity and masculinist bias remained dominant forces. In the 1990s this work had been extended and enhanced by Christopher Dean with his Glasgow-based company MCT, the acronym derived from the term 'Molly' which had been used since the early eighteenth century to describe an effeminate man and 'Collar and Tie' employed since the beginning of the twentieth century in reference to butch women. It was also the title of their first show. The work in progress, *Molly's Collar and Tie* (1996), was episodic in structure, interspersing confessional monologues with scenes from the lives of the gay men and lesbians from the past. Marion Sangster's account of her journey from schoolgirl crush to first love and betrayal, is augmented with reflections on the doomed relationship between James VI and Lord Lennox, tales from the Glasgow's sixties gay scene, and the tale of Murray Hall, who lived her adult life as a man in nineteenth-century America. Dean's *Smells and Bells* (1998)—the title a vernacular reference to Catholic ritual—exposed the sexual hypocrisy of the church, among other things with a scene of male on male fellatio in a confessional.

In 2019 the Traverse initiated the country's first LGBTQ+ playwriting festival Pride Plays, which has since premiered work by is a decidedly filthy comic romp that follows its hero Calvin as he attempts to leave an abusive boyfriend while at the same time learning to drive. His instructor Thelma is a bisexual, polyamorous, former psychotherapist, and the arrival of Wilf, a Volkswagen which has had seven previous owners, initiates a road trip which takes many dark and hilarious turns. Commissioned by the Traverse and directed by its Gareth Nicholls, *Wilf* is a work of real distinctiveness and confidence, and it was followed by *Ode To Joy (How Gordon got to go to the Nasty Pig Party)* (2022) which explores a darker and more sexually explicit side of gay culture. Ley has been commissioned by the NTS to adapt Damian Barr's misery memoir *Maggie & Me*, about growing up as a gay child in Thatcher's Britain, for a tour in early summer 2024.

Although still peripheral, gay and lesbian representation on Scottish stages, and in the sector more widely, has echoed trends in Scottish culture towards greater inclusion. The infamous Section 28 (more accurately Section 2A of the relevant Scottish legislation) was repealed by the Scottish Parliament in June 2000, and consequently removed from the statute books in Scotland earlier than elsewhere in the UK. Scotland has also led, or at least attempted to lead, the development of legislation to make it easier for trans people to change their legal sex. Since 2004, the Westminster Gender Recognition Act (GRA), to which the

Scottish Parliament consented, has facilitated this process but has been increasingly criticised for being out of step with international standards by placing too much emphasis on psychiatric assessment and medical transition. Consultations conducted by the Scottish Government between November 2017 and March 2018, and again between November 2019 and March 2020, found majority support for reforming the legislation and removing most of the existing and unnecessarily intrusive requirements. The Gender Recognition Reform (Scotland) Bill, which lowers the age a person can change their legal gender from 18 to 16, removes the requirement of a medical diagnosis of gender dysphoria, and reduces the waiting time from two years to six months of living in an acquired gender, was voted on by the Scottish Parliament on 22 December 2022 and passed by a majority of 86 to 39. The legislation is similar to that already in place in Belgium, Denmark, Finland, Iceland, Ireland, Luxembourg, Malta, Norway, Portugal, Spain and Switzerland. In January 2023, the Scottish Secretary Alister Jack, made an order under Section 35 of the Scotland Act (1998), vetoing the bill, the first time royal assent was not granted to a bill passed by the Scottish Parliament since its establishment in 1999. Jack's reasoning was that responsibility for equality legislation was reserved for Westminster under the Scotland Act and that the Scottish bill would put the country out of step with the rest of the UK.

This is not to suggest that all of the opposition to the bill came from outside Scotland. The legislation was opposed by the Scottish Conservatives, the trans-exclusionary LGB Alliance, the Catholic Bishops Conference and various organisations arguing vociferously, and typically using misinformation, that trans rights are somehow in conflict with women's rights. This situation has not only made the public sphere an increasing hostile place for trans people, but has also revealed fractures within the feminist community. As Sara Ahmed has observed, the 'policing of the boundaries of "women" has never not been disastrous for feminism' and such activity, however unconsciously, effectively does the work of the patriarchy by insisting on the ultimate authority of biological essentialism (2016: 31). The prevalence of trans-phobic rhetoric in contemporary culture threatens progress for LGBTQ+ people, then, but it also demonstrates that progress was always contingent on the tolerance of a heteronormative culture that remains dominant. Work made in Scotland by trans artists has been particularly instrumental in revealing and challenging this dominance.

First staged in 2009 at the Tron Theatre, Glasgow, Jo Clifford's pioneering *The Gospel According to Jesus, Queen of Heaven* was picketed by trans-exclusive campaigners and conservative Christians, who objected vociferously to its depiction of Jesus Christ as a trans woman. Written and performed by Clifford herself, the performance imagines Jesus reincarnated as a trans woman and involves a series of reworkings of parables from the New Testament and the Beatitudes from the Gospel according to Matthew, and a recreation of the Eucharist in which the audience is invited to share bread and wine with Clifford. In spite of the controversy, *Queen of Heaven* has been restaged on multiple occasions and various locations across the UK and internationally. In 2015, as Stephen Greer notes, following a revival at the Fringe as part of the Made in Scotland showcase, it 'was translated into Portuguese by director Natalia Mallo and re-imagined in a version performed by trans actor and activist Renata Carvalho that sees Jesus embodied in the present as a travesti woman from Sao Paulo' (Greer 2023: 166). In 2019, a festival organised to celebrate *Queen Jesus*' tenth anniversary, featured the Scottish premiere of the Brazilian production performed by Carvalho which was accessible alongside Clifford's version for the first time. In an essay titled 'Trans Women Onstage: Erasure, Resurgence and #notadebate', trans performance maker Emma Frankland, calls attention to the 'very different energy' Carvalho 'brings to the piece' and welcomes the opportunity to see 'two versions of the same show that are radically different and where the performer's identity impacts hugely on the experience' (2020: 297).

In *Feeling Backward: Loss and the Politics of Queer History*, Heather Love explains how 'the emphasis on damage in queer studies exists in a state of tension with a related and contrary tendency – the need to resist damage and to affirm queer existence' (2009: 3). Specifically in relation to *Queen of Heaven*, Greer sees this insight as particularly useful when thinking about 'intergenerational practices that evidence the forms of solidarity enabled by historical (dis)continuities of queer experience' (2023: 166). In spite of an increasingly hostile public sphere Clifford continues to make herself visible to young queer people in ways that are simultaneously tender and brave. Her solo testimonial performance *Eve* (2017) testifies to this commitment. As she writes in her Preface to the published text:

> When I began to live as a woman there was a huge emphasis on 'passing'. I was given voice lessons so I could sound like a woman and encouraged

to learn to sit and walk like a woman. The assumption being that people would hate and despise me if they discovered I was trans ... the abuse I suffered in those early days when I went out my front door and the hatred I provoked when I performed my *Gospel According to Jesus Queen of Heaven* seemed to confirm the good sense of this ... But it also made it all the more important to resist. (2017: 4)

Speaking as a playwright, translator, performer, father and grandmother, Clifford reflects on her life in largely elegiac tones in *Eve*, which was loosely paired with Frances Poet's *Adam* (2017)—both were commissioned by the NTS—another narrative of transition, which is more straightforwardly celebratory. The latter play featured Adam Kashmiry playing himself as the eponymous hero of the piece, accompanied by Nesha Caplan who represented Adam before his transition. These two Adams play various other characters and are accompanied by a digital choir of more than a hundred transgender and non-binary people from across the globe. Kashmiry had arrived in Glasgow as an asylum seeker in 2010, and the largely autobiographical show he created with Cora Bisset and Poet traces his gender dysphoria in childhood, his struggle for settled status in the UK, and his journey towards transition. 'Is it possible' he asked, 'for the soul of a man to be trapped in the body of a woman? The answer is yes' (Poet 2017: 49). *Adam* garnered excellent reviews and was later filmed by the NTS for digital distribution and also screened by BBC Scotland.

Rosana Cade and Ivor MacAskill's *The Making of Pinocchio* (2018–), a show created alongside and in response to Ivor's transition, began life in Glasgow at Take Me Somewhere in 2018, and has since toured nationally and internationally, most recently to London, Munich and Frankfurt in 2023. Like *Eve* and *Adam*, *The Making of Pinocchio* features direct and personal address to the audience and is, at least in part, a testimonial performance. In *Passionate Amateurs: Theatre, Communism and Love* (2013), Nicholas Ridout discusses the political potentials of the modes of attentiveness common to theatre and performance, arguing that these are heightened in dramaturgies that employ personal address, where:

> ... we are simply invited to give our attention, to assist, by means of our presence, at the making public of what otherwise might have been thought and imagined in solitude, in the hope, perhaps, that the simple but difficult act of making it public in this way, the act of offering it for the attention of others, might place that solitude in new relations. (2013: 154–155)

The Making of Pinocchio is not a solo piece, but it does make public an essentially personal and private experience and, in so doing, figures the experience of trans people and those who love them in new relations. The digital version of the show, which I reference here, begins with a cricket—which is of course a prominent character in Disney's animated version of *Pinocchio* (1940)—announcing itself as a kind of eternal story teller: 'A long, long, long time ago and also yesterday, and at the turn of every century and before the dawn of time, and after the end of time there was, and is, and always will be, a man and the man lives here, in the real world' (Cade and MacAskill 2021). Shortly after this introductory sequence, which also introduces Geppeto and the Pinocchio narrative, MacAskill introduces himself directly to the audience: 'My name is Ivor MacAskill. I'm a live artist and theatre maker based here in Glasgow. I'm 40 years old, nearly 41. What else to say? My pronouns are he/him or they/them. I'm one of the creators of Pinocchio and not far away is my co-creator and real-life partner Rosana Cade. Can you say hi darling' (2021). They then explain that they have been working on the show since 2018, when Ivor came out as trans, and began his journey to, like Pinocchio the puppet, become a real boy. Before that, Cade notes wryly, they had 'quite a solid lesbian identity' (2021). In what follows Cade and MacAskill tell the story of Ivor's transition, while incorporating Cade's non-binary identity and their role as supportive partner, through the frame of their process as artists creating a new version of Pinocchio. The result is a beautiful, tender, funny and amusing show that, 'testifies to an evolving, continually transforming love between partners, a love for making things and oneself' (Hawking 2022). Cade and MacAskill examine questions relating to bodily autonomy and its attendant challenge to heteronormativity in a performance space of multiple possibilities, from puppet workshop to Pleasure Island, to the belly of a whale, to a film studio, transitioning from female to male and even to donkeys in the process. At one point Ivor sings 'When you Wish Upon a Star' accompanied on film by his pre-testosterone, pre-top surgery self. *The Making of Pinocchio* is consequently marked, however gently, by a kind of queer anarchism that brings into question the borders and boundaries that underwrite official 'interpretation of gender and sexuality' which 'are assumed to be static, fixed, and conforming to clear borders' (Heckert et al. 2015: 749). The recent moral panic surrounding the very existence of trans people points to an over-investment in the tidy borders of male/female, hetero/homo, with the result that trans people are now placed at the bottom of a sexual minority hierarchy. In Cade and MacAskill's queer anarchist performance, it is the hierarchy itself which is productively called into question. Arguably, theatre has always dealt with questions of human agency under pressure from societal forces and other, equally urgent, questions have also preoccupied Scottish theatre-makers in recent years, particularly those that relate to the unforeseen impacts of rapid advances in technology and the climate emergency.

In Morna Pearson's short play *Darklands* (2019), an infertile couple, Brie and Logan, is offered the opportunity to pioneer a new technology. At the expense of their employer, and upon signing a legally binding agreement, they are informed, their baby will be 'incubated in an artificial womb' (Pearson et al. 2019: 26). They will be able to 'watch it grow on a twenty-four-hour live feed' and their daughter, they are assured, will be comprised of '88 – 93 per cent organic matter' derived from a 50/50 split of their DNA (26, 28). Brie is more troubled by the offer than Logan, although both welcome the prospect of respite from their mundane jobs. The disembodied female voice of what we take to be a central computer explains:

> Neither of you will be required to carry on working in your current roles after the gestation period. Your job will be to raise your child as per the agreement. Her progress will be monitored extremely closely, especially at first. As time goes on you'll be expected to make a daily report of any glitches, in case our monitoring methods don't pick them up. (30)

Having taken time to consider the more troubling aspects of the proposed arrangement, Brie refuses to sign the agreement but, in a plot twist that highlights her lack of agency, the experiment goes ahead without her consent.

Darklands was commissioned by the NTS and performed in March 2019—immediately before the first COVID-19 lockdown was imposed in the UK—as part of a trilogy of short plays advertised and published under the umbrella title *Interference*. All three imagine a near-future-world in which digital technologies have transformed work, human interaction and governance. Hannah Kalil's *Metaverse* (2019), the second play in the trilogy, stages an explicitly post-climate catastrophe world in which a female scientist is recruited, again by a powerful and faceless company, to work on the development of a virtual reality technology so tactile as to be indistinguishable from real world interaction. The project's progress is charted largely via a series of unsatisfactory virtual interactions between the scientist and her daughter. The trilogy closes with Vlad Butucea's *Glowstick* (2019) which is significantly more utopian in its figuring of the interaction of humans with technology, in this instance artificial intelligence (AI). *Glowstick* details the evolving relationship between a severely disabled woman living in a care facility and IDA, an android assigned to her care. As well as focusing on new technologies, each playwright imagines an outside world in which natural resources and biodiversity have been severely depleted or obliterated by the climate emergency, and from which humans have withdrawn into a controlled living environment. Elsewhere playwrights have taken a different, more oblique and satirical approach to commenting on the environmental crisis.

Stef Smith's *Human Animals* (2016) builds a disturbing vision of a London so plagued by foxes, mice and pigeons that roads are closed, parks burned and curfews imposed. Smith gives no indication of what is causing this plague. The action begins innocently enough with a pigeon crash-landing through an urban window and lying smeared across the living-room floor of a flat shared by a young couple, Jamie and Lisa. What follows is comprised of a series of short scenes between the lovers; between Nancy and John, a pair of neighbours/friends in late middle-age; between Nancy and her daughter Alex, who has just returned from a gap year; and less frequently involving a more shadowy figure named Si who seems to be Lisa's boss and tries to pick John up in the local pub. In Smith's play, the familiarity of the domestic setups is disrupted by the force of the external crisis under which the existing moral order is disintegrating. Things deteriorate rapidly and before long extermination squads are roaming the streets and phone lines are being cut. Some of the characters are alarmed by unfolding events, some see them as an opportunity for financial gain, and some, including Lisa and Nancy, determinedly ignore them, preferring to believe that the authorities have the situation under control and that things will imminently return to normal.

Human Animals is replete with images of the outside world bearing down inexorably on its mostly domestic interiors. Foxes drop dead, but not before spreading disease, mice chew themselves to death, birds congregate in troubling numbers, lions escape from the zoo and wander the streets. Houses are burnt down because sparrows are found nesting on the roof. Smith's imagery is consistently grotesque. The play is a kind of grim satire, then, in which public space is abandoned and a very disturbing picture of the non-human world's reprisal against the continued pollution and exploitation of the environment is constructed. Elsewhere, Kieran Hurley's *Heads Up* (2016) takes the form of four intersecting monologues in which an office worker, a school girl, a barista and a rock star deal with the imminent end of the world and Zinnie Harris' *The Scent of Roses* (2022) features five characters walking a tight rope between survival and despair as the world around them spirals into full-blown climate collapse.

Epilogue

This book has been a relatively long time in the making and has been shaped by the ongoing cultural and political dramas precipitated by the 2014 Independence referendum and the 2016 Brexit vote, as well as global concerns around AI and environment. The 2014 vote launched a new set of political identifiers in Scotland—Yes and No voters—that show no sign of disappearing. The Yes campaign lost the vote, polling 45%, but as Ben Jackson observes 'the most remarkable feature of the referendum was the large increase in popular support for independence during the campaign' and then for the SNP at the British general election in 2015, 'when it polled 50% of the Scottish vote' (2020: 1). Devolution had transformed Scotland's political and cultural scene in ways not intended by the New Labour administration that set it in motion, and the SNP had affected an astonishingly rapid 'transition from being a small oppositional force, heavily dependent on voluntary activity, into a party of government' (Mitchel et al. 2011: 12). The referendum also marked a high point in democratic engagement, producing an unprecedented 84.6% turnout.

If truisms about great art emerging from periods of crisis and change do not always hold, there does nevertheless seem to be a concrete connection between the political and cultural reawakening precipitated by the constitutional debate and the flowering of Scotland's theatre culture in recent decades, however much the continuation of this flowering is now threatened by the ongoing funding crisis. Twenty-first-century Scotland continues to feel like an interesting place to be and performance has proved itself a medium highly suited to participate in the formation, transformation, and re-evaluation of contemporary Scottish identities. The aim of this book has been to think in a focused, if extended, way about how Scottish theatre as a critical as well as a creative project has been incorporated into the fabric of contemporary Scotland. My intention has been to show that the theatre and performance sector has been an exciting space in which (re)thinking of the relationship between politics, culture and nation, has demonstrably occurred. Through engaging with local, national and international questions in the context of a period of rapid and profound constitutional change, Scottish theatre-makers have worked to reconstitute the nation in socially constructive ways. In particular, and often through the mechanism of the dispersed model of the NTS, they have championed applied and participatory models that are purposefully geographically inclusive, and have sought to make work that reflects the lived experience of Scots in the diverse communities in which they live, work and play. As this last chapter demonstrates, theatre artists have also performed acts of hope in and age of precarity, uncertainty and rising intolerance, by insisting on staging dissonant and dissenting voices, and by asking Scotland to be more honest about its past, in order to pave the way for a more progressive future.

References

Ahmed, Sara (2016) 'An Affinity of Hammers'. *Transgender Studies Quarterly*, 3, pp. 22–34.

Ahmed, Sara (2004) *The Cultural Politics of Emotion*. Edinburgh, Edinburgh University Press.

Alston, David (2021) *Slaves and Highlanders: Silenced Histories of Scotland and the Caribbean*. Edinburgh, Edinburgh University Press.

Billington, Michael (2017) 'Flight Review: Miniature Models Tell Epic Refugee Story'. *Guardian*, 6 August.

Cade & MacAskill (2021) *The Making of Pinocchio*. Accessed 25 June 2021.

Centre for Racial Equality and Rights (2023). Available at: https://www.crer.org.uk/.

Clifford, Jo and Chris Goode (2017) *Eve*. London, Oberon Books.

Collins-Hughes, Laura (2018) 'Review: 'Flight' Has No Live Actors. But Its Story of Two Afghan Boys Feels So Real'. *New York Times*, 12 February.

Craig, Cairns (2001) 'Constituting Scotland'. *The Irish Review*, 28:1, pp. 1–27.

Creative Scotland (2018) 'Additional Funds to Enhance 2018–21 Regular Funding Network'. Available at: https://www.creativescotland.com/news-stories/latest-news/archive/2018/02/additional-funds-to-enhance-2018-21-regular-funding-network.

Crown Office and Procurator Fiscal Service (2022) 'Hate Crime in Scotland, 2021–22'. Available at: https://www.copfs.gov.uk/media/d3jnt5t2/hate-crime-2021-22-publication-final.pdf.

Darke, Paul Anthony (2003) 'Now I Know Why Disability Art Is Drowning in the River Lethe', in Sheila Riddell and Nick Watson (eds.) *Disability, Culture and Identity*. London and New York, Routledge, pp. 131–142.

Ferguson, Brian (2021) 'Float: Small Town Swimming Pool Is Stage for Scotland's Unexpected Love Story'. *Scotsman*, 5 September.

Ferguson, Brian (2023a) 'Unions Accuse "Big Six" Venues of Putting Jobs at Risk and Endangering Future of Scottish Theatre'. *Scotsman*, 1 August.

Ferguson, Brian (2023b) 'Creative Scotland Reveals £56m Gap After Deadline Passes for Long-Term Funding Bids'. *Scotsman*, 26 October.

Fisher, Mark (2019a) 'Nora: A Doll's House Review—Ibsen Gets Three Heroines in Feminist Rewrite'. *Guardian*, 28 March.

Fisher, Mark (2019b) 'The Panopticon Review—Intense and Brutal Tale of a Loveless Childhood'. *Guardian*, 13 October.

Fisher, Mark (2021) 'Ghosts Review—Writing the Enslaved Back into Glasgow's Past'. *Guardian*, 23 April.

Fisher, Mark (2022) 'Enough of Him Review—Master and Slave Square Off as Scotland Abolishes Bondage'. *Guardian*, 25 October.

Frankland, Emma (2020) 'Trans Women Onstage: Erasure, Resurgence and #notadebate', in Jan Sewell and Clare Smout (eds.) *The Palgrave Handbook of the History of Women on Stage*. Cham, Switzerland, Palgrave Macmillan, pp. 775–806.

Fuchs, Elinor (2014) 'Estrangement: Towards an Age Theory'. *Performance Research*, 9:3, pp. 69–77.

Greer, Stephen (2023) 'Ten Years of *The Gospel According to Jesus, Queen of Heaven*: Reflections on the History of Trans and Non-Binary Performance in Scotland'. *Contemporary Theatre Review*, 33:1–2, pp.165–170.

Hamilton, Christine (2020) *Where Are the Women? Part 2*. Christine Hamilton Consulting. Available at: https://www.creativescotland.com/__data/assets/pdf_file/0006/85497/Where-are-the-Women-Part-2-FINAL.pdf.

Harvie, Jen (2005) *Staging the UK*. Manchester, Manchester University Press.

Hassan, Gerry and Simon Barrow (2017) *A Nation Changed? The SNP and Scotland Ten Years On*. Edinburgh, Luath Press.

Hawking, Frey Kwa (2022) 'The Making of Pinocchio'. *Stage*, 1 July.

Hechter, Michael (1975) *Internal Colonialism: The Celtic Fringe in British National Development, 1536–1966*. London, Routledge.

Heckert, Jamie, Deric Shannon and Abbey Willis (2015) 'Queer Anarchism', in James D. Wright (ed.) *International Encyclopedia of the Social & Behavioral Sciences*, 2nd edition, Volume 19. Amsterdam, Elsevier, pp. 747–751.

Jackson, Ben (2020) *The Case for Scottish Independence: A History of Nationalist Political Thought in Modern Scotland*. Cambridge: Cambridge University Press.

Lavery, Hannah (2021) *Lament for Sheku Bayou*. London, Salamander Street Press.
Love, Heather (2009) *Feeling Backward: Loss and the Politics of Queer History*. Cambridge Massachusetts, Harvard University Press.
Macwhirter, Iain (2014) *Disunited Kingdom: How Westminster Won a Referendum but Lost Scotland*. Glasgow, Cargo Books.
McKean, Kathy (2011) 'Listen I Will Tell the Story to You/As I Have Been Told It: Memory and Identity in the Plays of Nicola McCartmney'. *International Journal of Scottish Theatre and Screen*, 4:1. Available at: https://ijosts.glasgow.ac.uk/volume-4/listen-i-will-tell-the-story-to-you-as-i-have-been-told-it-memory-and-identity-in-the-plays-of-nicola-mccartney/.
McMillan, Joyce (2021) 'EIF Theatre Review: Lament for Sheku Bayoh'. *Scotsman*, 26 August.
McMillan, Joyce (2022) 'Theatre Reviews: Enough of Him | Shirley Valentine'. *Scotsman*, 25 October.
Mitchel, James, Lynn Bennie, and Rob Johns (2011) *The Scottish National Party: Transition to Power*. Oxford, Oxford University Press.
Mullen, Stephen (2022) *The Glasgow Sugar Aristocracy: Scotland and Caribbean Slavery, 1775–1838*. London, University of London Press.
Nairn, Tom (1977) *The Break-Up of Britain*. London, Verso.
Nathan, John (2021) 'Theatre review: Flight'. *Jewish Chronicle*, 20 May.
Paterson, Lindsay (1994) *The Autonomy of Modern Scotland*. Edinburgh, Edinburgh University Press.
Pearson, Morna, Hanna Khalil, and Vlad Butucea. (2019) *Interference*. London: Methuen, 2019.
Poet, Frances (2017) *Adam*. London, Nick Hern Books.
Pollock, David (2020) 'Scenes for Survival'. *Stage*, 29 May.
Ridout, Nicholas (2013) *Passionate Amateurs: Theatre, Communism and Love*. Ann Arbor, University of Michigan Press.
Smith, Stef (2016) *Human Animals*. London, Nick Hern Books.
Smith, Stef (2019) *Nora: A Doll's House*. London, Nick Hern Books.
SNP Manifesto (2021) 'What We're Doing for Culture and Creativity'. Available at: https://manifesto21.s3-eu-west-1.amazonaws.com/Culture_and_Creativity.pdf.
Sumbwanyambe, May (2022) *Enough of Him*. London, Methuen.
Valluvan, Sivamohan (2019) *The Clamour of Nationalism: Race and Nation in Twenty-First-Century Britain*. Manchester, Manchester University Press.

Index

A
Adam, Henry, 19, 195, 196
  The People Next Door, 196
Advisory Council for the Arts in Scotland (AdCAS), 105
Agnew, Denis, 104
Ahmed, Sara, 225, 227
Alston, David, 222, 225
A Play, a Pie and a Pint, 140, 149, 194, 211
Arches, The, 17, 34, 79, 82–84, 144, 194
Archibald, David, 71, 72, 118
Arnold, Andy, 82
Arnott, Peter
  Group Portrait in a Summer Landscape, 200, 201
  The Monarch of the Glen, 40, 201
  The Signalman, 40, 202
  Tay Bridge, 202
  White Rose, 16, 40, 44, 45, 63
Arts Council of Great Britain (ACGB), 33
Aston, Elaine, 33
Augé, Marc, 91, 163

B
Balibar, Etienne, 7, 8
BECTU, 15
Behavior, 17
Berton-Charrière, Danièle, 197
Billington, Michael, 59, 125, 212
Binnie, John, 51, 225
  Killing me Softly, 51
Birds of Paradise, 82, 214, 217
Bisset, Cora, 101, 163, 164, 166, 210, 229
  Glasgow Girls, 163, 165–167
Bottoms, Stephen, 71
Brantley, Ben, 117
Bratchpiece, David, 82, 83
Brook, Peter, 86
  Mahabharata, 17, 32, 77
Brown, Ian, 12, 31, 61, 72, 111, 174, 189, 196, 198
Brown, Mark, 12, 50, 72, 165, 177
Bryden, Bill
  The Big Picnic, 78
  The Ship, 78
Bull, John, 113, 114, 191
Burke, Gregory

Black Watch, 18, 21, 96, 115–122, 129, 148, 152, 166, 180, 191, 192
  Gagarin Way, 12, 191, 192, 196
Burnett, Andrew, 109
Butucea, Vlad, 232
Byrne, John, 32, 37, 51, 69, 112, 163

C

Cade, Rosana, 82, 229–231
Calvinism, 73
Cameron, Alasdair, 43–45, 72, 77
  Scot Free, 45
Carner, Nicole, 146
Carter, Pamela, 71, 157
Catherine Wheels, 19, 107, 110, 152, 153, 156, 217, 218
  White, 153
Centre for Contemporary Arts (CCA), 79
Citizens Theatre, 15, 20, 35
civic nationalism, 18, 220
Clapp, Susannah, 89, 129
Clifford, Jo
  Eve, 228, 229
  Gospel According to Jesus, Queen of Heaven, 228
  Life is a Dream, 109, 203, 204
  Losing Venice, 16, 40, 43–45, 63
Clyde Unity, 51
Communicado, 16, 21, 47, 49–51, 61, 77, 107, 144
  Cyrano de Bergerac, 50
Cooper, Neil, 45, 79, 84, 141, 151, 201
Corbett, John, 47
Corrie, Joe, 111, 112, 148
Coveney, Michael, 16, 37, 38
Craig, Cairns, 34, 220
Cramer, Steve, 40, 56, 187, 199
Creative Scotland, 14, 83, 120, 142, 174, 216, 217, 219
Crichton, Mamie, 36
Critics' Awards for Theatre in Scotland (CATS), 188
Cullen, Mike, 11, 112
Cull Ó Maoilearca, Laura, 26
Cumming, Alan, 38, 97, 101, 112, 121, 122

D

Dean, Christopher, 226
de Jongh, Nicholas, 186
Devine, Tom, 45, 180
devolution, 2, 5, 6, 8, 11–13, 18, 22, 24, 32, 75, 104, 119, 131, 149, 164, 174, 177, 180, 195, 212, 216, 221, 233
Diamond, Elin, 175
Di Mambro, Ann Marie, 53
  Tally's Blood, 53
Disaster Plan, 54
  Move, 54
Dixon, Steve, 138
Dolan, Jill, 166
Drummond, Rob, 19, 82, 194
  Bullet Catch, 192, 193
Dudley Edwards, Owen, 20
Duncan, Ian, 22, 23, 75
Dundee Repertory Theatre (Dundee Rep), 13, 15, 46, 104, 143, 194, 195, 211, 214
DV8 Physical Theatre, 80
  Dead Dreams of Monochrome Men, 80

E

Eades, Alex, 27
Eatough, Graham, 21, 23, 24, 56, 79, 85, 95, 107, 110
Edgar, David, 184
Edinburgh Fringe, 4, 89, 102, 210

INDEX 239

Edinburgh International Festival (EIF), 20, 27, 49, 61, 77, 79, 91, 95–97, 101, 113, 127, 131, 176, 181, 185, 188, 211, 222
Emmanuel, Oliver, 157, 211
  Flight, 211
Enlightenment, 75
epistemic community, 12, 13, 18, 19, 26
European City of Culture, 49, 77
Expo fund, 20

F

Featherstone, Vicky, 105, 107, 111, 112, 120, 127, 132, 149, 152, 176, 188
Federation for Scottish Theatre (FST), 13, 104
Ferguson, Brian, 15, 210, 216
Findlay, Bill, 47, 63
Findlay, Richard, 10, 105
Findlay-Walsh, LJ, 83
Finlay McLeod, Iain, 149
Fischer, Kai, 93, 204
Fisher, Mark, 6, 60, 126, 161, 163, 167, 197, 202, 203, 209, 218, 224, 225
Fletcher-Watson, Ben, 156
Forced Entertainment, 21, 80
Frankland, Emma, 228
funding
  funding crisis, 19, 233
  funding cuts, 2
  funding mechanism, 12, 87

G

Gaelic drama, 150
Gardner, Lyn, 83, 114, 116, 117, 176, 199
Gender Recognition Reform, 227
Gifford, Douglas, 34

Glover, Sue, 32, 52, 53, 60, 210
  Bondagers, 52, 53, 60
  The Seal Wife, 52
Gray, Alasdair, 20–24, 26, 27, 34, 79
  Lanark: A Life in Four Books, 20
Greer, Stephen (Steve), 72, 81, 82, 228
Greig, David
  American Pilot, The, 159, 183
  Bacchae, The, 21, 38, 121
  Caledonia Dreaming, 1–6, 17, 56
  Caledonia Dreaming, 179
  Damascus, 55, 183
  Dunsinane, 21, 122–127, 140, 148
  Europe, 21, 55–59, 62, 159, 179, 184
  Events, The, 21, 193
  Lanark: A Life in Three Acts, 20, 27
  Midsummer, 21, 148, 183, 184
  Monster in the Hall, The, 158, 160–162
  One Way Street, 17, 56, 159
  Outlying Islands, 55, 180, 181
  Pyrenees, 159, 181–183
  San Diego, 21, 97, 159, 181–184
  Speculator, The, 17, 21, 55, 56, 97, 174
  Strange Undoing of Prudencia Hart, The, 21, 130, 131, 148, 183
  Suppliant Women, The, 21, 193
  Victoria, 17, 56, 179–181
  Yellow Moon: The Ballad of Leila and Lee, 158
Gridiron
  Muster Station, 91, 92
  Roam, 90, 91, 95, 110, 119
  The Bloody Chamber, 88
Grierson, Sandy, 21, 23–25

H

Haas, Peter, 13
Haedicke, Susan, 163, 164
Halliday, Kirstin, 83
Hames, Scott, 2, 4, 5, 147
Hamilton, Christine, 131, 143, 144, 210, 211
Hannan, Chris
  Elizabeth Gordon Quinn, 16, 40, 41, 45, 46, 63, 111
  Shining Souls, 17, 61, 62
Harman, Paul, 152
Harpin, Anna, 114, 168, 186, 190
Harrison, Ben, 88–90, 92, 201
Harris, Zinnie
  Duchess of Malfi, The, 177
  Further than the Furthest Thing, 173, 175
  How to Hold Your Breath, 176
  Meet Me at Dawn, 176, 211
  Midwinter, 175, 176
  Scent of Roses, The, 233
  This Restless House, 173, 177, 211
  Wheel, The, 175, 176
Harrower, David
  Blackbird, 97, 185–187
  Calum's Road, 18, 144, 146
  Ciara, 187, 188
  Knives in Hens, 17, 55, 59, 60, 62, 75, 187
Hart, Katie, 176
Harvie, Jen, 27, 97, 103, 108, 140, 193, 216
Hassan, Gerry, 147, 220
Havergal, Giles, 16, 35–38, 70, 74
Hawking, Frey Kwa, 230
Hechter, Michael, 221, 222
Heddon, Deirdre, 79
Heggie, Iain, 51, 52, 225
  A Wholly Healthy Glasgow, 51, 52
Hoggett, Steven, 116, 117, 152
Hogg, James, 69, 71, 73–76
Holdsworth, Nadine, 103, 175, 179, 180, 183
Holyrood, 14, 220
Horvat, Ksenija, 47, 51
Howard, Philip, 55, 62
Hurley, Kieran
  Heads Up, 195, 233
  Hitch, 195
  Mouthpiece, 195
  Rantin, 18, 144, 146–149, 194, 195
Hutchison, David, 35, 37, 55

I

Imaginate, 156, 157, 214
Independence Referendum, 8, 127, 128, 139, 200, 201, 233
Innes, Christopher, 38
Innes, Kirstin, 82, 83

K

Kalil, Hannah, 231
Kelly, Muireann, 19, 151
Kershaw, Baz, 32
Killick, Jenny, 39
Klein, Jennie, 79, 81
Kruger, Loren, 127

L

Laing, Stewart, 71, 72, 95, 107, 110, 158
Lavery, Hannah, 102, 210, 222, 223
  Lament For Sheku Bayoh, 102, 222, 223
Lenton, Matthew, 92, 94, 107–109
Lepage, Robert, 79
Letts, Oliver, 116
Levick, Jemima, 211
Ley, James, 226
Lichtenfels, Peter, 39

Live Art in Scotland, 72
Loan, Eilidh, 162, 210
   Moorcroft, 162
Lochhead, Liz
   Jock Tamson's Bairns, 49, 77
   Mary Queen of Scots Got her Head Chopped Off, 16, 46, 47, 49, 63, 111
   Medea, 49, 97, 101, 102, 104
   Tartuffe, 47
Love, Heather, 228
Lung Ha, 217
Lyceum Theatre, 20, 24, 56

M

MacAskill, Ivor, 230
   The Making of Pinocchio, 229, 230
MacDonald, Robert David, 16, 35, 46
MacDonald, Sharman, 52, 53
   When I Was a Girl I used to Scream and Shout, 52, 54
Macleod, Michelle, 150, 151
Macrae, Alasdair, 94, 144, 145
Macwhirter, Iain, 164, 220
Maguire, Tom, 53, 177
Maloney, Paul, 46, 166
Manley, Andy, 153–156
Maxwell, Douglas, 88, 97, 166
   Decky Does a Bronco, 88, 89
Mayfest, 79
McArthur, Isobel, 167, 210
McCartney, Nicola, 92, 112, 174, 210, 217–219
McCleary, Nat, 97
McCrone, David, 5, 10, 11, 179
McDonald, Jan, 39
McGrath, John, 4, 31, 53, 61, 77, 112, 115, 144, 165
   The Cheviot, the Stag and the Black, Black Oil, 4, 31, 112, 115, 144, 165

McGrath, Tom, 31, 80
McLaren, Graham, 111, 112, 132, 148
McLennan, David, 112, 140, 194
McMillan, Joyce, 2, 15, 27, 39, 49, 50, 61, 97, 105, 110, 112, 115, 128, 129, 131, 145, 156, 157, 166, 198, 201, 204, 224
McMillan, Joyce", 107
McNair, Gary, 82, 83, 166, 194
   Dear Billy, 166, 167
Millican, Nikki, 80–82
Milling, Jane, 32, 33
Moireach, Dòmhnall S., 150
Morgan, Fergus, 54
Mulgrew, Gerry, 21, 50, 51, 144
Mullen, Stephen, 222
Müller, Anja, 56
Munro, Rona
   James IV: Queen of the Fight, 101, 199
   James Plays, The, 21, 97, 127, 129, 130, 140, 148, 198
   James V: Katherine, 199
   Last Witch, The, 97, 199
   Maiden Stone, The, 53, 199
Murray, Neil, 105, 132, 150

N

Nairn, Tom, 131, 167, 174, 221, 222
Nationalism, 7, 8, 18, 35, 53, 103, 120, 131, 168, 201, 212, 220, 221
National Library of Scotland, 60, 218
National Lottery, 14, 87
National Review of Live Art (NRLA), 79–82
National Theatre of Scotland (NTS)
   Burn, 97, 101, 102, 104
   Five Minute Theatre, 18, 137–141
   Granite, 18, 142, 144

Great Yes No Don't Know 5 Minute Theatre Show, The, 139
Home, 18, 95, 106, 107, 109, 119, 132, 137, 142, 143
Ignition, 18, 142, 144
Macbeth, 121–125, 173
Scenes for Survival, 19, 213–216
Transform, 151, 152
Neilson, Anthony
 Realism, 18, 96, 97, 112–115, 188, 189, 191
 Wonderful World of Dissocia, The, 188

O
O'Loughlin, Orla, 101, 197, 225
Oliver, Cordelia, 46, 47
Onashile, Adura, 49, 224
Òran Mór, 139, 149, 194
Overend, David, 147

P
Paterson, Lindsay, 49, 220
Pattie, David, 5, 115, 174, 192
Pearson, Morna
 Darklands, 231
 The Artist Man and the Mother Woman, 197
Peebles, Alison, 49, 50, 61, 70, 74, 107, 110, 111
Pitlochry Festival Theatre, 15, 40, 101, 143, 200, 201, 211
Pittock, Murray, 75
Playwrights' Studio Scotland (PSS), 174
Poet, Frances, 102, 151, 210, 229
Powell, Nick, 21, 85, 86
Power, Cormac, 74
Price, Victoria, 123
Prowse, Philip, 16, 35, 37, 38, 72

R
Rebellato, Dan, 87, 182
Reekie, Tony, 156
Rees-Mogg, William, 33
Reid, Trish, 102, 138, 160, 191
Reinelt, Janelle, 7, 8, 59, 180, 183
Reizbaum, Marylin, 48
Riach, Alan, 111
Ridout, Nicholas, 229
Robertson, Gill, 110, 152, 153
Robinson, Jo, 143, 144
Robinson, Rebecca, 104, 120
Robson, Mark, 58
Rockvilla, 132
Rodríguez, Verónica, 57, 58, 178, 179
Roper, Tony, 46, 112
 The Steamie, 46, 112
Royal Conservatoire of Scotland, 81, 84
Royal Scottish Academy of Music and Drama, 81
Runcie, Charlotte, 129
rural touring, 142, 143

S
Sansom, Laurie, 95, 127, 129, 130
Schaaf, Jeanne, 56
7:84 Scotland, 4, 46, 50, 85, 140, 147, 194
Scott, Ian, 85, 86
Scottish Arts Council (SAC), 13, 39, 69, 84, 104, 120
Scottish Government, 13–15, 18, 20, 21, 120, 121, 132, 146, 147, 164, 216, 219, 220, 227
Scottish National Party (SNP), 8, 9, 11, 120, 219–221, 233
Scottish Parliament, 5, 8, 12, 24, 104, 110, 112, 164, 174, 218, 220, 226, 227
Scottish Television (STV), 15

Scullion, Adrienne, 12, 36, 39, 46, 51, 72, 131, 143, 144, 173, 174, 189
Sierz, Aleks, 119, 184, 188
Six, Anna, 188
slave trade, 101, 222, 224, 225
Śledzińska, Paula, 143, 145, 149, 151
Smith, Alexander, 5
Smith, Donald, 33, 155
Smith, Stef
  Human Animals, 232
  Nora: A Doll's House, 209
  Roadkill, 210
Society for Scottish Playwrights, 15
Spencer, Charles, 186
Starcatchers, 153, 156
Stein, Peter, 185, 186
Stellar Quines, 210, 211, 214, 217
Stevenson, Randall, 31, 45, 47, 48
Stewart, Ena Lamont, 41
Sumbwanyambe, May, 101, 224, 225
  Enough of Him, 101, 104, 224, 225
Summerhall, 69, 73, 214
Suspect Culture
  8000m, 21, 86
  Airport, 21
  Escapologist, The, 86
  Futurology, 86
  Lament, 21, 85, 86
  Mainstream, 21, 85, 91
Svitch, Caridad, 184

T
TAG Theatre Company, 20, 111
Take me Somewhere, 17, 79, 83, 229
Taudevin, Julia, 54, 82, 147, 210
Taxidou, Olga, 78
Taylor, Paul, 59, 128
Test Department, 78, 87
  The Second Coming, 78

Thatcherism, 10, 11, 16, 32, 34, 45, 78
Thatcher, Margaret, 9–11, 22, 32, 39, 41, 42, 48, 226
Theatre Gu Leòr, 151
Theatre in Schools Scotland (TiSS), 157
Third Eye Centre, The, 17, 80
Tiffany, John, 18, 79, 106, 110, 115–118, 121, 152, 191
Todd, Richard, 34
Tomlin, Liz, 76, 87, 107, 152
Tompkins, Joanne, 103, 104, 149
Tramway, 17, 32, 34, 49, 52, 55, 76–79, 86, 96, 121, 177, 179, 209
Traverse theatre, 15, 39, 52, 62
Treaty of Union, 73
Tron Theatre, 15, 106, 123, 188, 211, 214, 228
Turner, Cathy, 78

U
Untitled Projects
  Paul Bright's Confessions of a Justified Sinner, 27, 70, 76, 97
  The End of Eddy, 157

V
Valluvan, Sivamohan, 225
Vanishing Point
  Destroyed Room, The, 94, 97
  Interiors, 93–95, 97
Visible Fictions, 19, 153, 155, 156, 217
Vox Motus, 27, 97, 211, 212
  Dragon, 27, 97

W

Wallace, Clare, 4, 6, 56, 58, 85, 86, 124, 127, 160, 178, 179, 182, 184, 186, 187
Walmsley, Ben, 143
Watson, Ariel, 103, 104, 118, 123, 129
Weight, Richard, 34
Whyte, Christopher, 24
Wildcat
  Border Warfare, 77
  John Brown's Body, 77
Wilkie, Fiona, 87, 88, 107
Wilson, Wils, 108, 109, 131, 142, 204
Winter School, 81, 82, 84
Wooster Group, The, 21, 79
Wright, Allen, 36
Wylie, Jackie, 82, 83, 95, 210

Y

Young, Morna
  Lost at Sea, 198

Z

Zajac, Matthew, 196
Zaroulia, Marilena, 181
Zenzinger, Peter, 5, 53, 188
Zerdy, Joanne, 115

GPSR Compliance

The European Union's (EU) General Product Safety Regulation (GPSR) is a set of rules that requires consumer products to be safe and our obligations to ensure this.

If you have any concerns about our products, you can contact us on

ProductSafety@springernature.com

In case Publisher is established outside the EU, the EU authorized representative is:

Springer Nature Customer Service Center GmbH
Europaplatz 3
69115 Heidelberg, Germany

www.ingramcontent.com/pod-product-compliance
Lightning Source LLC
LaVergne TN
LVHW021957060526
838201LV00048B/1598